Institutions and Economic Change in Southeast Asia

Institutions and Economic Change in Southeast Asia

The Context of Development from the 1960s to the 1990s

Edited by

Colin Barlow

Visiting Fellow, Research School of Pacific and Asian Studies, Australian National University, Australia

Edward Elgar
Cheltenham, UK • Northampton, MA, USA

Published by
Edward Elgar Publishing Limited
Glensanda House
Montpellier Parade
Cheltenham
Glos GL50 1UA
UK

Edward Elgar Publishing, Inc.
136 West Street
Suite 202
Northampton
Massachusetts 01060
USA

A catalogue record for this book
is available from the British Library

Library of Congress Cataloguing in Publication Data

Institutions and economic change in Southeast Asia : the context of
    development from the 1960s to the 1990s / edited by Colin Barlow.
        Includes index.
        1. Asia, Southeastern—Economic conditions. 2. Asia,
    Southeastern—Economic policy.   I. Barlow, Colin.
    HC441.I57   2000
    338.959—dc21   99–41670
                                                         CIP

ISBN 1 85898 726 1

Printed in the United Kingdom at the University Press, Cambridge

Contents

Contributors   *vii*
Preface and Acknowledgements   *x*

PART I.   GENERAL

1.   Introduction
     Colin Barlow   3
2.   An Economic Theory of Institutional Change
     Justin Yifu Lin   8

PART II.   INSTITUTIONS IN PARTICULAR MARKETS

3.   Institutions of Change in Rural Development: Mediating Markets for
     New Crop Technologies in Sumatra
     Colin Barlow   25
4.   Labour Institutions: The Case of Indonesia
     Chris Manning   42
5.   Industrial Institutions: The Case of Malaysia
     Tham Siew-Yean and Mahani Zainal-Abidin   55
6.   Entrepreneurship and Institutions: The Southeast Asian Experience
     Jamie Mackie   72
7.   The Economics of Institutional Change: Making Economic Policy in
     Thailand
     Medhi Krongkaew   85

PART III.   INSTITUTIONS IN NATIONAL AND INTERNATIONAL
            ECONOMIC CHANGE

8.   Government and Deregulation in Indonesia
     Hadi Soesastro   105
9.   The Institutions of Transition from Central Planning: The Case of
     Vietnam
     Adam Fforde   118

10. Executive–Legislative Relations in the Philippines: Continuity and
    Change
    Emmanuel S. de Dios   132
11. Global Economic Institutions from the Southeast Asian Perspective
    David Vines   150

PART IV. CONCLUSIONS

12. Conclusions
    Colin Barlow   167

References   181
Index   197

Contributors

Colin Barlow is a Visiting Fellow in the Research School of Pacific and Asian Studies at the Australian National University, Canberra. He has worked on rural economic and social development in many Southeast Asian countries, focusing on the production and marketing of cash crops and ways in which public and other interventions are best organized to secure adoption of new techniques. He is the author (with Sisira Jayasuriya and C. Suan Tan) of *The World Rubber Industry* (Routledge, 1994) and co-editor (with Joan Hardjono) of *Indonesia Assessment, 1995. Development in Eastern Indonesia* (Institute of Southeast Asian Studies, 1996).

Emmanuel S. de Dios is a Professor of Economics at the University of the Philippines, School of Economics. He has gained recognition for his works on the causes of the economic crisis under the Marcos regime, as well as on poverty, fiscal policy, exchange-rate management and human development. He served briefly in the Office of the President during the Aquino administration, and has occasionally worked as a consultant to non-government organizations, labour unions, various official agencies and international bodies.

Adam Fforde is an economist working both as a consultant (as head of the Canberra-based ADUKI Pty Ltd), and academic researcher (as Visiting Fellow in the Research School of Pacific and Asian Studies, Australian National University). His work has centred on issues of transition, especially the role of policy in systemic change. He has wide experience in the management and analysis of aid policy, including rural development policies in transition, aid project redesign, macroeconomic management and problems of institutional change. His most recent published works are: *Doi Mo – Ten Years After the 1986 Party Congress* (ed., Political and Social Change Monograph 24, Australian National University, 1997), *From Plan to Market: The Economic Transition in Vietnam* (with Stefan de Vylder, Westview, 1996), and *From Centrally Planned to Market Economies: The Asian Approach* (Volume III, Part 3: Vietnam, with Stefan de Vylder, Asian Development Bank/Oxford University Press, 1996).

Medhi Krongkaew is Director of both the Institute of East Asian Studies and the Thai APEC (Asia Pacific Economic Cooperation) Study Center at Thammasat University in Bangkok. He also teaches at the Faculty of Economics at

Thammasat, and has served in many international institutions including the World Bank and various United Nations agencies. He has worked on Thailand's public policies since the early 1970s, concentrating on issues of poverty and income distribution. He is the editor of *Thailand's Industrialisation and its Consequences* (Macmillan, 1995).

Justin Yifu Lin is the Founder and Director of the China Center for Economic Research, and a Professor of Economics in the Department of Economics at Peking University. He is also a Reader at the Hong Kong University of Science and Technology. He belongs to several key academic bodies in China, North America and Europe, and has published widely in both Chinese- and English-language academic literature. He is the author of *Institutions, Technology and Agricultural Development in China* (Shanghai Sanlian Sudian, 1992) and *Farming Institutions and Agricultural Growth in China: A Contribution to New Institutional Economics* (Johns Hopkins University Press, 1996).

Jamie Mackie is a Visiting Fellow at the Research School of Pacific and Asian Studies, Australian National University. Professor Mackie has been researching and writing on Southeast Asia, particularly Indonesia, since the 1950s. He was Research Director at the Centre of Southeast Asian Studies, Monash University, from 1968 to 1978, and Foundation Professor of the Department of Political and Social Change in the Research School of Pacific and Asian Studies of the Australian National University until 1989. His publications include: *Konfrontasi: the Indonesia–Malaysia Dispute, 1963–66* (OUP Malaysia, 1974), *The Chinese in Indonesia: Five Essays* (co-editor with Thomas Nelson; Australian Institute of International Affairs, 1976) and *Balanced Development: East Java under the New Order* (co-editor with Howard Dick and J.J. Fox; OUP Malaysia, 1993).

Mahani Zainal-Abidin is an Associate Professor at the Department of Applied Economics, Faculty of Economics, University of Malaya, and Associate Fellow at the Malaysian Institute of Economic Research (MIER). Her work has been mainly on industrial policy and multilateral trade arrangements. She is a member of the Working Group instrumental in producing the important Malaysian government policy document, *National Economic Recovery Plan. Agenda for Action* (National Economic Action Council, 1998), setting out measures to overcome the effects of the recent financial crisis.

Chris Manning is a Research Fellow in the Economics Department and Indonesia Project, Research School of Pacific Studies, Australian National University. His major research interests are Indonesian and Southeast Asian labour and welfare. He has published a range of articles and edited several books on aspects of Indonesian labour – most recently *Indonesian Labour in*

Transition: An East Asian Success Story? (Cambridge University Press, 1998). He also has had a long-standing interest in general and regional economic development in Indonesia, especially in the province of Irian Jaya. He is currently working on two projects: international labour migration and structural adjustment in East Asia, and labour market adjustment to economic boom and crisis in Southeast Asia.

Hadi Soesastro is the Executive Director of the Centre for Strategic and International Studies in Jakarta, and Chairperson of the Asia Pacific Economic Community Cooperating Group. He is a macroeconomist with special interests in trade, technology and international political economy, and has published extensively on the Indonesian economy in particular. His well-known works include *Technological Challenge in the Asia-Pacific Economy* (Allen and Unwin, 1990), and *Indonesia 2020* (co-edited with Iwan Hutajulu, 1996).

Tham Siew-Yean is Associate Professor in the Faculty of Economics of the National University of Malaysia (UKM), and in 1998 was also appointed Associate Fellow at the Institute of Malaysian and International Studies (IKMAS). She obtained her PhD from the University of Rochester in 1988. Her research interests are mainly in foreign direct investment and in trade and industry studies.

David Vines is the Director of the Global Economic Institutions Research Programme of the British Economic and Social Research Council. He is a Fellow in Economics at Balliol College, Oxford and a Research Fellow at the Oxford Centre for Economic Research. During 1991–7 he was Adjunct Professor of Economics at the Research School of Pacific and Asian Studies at the Australian National University.

Preface and Acknowledgements

The idea of this book first emerged in 1992, during a series of stimulating seminars on the economics of institutional development which I organized at the Australian National University, Canberra. Then other events intervened, and little was done until 1997 when I began seriously to marshal contributors for the present volume. Now only Justin Lin, Chris Manning, Medhi Krongkaew, Jamie Mackie, David Vines and myself remain as authors from the original sixteen participants, and our contributions have been largely rewritten. Fortunately five other distinguished scholars subsequently agreed to write chapters for the volume. I would note that my introductory Chapter 1 and concluding Chapter 12 reflect solely my personal opinions, and were not written in consultation with the other contributors.

I wish to thank the Departments of Economics and of Political and Social Change in the Research School of Pacific and Asian Studies at the Australian National University (ANU) for providing facilities allowing this project to be undertaken. I particularly want to acknowledge the original impetus for this effort from Ross Garnaut and Ben Higgins, both of whom encouraged me greatly, provided important intellectual stimulus in the original seminars, and threw much light through their own works on the role of institutions in development. I am also grateful to the President and Fellows of Wolfson College, Oxford, where I finally completed the volume during a period as a Visiting Scholar in late 1998. I would also especially mention George Peters and Barbara Harriss of Queen Elizabeth House, Oxford, who were my main sponsors at that University. I am indebted to the staff of Edward Elgar Publishing for their able and efficient assistance in the production of the book.

Several authors wish to add their special thanks to people and groups who assisted them with their chapters. Colin Barlow acknowledges the cooperation and support of the farmers, managers and entrepreneurs engaged in the organizations which he analyses in Chapter 3. Tham Siew-Yean and Mahani Zainal-Abidin are indebted to Mr Kong Ping Yee of the Malaysian Rubber Products Manufacturers Association, who gave them valuable insights into the case of the Malaysian rubber products industry. Adam Fforde would like to thank many colleagues in Vietnam and elsewhere for their support, and also for the discussions on which his chapter draws. David Vines is grateful for helpful discussions on his material with Heinz Arndt, John Braithwaite, Geoffrey Brennan, Ian Clark, David Currie, Paul David, Peter Drysdale, Barry Eichengreen, Ross

Garnaut, Chris Gilbert, Anne Krueger, Warwick McKibbin, Marcus Miller, David Robertson, Gary Sampson, André Sapir, Hadi Soesastro, Yongzheng Yang and Steven Woolcock.

I should finally like to express my huge appreciation for the continued support and help of Lulu Turner, who assisted me greatly with editing and made certain that drafts going to press were properly presented and met the requirements of the Elgar house style.

I would note that all values in the book are quoted in United States dollars at concurrent exchange rates.

PART I

General

1. Introduction

Colin Barlow

This book addresses the role of institutions in the development of Southeast Asia[1] – one of the most dynamically growing international regions in the three decades up to the massive financial crisis of 1997 which created such widespread bankruptcy and poverty. It seeks to determine the significance of institutional arrangements and structures to the progress of economic and social improvement, and to examine how these vehicles have adapted to demands imposed by dynamic change. The book also throws light on a part of the world where traditional societies have adapted vigorously to the challenges of advance, but where underlying social structures and arrangements have been little investigated. It reviews the characteristics of institutions in the spheres of rural society, labour markets, manufacturing industry, national governance and relevant parts of international finance, checking key features and reactions to change, and ways in which particular experiences provide guidance for institutional development elsewhere.

The agricultural economist, Theodore Schultz, wrote that 'an institution can be perceived as a set of behavioural rules commonly observed by individuals in a society' (Schultz 1968, p. 115). Institutions so defined cover a multitude of behavioural arrangements, including families, firms, governments, universities, money markets, values, customs and ideologies, all of which perform key economic, social and other tasks in governing and facilitating human activity. There are also well-defined subsets of arrangements within broader institutional categories, as where government, for example, includes subsets for formulating legislation, policy-making and policy implementation. The benefits conferred by institutions include the economic advantages of returns to scale and internalizing of externalities, and the social advantages for participating individuals of helping them overcome limitations imposed by bounded rationalities and life-cycle exigencies. These benefits are addressed in detail by Justin Lin who explores basic ideas concerning institutional change in Chapter 2.

Looking at the institutional element in behaviour is not a new branch of social science, with antecedents stretching back both to the classical economists and other scholars including Karl Marx (1858), Thorstein Veblen (1919), John Commons (1934) and Clarence Ayres (1944). While Marx included institutions

3

in his wide canvas of human society and recognized their key role in society at large, Veblen, Ayres and Commons mainly described and analysed legal and operational aspects of selected bodies, with prime concern over how they reacted to technical change.

The economic and social dimensions of institutions have subsequently been further analysed by numerous scholars, many of whose contributions are quoted in this volume. These later studies have once more addressed different arrangements and structures, looking at ways in which they adapted to miscellaneous changes and at how they were constrained. They have also examined how separate institutions have interacted with one another, and how individual organizations related to the overall institutional structure. The studies have further focused on 'transactions and information cost' economics, scrutinizing how expenditures may be reduced and efficiency enhanced through appropriate institutional configurations and adjustments. They have also looked at the crucial topic of 'collective action', entailing the manner in which groups of persons are organized to work together towards certain goals, and the means whereby some institutional forms permit this to be undertaken more effectively than others.

Both earlier and later exponents of institutional economics have been concerned with how this branch of inquiry connects with the broad theory of neoclassical economic theory. That theory commonly takes institutions as given and assumes well-defined property rights, perfect information and frictionless transactions. Later scholars have worked on linkages to this theory, attempting to show how emerging understandings of institutions can be used to complement it, enabling a better explanation of human behaviour and development. Yet, while some scholars have gone so far as to distinguish between 'old' and 'new' institutional economics, with the former comprising the largely descriptive earlier approaches and the latter the rather more theoretical and analytical vein of later work, this writer can see little value in making precarious distinctions between supplementary and overlapping strands of thinking. Institutional economics in this book is accordingly regarded as a coherent body of thought, with no division between successive stages.

This book adopts an approach of studying institutions through selected case studies, following the practice of other recent volumes. The latter include the edited works by Nabli and Nugent (1989) addressing applications in Tunisia, by Harriss, Hunter and Lewis (1995) looking at key institutions in poorer countries, and by Dorward, Kydd and Poulton (1998) concerning institutions in smallholder cash-crop agriculture. This case-study approach has the well-recognized merit of enabling basic ideas – in this instance, those of institutional economics – to be tested in practical contexts. Such testing often provides new insights for modifying and elaborating those ideas, while the fact that a variety of contexts is addressed enables differing implications for the same idea to be observed. Empirical scrutinies of institutions usually bring out the complexity of real-life circumstances, with a diversity of actors and influencing factors being involved. This is certainly true both of the studies quoted above and of the present book. Hence a main goal of this book is to use the case studies in successive chapters to examine and compare how institutions have performed in specified areas of economic and social improvement.

The editor of this volume was fortunate in assembling a distinguished panel of contributors from various countries, permitting the role of institutions to be explored in a range of contexts. First, Justin Lin in Chapter 2 sets out a broad economic theory of institutional change, also giving references to other pertinent studies and providing a framework to which subsequent chapters and discussions can be related. Then Colin Barlow in Chapter 3 scrutinizes the mediation of new agricultural technologies in Sumatra, where this was done by the institution of private firms on the one hand, and government development organizations on the other. He compares the effectiveness of the two very different approaches to improvement, also analysing factors conducive to institutional change in a traditional society.

Chris Manning in Chapter 4 examines and discusses the economic efficiency of important Indonesian labour market institutions, doing this against the political background of Suharto's 'New Order' which ended in 1998. He contrasts industrial labour institutions chiefly imposed and controlled by a dictatorial state with rural labour institutions arising largely from market forces affected by the technological change of the 'green revolution'. He carefully scrutinizes the economic, social and political consequences of each of the arrangements. Tham Siew-Yean and Mahani Zainal-Abidin in Chapter 5 investigate the recent circumstances of industrial institutions in Malaysia, especially addressing the development of integrated clusters of firms favoured by an interventionist government as a means of lowering industrial transactions costs and promoting technological change. Such development is compared for the sectors of electronics, rubber products and automobiles, each of which embodies different kinds and extents of linkages. The nature of input and output markets differs in each case, with consequently diverging needs for clusters.

Jamie Mackie in Chapter 6 reviews the entrepreneurial role of the Chinese in Southeast Asian economic development, looking at how this vital aspect of behaviour is expressed and how it relates to the institutional features of family organization, ethnic networks and forms of business enterprise. In addition, he touches on the institutional and economic preconditions for the emergence of entrepreneurship, their variation between countries, and the challenges arising from the radically altering institutional environment of modern commerce where family firms have often been replaced by much larger organizations. Medhi Krongkaew in Chapter 7 moves the debate to the institutional underpinnings of Thai policy-making, checking the organizational and political backgrounds of those 'supplying' policy and the effects of this on policy formulation. He further explores the perennial and institutionally channelled conflict between bureaucratic and business interests, looking at this specifically in relation to policies of public enterprise privatization, automobile development and control of the sugar trade.

Hadi Soesastro in Chapter 8 begins the part of the book with a wider canvas, in the sense of reviewing the interrelated roles of many different and complementary institutions in processes of development. He addresses the evolution of economic and government institutions in Indonesia against the altering political background, checking the effects of such change on economic and social progress. He demarcates three distinct phases in this evolution over the 30 years of the New Order, with an initial strengthening of the bureaucracy and the introduction of centralized economic management being followed in the 1980s by deregulation and finally in the 1990s by general stagnation and reversed deregulation accompanied by rampant cronyism. Adam Fforde in Chapter 9 examines institutional change in the economically pre-eminent rural sphere of communist Vietnam from the late 1950s, highlighting the successive economic development stages of a collectivized rural economy, a 'transitional model' to freer markets in the 1980s, and an almost complete deregulation in the 1990s. He gives special attention to the intriguing phenomenon of how official policies were altered in response to spontaneous institutional adjustments springing from economic and political pressures.

Emmanuel de Dios in Chapter 10 surveys the institutional organizations of Philippine governance in the period since independence, and their influence on economic growth and development. He looks at models of behaviour contained within the respective legislative and executive branches of national government, and at how the constituent processes and policy outcomes within these institutional frameworks were influenced towards change by altering political scenarios and balances of power. David Vines in Chapter 11 turns to the organization and operation of global financial and trade institutions, concentrating on ways in which these relate to Southeast Asia. He analyses what he judges to be the key roles of the International Monetary Fund, the World Bank and the World Trade Organization, exploring what have now become urgent needs for adjustment of those bodies in light of the recent financial crisis. He further addresses, in relation to trade liberalization, the collective East Asian institutional approach of 'open regionalism', contrasting this with the trade bloc system exemplified by the European Union and the North American Free Trade Agreement, and assessing its merits as a strategy of adjustment in the period ahead.

Finally, Colin Barlow in Chapter 12 draws the discussions of individual chapters together, assessing the experiences and analyses of the case studies in relation to the theoretical framework presented by Justin Lin. He identifies further aspects of institutional development and change emerging from the cases, also summarizing basic indications arising from the book and indicating desirable directions of future institutional development in Southeast Asia.

This book makes a valuable contribution to the institutional debate, not only in helping to elucidate and inform aspects of institutional theory but also in discussing key issues of institutional development in Southeast Asia and beyond. All chapters do indeed denote the critical role of institutions in economic and social events, and the significance of institutional change to the progress of societies involved. The analyses of national cases illustrate the characteristics and contributions of particular types of institutions across a variety of contexts, lending themselves to useful comparisons. The revealed failure of some institutions to contribute to economic and social progress and the reasons underlying this are also useful features of the discussion, being aspects whose significance for study is emphasized dramatically by the institutional deficiencies made evident by the recent crisis.

The widespread current resurgence of interest in the economic, social and other roles of institutions may be seen as overdue recognition of the vital function exercised by these bodies in peoples' affairs. This book is offered as a further contribution towards increasing understanding of the part played by these arrangements of society, and the ways in which they may be influenced towards more effective performance in the pursuit of human welfare.

NOTE

1. This is the region encompassing ten countries: Indonesia, the Philippines, Vietnam, Thailand, Malaysia, Singapore, Cambodia, Laos, Burma and Brunei. This book focuses chiefly on the first five of these countries.

2. An Economic Theory of Institutional Change[1]

Justin Yifu Lin

The relevance of institutions and institutional changes to economic development has been realized in the writings of classical economists such as David Hume, Adam Smith and John Stuart Mill. However, attempts to focus on more mathematically tractable topics have caused most neoclassical economists to take a simple approach to institutions and institutional changes. In their construction of economic models, the market institutions of modern Western economies are often taken as given, and include well-defined property rights, perfect information and frictionless transactions. Alternative institutional arrangements are irrelevant in this context, because the market performs the function of resource allocation more efficiently than other institutional arrangements. Government interventions are warranted only when market failures occur.

Nevertheless, different institutions exist side by side with markets even in the most advanced economies. For example, large modern hierarchical business enterprises compete with markets as alternative institutions in coordinating production and allocating resources. The above neoclassical assumptions are particularly inadequate for analysing many economic problems in underdeveloped areas, where factor and output markets are imperfect. They mean that the applicability of modern economics to analysing and solving a variety of economic issues in less developed countries (LDCs) is limited.

Fortunately, there is growing realization of the limitations of mainstream neoclassical economics in treating ideal market institutions as implicitly or explicitly given. A number of economists have attempted to extend the neoclassical framework to endogenize the choice of institutions. Attention has been increasingly given to the role of costs of information and transactions in determining efficient institutions in market economies (Arrow 1974; Williamson 1975, 1985), rural economies (Binswanger and Rosenzweig 1986) and primitive societies (Posner 1980). The same analytical framework has also been extended to explain the change of institutions over time (Schultz 1968; Davis and North 1970; North and Thomas 1970; North 1981; Hayami and Ruttan 1971; Binswanger and Ruttan 1978; Hayami and Kikuchi 1982).

This chapter draws on these recent ideas to analyse the functions and choices of institutions. The purpose is to show that institutions provide useful services, and that their choices and changes can be analysed in a demand-and-supply framework. Special attention is given to the role of the state in the process of institutional change in an economy.

THE FUNCTIONS OF INSTITUTIONS

The Need for Institutions

In the most general sense, an institution can be perceived as a set of behavioural rules commonly observed by individuals in a society.[2] The reasons why institutions are indispensable for human beings need to be explained in terms both of the limitation of human ability and of the environment in which human beings live.

One of the most robust assumptions in economics is that 'men are rational'. By 'rationality', economists mean that individuals, when confronted with real choices in exchange, will choose 'more' rather than 'less'. This approach to human behaviour, according to Becker, distinguishes economics from other social sciences (Becker 1976, Chapter 1). Following Becker's approach, it is assumed that individuals have stable preferences 'defined over fundamental aspects of life, such as health, prestige, sensual pleasure, benevolence, or envy', which are denoted as 'commodities' (p. 5).[3] An individual uses purchased goods as well as personal time to produce those commodities which maximize personal preference. Therefore an individual is not solely concerned with material gains or money income. Although an individual is rational, that rationality is limited or bounded: first, by a neurophysical ability to receive, store, retrieve, and process information and a language ability to make knowledge or feelings understood by others (Williamson 1975, Chapter 2); and second, by the costs of collecting information to make decisions for every contingency.

Bounded rationality explains the need for behavioural rules, but does not explain why the rules should be commonly observed by individuals in a society. The latter follows, on the one hand, from the cycle of individual life, uncertainties from health and the production process, and disasters from nature, and on the other, from gains secured through technological economies of scale and internalizing externalities. Because of life-cycle aspects, human beings need institutions to facilitate cooperation with others, to make provisions for security when they are young and old, to even out income and consumption over time, and to insure against the consequence of risks and disasters. These are referred to as the 'security functions' of institutions. Again, because an individual as a unit of production is too small to secure the above economies, collective actions enabled by institutions are required. These are referred to as the 'economy functions' of institutions. Security and economy are the basic reasons for the existence of institutions.

An Economic Inquiry into Institutions

Before further investigation, it is pertinent to distinguish two related concepts concerning institutions.

An 'institutional arrangement' is defined as a set of commonly observed behavioural rules that governs a specific pattern of actions and relationships. An institutional arrangement can be formal or informal. Examples of formal institutional arrangements are families, firms, labour unions, hospitals, universities, governments, money, future markets and so on. Examples of informal institutional arrangements are values, ideologies and customs.[4] When the term 'institution' is used by economists, it generally refers to an institutional arrangement. A second concept is the 'institutional structure', which is defined as the totality of institutional arrangements, both formal and informal, in a society. As will become clear in the next section, an institutional change usually only refers to the change in a particular institutional arrangement, with other arrangements in the structure remaining unchanged. Failure to distinguish between these two concepts has caused some controversy in the literature about the possibility of endogenizing institutional change (Field 1981).

Institutional arrangements are means of achieving the benefits of collective actions, having the fundamental justifications of security and economy. Yet, since individual rationality does not necessarily imply group rationality, it is in the interest of each individual to seek the most favourable personal result. Conflicts of interest may arise, with collective actions creating problems that do not exist when individuals work alone. Among these problems are cheating, shirking, free-riding[5] and moral hazard.[6] Again, individuals in a group often have to assess the quality of other people's work or contributions, with information about quality in many circumstances being very costly, uncertain or even impossible to obtain. To alleviate these problems, institutional arrangements are created to perform the functions of monitoring, enforcement and so forth. Laws, social mores and ideology are some institutional arrangements in this regard.

Prominent among economy institutions are property-rights institutions, which have the function of internalizing externalities (Alchian 1995; Demsetz 1967). Property rights are formal or informal rules that delimit an individual's or group's rights over their assets (including their own labour), incorporating rights to consume, obtain income from, and alienate the assets. The gains from exchanges of goods, services and assets among different agents resulting from such property rights can both improve resource allocation and smooth consumption patterns over time. Property rights embody a crucial economic institution; they also illustrate the importance of the redistributive function of an institution. These rights are seldom neutral with respect to distributing the gains of specialization and exchange. Distribution may in fact be the dominant role for many institutional arrangements.

Institutions Matter

Institutions perform several different functions in an economy. At a very early stage of human history, basic functions were probably all internalized in a few institutions, such as the family, tribe or kinship relations. In these institutions, every individual had a fair amount of knowledge about other persons involved. Production techniques were simple. Most exchanges were personal and repeating. Opportunistic behaviour was rare because it was easily detected. As an economy develops, however, production and exchange become increasingly complex and the institutional structure changes accordingly. Each arrangement tends to have a more well-defined and more specialized function. Moreover, a similar function can often be performed by several competing institutional arrangements. Institutions are interesting subjects for study in development economics precisely because of this, and different arrangements may have divergent implications for economic growth and distribution.

The efficiency of an institutional arrangement depends on many factors: these include the technical nature of the production process, the existence or absence of other auxiliary institutions having the function of mitigating opportunism, and so on. Some economists assume that competition – actual or potential – among alternative arrangements assures the emergence of efficient institutions, and that existing institutions in an economy must therefore be efficient. For this proposition to be true in all cases, several preconditions are required: first, at the beginning of every production cycle, institutions must be adjusted anew according to such conditions as changes in technology and factor endowments; and second, changes in institutions must be costless. Matthews (1986) has pointed out that if these two conditions are met, institutions are in continual and quick adaptation, and institutional change is a necessary concomitant to economic growth. It is not in these circumstances meaningful to consider institutional change as an independent 'determinant' of economic growth.

Another more likely scenario is that institutions may not always evolve 'efficiently'. Basu, Jones and Schlicht (1987) have suggested it is quite possible that some institutional alternatives are eliminated from the feasible institutional choice set by historical precedent. Moreover, some existing institutions may not be efficient and this is known to their members, yet such people may not have sufficient motivation to do anything about it if each fears being penalized (by ostracism or otherwise) for not adhering to existing institutional rules. If institutional inertia can persist even when no member of society benefits from it, it should not be surprising that such inertia frequently exists when only some members of society are disadvantaged by it. Last but by no means least, an efficient institutional arrangement may be excluded from the individual agents' choice set by the restrictive policies of government or the prohibitions of customs and conventions.

How effectively an institutional arrangement performs its intended function depends on how well it copes with the likely opportunism of agents operating within it. It is likewise true that the seriousness of agents' opportunistic behaviour may vary according to the existence and strength of other institutional arrangements in the institutional structure. For example, the managerial discretionary behaviour in modern corporations is greatly mitigated by the existence of competitive product markets, managerial labour markets and stock markets (Alchian and Demsetz 1972; Fama 1980). A corporation may be expected to perform differently depending on whether it is with or without these markets. Similarly, the effectiveness of constitutions, laws, property rights and political systems also depends on the function of other arrangements. It is indisputable that the constitution of the United States of America has made great contributions to its economic development since its independence. However, although a similar constitution was adopted in many Latin American countries after their independence in the nineteenth century, it did not produce the same effect as in the United States (North 1990, Chapter 11). Again, while the property rights systems of Western countries have been introduced to many less developed countries, they have not brought out the expected efficiencies. In all these cases, the written rules of an institutional arrangement – be it the modern corporation, constitution or property rights – are almost exactly the same, but enforcement mechanisms, behavioural norms and ideologies of actors are different. It thus appears that the performance of a specific institutional arrangement does not depend only on its formal written rules but also on the functions of other arrangements in the institutional structure. An apparently common institutional arrangement can accordingly lead to dramatically different outcomes in societies where there are subtle differences in other arrangements of their institutional structures.

This discussion indicates that the phrase 'institutions matter' has two important implications: (a) differences in the institutional arrangements of an economy will cause its economic performance and rate of economic growth to diverge; and (b) the effectiveness of a specific institutional arrangement depends on the functions of other arrangements in the institutional structure. Because 'institutions matter', there is important motivation to reform inefficient institutional arrangements in an economy. Nonetheless, it is also evident that an institutional reform is not a simple matter of transplanting some successful arrangement in one economy to another, without first considering the functions and characteristics of other arrangements in the institutional structure.

AN ECONOMIC APPROACH TO INSTITUTIONAL CHANGE

A number of institutional arrangements can perform a given institutional service, and the choice of an arrangement thus involves the calculus of costs and benefits. In conventional cost-benefit analysis only production costs are taken into account, and optimality is obtained when the values of marginal products of each input are equalized. Yet the costs in the choice of an institutional arrangement additionally include those of organizing, maintaining and enforcing the rules of the particular arrangement. These latter items are referred to as 'transactions costs'.

Theoretically it is easy to say that, with given production and transactions costs, one institutional arrangement is more efficient than another if it provides more services. Alternatively, for two institutional arrangements that provide the same amount of service, the one with lower costs is the more efficient. The two different types of factor that affect the efficiency of an institutional arrangement are accordingly those affecting production efficiency and those determining transaction efficiency, both fundamentally functions of technology. Since an institutional arrangement is embedded in an institutional structure, its efficiency further depends on how well other institutional arrangements perform their functions.

The study of an institutional arrangement's performance requires specific knowledge of its history as well as of the region and institutional structure within which it is situated. In the absence of such understanding, discussion of the efficiency of a particular arrangement is without substance. The direction and scope of institutional change are not random, and can be subjected to rigorous economic analysis. A profitable approach in this context is to investigate why new institutional arrangements are innovated, and how they are adopted.

Sources of Institutional Disequilibrium

An institutional arrangement will be chosen from a set of possible arrangements if it is more efficient than the other arrangements in this choice set, taking both production and transactions costs into account. For an induced institutional change to occur, there must be profitable opportunities that arise from institutional disequilibrium; for some reason the existing institutional arrangement is no longer the most efficient in the choice set. Starting from an original equilibrium point, institutional disequilibrium can arise from four different sources: (a) changes in the institutional choice set; (b) changes in

General

technology; (c) long-run changes in relative factor and product prices; and (d) changes in other institutional arrangements. Each of these four sources, in turn, consists of several different factors.

Changes in the institutional choice set

Just as the set of feasible production technologies is a function of knowledge in physics, chemistry and other natural sciences, the set of feasible institutional arrangements for a particular institutional services depends on knowledge in the social sciences. Ruttan (1984) has argued forcefully that the demand for knowledge in economics and other social sciences, as well as in related professions such as law, business and social services, is derived primarily from a desire for institutional change and improvements in institutional performance. Advances in the social sciences improve the bounded rationality of the human mind, and therefore increase individuals' ability not only to manage existing institutional arrangements but also to perceive and innovate new ones.

An institutional choice set may also be enlarged by contacts with other economies, paralleling the way in which such contacts may increase the available technological choice set. Bauer (1984, p. 12) has emphasized the roles of individual traders in bringing new technology and institutional arrangements, as a result encouraging people to 'question existing habits and mores, and promoting the uncoerced erosion of attitudes and customs uncongenial to material progress'. The achievement of institutional change through borrowing other societies' institutional arrangements greatly decreases the costs of investment in basic social science research. However, as the efficiency of an institutional arrangement depends on other related arrangements, adaptations are often required for a transferred arrangement to perform its functions effectively.[7]

Finally, the institutional choice set can be enlarged or contracted by a change in government policies. When government places a new constraint on the institutional choice set and this constraint is binding, institutional disequilibrium will result, and a less efficient arrangement may become dominant in the restricted set. Thus the emergence of subtenancy in Philippine villages surveyed by Hayami and Kikuchi (1982) is a result of the restriction of rent by the land reform law. On the other hand, removing a restrictive government policy has the same effect as enlarging the choice set.

Changes in technology

Marx's view that the institutional structure of a society is fundamentally conditioned by technology (Marx and Engels [1818–83] 1968, pp. 182–3) is shared by the author. Changes in technology will also alter the relative efficiencies of particular institutional arrangements and make other arrangements inoperative. The impacts of technological change can be analysed through their effects on both production and transaction aspects.

Regarding production, new institutional arrangements are often required to take advantage of new potential externalities or to modify the partitioning of new income streams among factor owners and economic sectors. An example of the first case is the dominance of modern firms over traditional family workshops in manufacturing industry, which is a response to the size demanded by the use of machinery in the production process (Brewster 1950). An example of the second case is the effect in the Philippines of new high-yielding varieties of rice and increased availability of labour in causing the replacement of the *hunusan* by the *gama* contract. The former gives all villagers the right to participate in harvesting and receive one-sixth of the yield, while the latter gives an exclusive right of harvesting for the same share to restricted workers who do weeding without receiving a wage (Hayami and Kikuchi 1982, Chapter 5). The innovation of the *gama* system is clearly induced by the desire to modify the partition of the new income stream between landowners and labourers.

Regarding transactions costs, changes in technology may affect these and make originally inoperative institutional arrangements operative. This is illustrated by the sphere of private property rights whose establishment requires, among other things, that the benefits to the owner from the rights are greater than the costs of excluding others from using the property. When these costs are too high, property will be commonly owned, as is generally true of grazing land owing to high charges for fencing. The innovation of low-cost barbed-wire fencing, however, resulted in private ownership and leasing of public grazing land in the American West (Anderson and Hill 1975). Again, property managements are affected by the innovation of tractors and other farm machinery, which greatly reduce costs of supervision, since it is easier to supervise one driver than many manual workers; hence there is a tendency when such innovation occurs to shift from sharecropping to owner operating or to operating with wage workers (Day 1967).

Long-run changes in relative factor and product prices

There are major reasons behind many alterations in historical property-rights arrangements. A rise in the relative price of a factor makes ownership of that factor relatively more profitable compared with other factors. A rise in the price of a product likewise makes exclusive use of factors used to produce this product more attractive. North and Thomas (1973) suggest that the shift from property rights in man to property rights in land in medieval Europe was a result of an increase in population and in land scarcity, which increased the relative price of land. Feeny (1982) likewise finds that the transfer from property rights in man to property rights in land in Thailand between the mid-nineteenth century and early twentieth century can be explained by increases in population and in export demand for rice during that period. Again in England, increases in the price of food made enclosure of open fields and common pasture into private units profitable. McCloskey (1975) estimates that, despite high costs of fencing, such enclosure yielded a yearly rate of return of the order of 17 per cent.

Changes in other institutional arrangements

As previously indicated, the performances of institutional arrangements within a structure are interdependent, with a change in a particular arrangement sometimes resulting in changes in the demand for the services of other arrangements. Thus the sense of honour, which was such a prominent trait in primitive and ancient societies, can be explained by the lack of a formal law-enforcement arrangement. It increased the probability of retaliating, and was therefore an important device for keeping society in order (Posner 1980). However, once the modern state became the sole legitimate institutional arrangement with the right to use coercive force and retaliation, and once duels were forbidden, honour became less significant although it was still valued. Again, the 'subsistence ethic' in pre-industrialized society can be explained by the low level of agricultural productivity and limited potential size of market. As well, the patron–client relationship is a mutual-help and transactions-cost-saving device which is a substitute for a set of specialized markets in labour, land, credit and insurance (Hayami and Kikuchi 1982, Chapter 2). This relationship is then restricted by the expansion of markets (Polanyi 1944).

The Dynamics of Induced Institutional Change

New institutional arrangements will be introduced to take advantage of profitable opportunities arising from the institutional disequilibria discussed above. However, the rationality of the human mind is bounded, and it is beyond its capacity to perceive all necessary changes and design all optimal arrangements at the same time.

Setting up a new institutional arrangement is also a time-, effort- and resource-consuming process. Individuals with different experiences and roles in the structure will furthermore have different perceptions of the degree and source of disequilibrium. They will also seek different ways of partitioning gains from the change. For a new set of behaviour rules to become commonly accepted and adopted, negotiation and agreement among individuals are required. It is hence likely that when disequilibrium occurs, the process of institutional change will start from one arrangement and spread only gradually to other arrangements. The process will take place in a historically determined political and social structure, and be conditioned by this structure. Consequently, some arrangements favourable from an abstract theoretical point of view will not be viable because of incompatibility with other existing arrangements in the structure. The process can be seen as path-dependent (North 1990, Chapter 11), with institutional change being an evolutionary process subject to a number of factors (Alchian 1950; Nelson and Winter 1982).

Society as a whole gains from a new institutional arrangement that captures profitable opportunities arising from institutional disequilibrium.[8] Whether such innovation takes place, however, depends on expected gains and costs to individual innovators. The costs to innovators include not only the time, effort and other resources involved in creating the new rules and getting them to be commonly accepted, but also likely social pressures on them for 'violating' existing social rules.

Innovations in an institutional arrangement will generally encounter both externality and free-rider problems. The externality problem may arise because the arrangement is not patentable; when it is innovated, other groups of individuals can imitate it and dramatically reduce their costs of organizing and devising it. This means that returns to the innovator are less than returns to society as a whole. Because of this problem, the intensity and frequency of institutional innovations will be less than the optimal number for society as a whole, with institutional disequilibria resulting as a consequence.

The free-rider problem may occur because an institutional arrangement is a public good. Once it is innovated and instituted, all individuals governed by it will receive the same service whether or not they were engaged in its introduction. Yet the free-rider problem will also be attenuated by the ideological convictions of individuals; if the new arrangement is in conformity with their ideas of a fair world, the premium required for them to free-ride will be larger. The free-rider problem will also depend on how the group of individuals is related; if the mobility of members is high, for example, free-riding is more likely to happen because a given person's behaviour is less likely to be detected. It will further hinge on group structuring, where, in a tightly structured community, 'people are less individualistic and conform to social norms more closely' with free-riding problems being less severe (Hayami and Kikuchi 1982, p. 36).

The free-rider problem means that the role of political or institutional entrepreneurs is especially crucial in innovating institutions. A political entrepreneur is someone 'who is generally trusted (feared), or who can guess who is bluffing in the bargaining, or who can simply save bargaining time and can sometimes work out an arrangement that is better for all concerned than any outcome that could emerge without entrepreneurial leadership or organization' (Olson 1965, p. 176). Institutional disequilibrium may affect individuals differently so that the success of a political entrepreneur depends, among other things, on the ability to design a partitioning of potential profits that seems to make everyone better off and appears to be in conformity with people's own ideologies.

The political entrepreneur will articulate new goals and set up new rules if the resulting gains are believed to be greater than the costs. These gains are not necessarily material and can, for example, comprise social prestige or political support. The costs to the entrepreneur will be smaller if that person can mobilize political support from government agencies or local vested-interest groups (Hayami and Kikuchi 1982, Chapter 2). However, getting such support implies that the new institutional arrangement may be detrimental to some individuals, because once coercive power is applied, consensus is no longer a necessary condition for the innovation.

THE POLITICAL ECONOMY OF INSTITUTIONAL CHANGE

Because an institutional arrangement is a public good and the free-rider and externality problems are intrinsic to the innovation process, the state has a potential role as an intervenor in institutional change. But intervention also incurs costs and benefits, and there is no certain guarantee that the state will take the initiative or that its policies will succeed. The state can fail either because it does too little or too much. Unless the behaviour of the state can be explained, however, the process of institutional change cannot be fully analysed.

Economic Approaches to the State

The state, according to Weber's definition (Frohlich and Oppenheimer 1974, p. 4), is the institutional arrangement that has a monopoly over legitimate use of coercion in a given area. The basic functions of the state are to provide law and order and protect property rights, in return for tax payments. Normatively, the most desirable state might be a minimal one 'limited to the narrow functions of protection against force, theft, fraud, enforcement of contracts, and so on' (Nozick 1974, p. ix). In reality however, the state – in its role of a monopolist in the legitimate use of coercive power – can extend its sphere of influence well beyond these functions. A more interesting question is whether the state has the incentive and ability to design and set up suitable institutional arrangements when these cannot be provided by the induced innovation process.

According to Findlay (1990), states currently existing in the less developed countries of Asia, Africa and Latin America range from traditional monarchies through traditional dictatorships, right-wing and left-wing authoritarian regimes, to democracies. Each state has its unique ideology and political organization. Almost all states in less developed countries, however, tend to dominate civil society and have substantial autonomy in policy-making. A useful framework for studying the behaviour of autonomous states in such countries is, therefore, the multiple-level, principal–agent framework.

At the first level of such a framework, the head of the state – the ruler – can be treated as the agent of either the people, as in Locke or Rousseau, or the ruling class, as in Marxian variants. The ruler (king, dictator, president, prime minister, or behind-the-scenes supreme leader) is a rational person. Within such a framework the problem of principal–agent analysis is that of monitoring the activities of the ruler to see whether or not the implicit social contract is being adhered to. The problem is compounded by the fact that the ruler is empowered with a legal monopoly on the use of force, having a substantial degree of autonomy in pursuing personal preferences in policy decisions within constraints determined by the legitimacy surrounding the head of state, the legal tradition of the society and other cultural endowments.

Since the power, prestige and wealth of the ruler depend ultimately on the wealth of the state, a rational person in this position has an incentive to maintain a set of institutions including: (a) property rights arrangements that facilitate production and trade; (b) a judicial system for settling disputes and enforcing contracts; and (c) weights and measures that reduce measurement costs and potential for rent dissipation (Barzel 1982; Cheung 1974). Since the compliance costs of the political system depend on the perceived legitimacy of the ruler, that person will invest in ideological education to promote this amongst constituents.

At the second level of the principal–agent framework, the ruler has to employ bureaucrats as agents to assist in implementing law and order, collecting taxes, inflicting punishments, securing national sovereignty and providing other public services. An efficient bureaucracy enables the ruler to govern. Nevertheless, bureaucrats are rational individuals whose interests will not completely coincide with those of their principal, and they will attempt to use the authority delegated to them to benefit themselves at the expense of the ruler or state. Since the costs of supervising a bureaucrat's discretionary behaviour are convex, the ruler can reduce these by implementing a reward system that promotes loyalty and inculcates an ideology that encourages honest and unselfish commitment to office.[9] However, since discretionary behaviour by bureaucrats cannot be completely eliminated even in totalitarian states, the power of ruling is shared between ruler and bureaucrats.

Sources of Policy Failures

As the economy develops, existing property rights, laws, norms and other institutions may become inefficient. Although some disequilibria will be removed

by private initiatives, some will persist because of divergences between private
and social benefits and costs. Here the state can play an essential role in restoring
institutional equilibrium. Most politicians also see institutional change as a source
of economic development, because they have a comparative advantage in
bringing about such change (Matthews 1986). However, states in less developed
countries often fail to introduce institutional reforms which result in sustained
economic growth. The principal–agent model suggests several alternative
explanations for what will be referred to as 'policy failures'.

One explanation for such failures flows from the preferences and bounded
rationality of the ruler. The latter may not promote institutional adjustment owing
to expectations of lower personal benefits and higher transactions costs, as well
as to an inability either to comprehend the disequilibrium or institute the
necessary new arrangements. It may be too that the ruler prefers military or
other kinds of prestige over nationally desirable institutional adjustment. Another
explanation for failures may be ideological rigidity, flowing from the ruler's
perception that introducing new institutional arrangements will undermine
accepted doctrine with its important function of legitimizing the *status quo*. In
these circumstances it may be seen as best to maintain old inefficient
organizations.

Bureaucrats employed by the ruler may be expected to oppose institutional
reform if it runs counter to their interests. If bureaucratic losers in a change do
not receive compensation, and this is usually the case, they will obstruct reform,
and the ruler who fears reduced political support will not pursue it. Furthermore,
the monopoly power of the ruler is constrained by potential rivals within or
without the state, who can provide the same set of services. Groups of constituents
having good access to such rivals possess high bargaining power, and change
will not be effected if the ruler sees it as driving groups into other camps while
benefits from remaining constituents do not compensate for harm thus incurred
(North 1981, Chapter 3). Failures to make efficient institutional reforms may
further be attributed to the promotion by powerful groups of new arrangements
redistributing income towards themselves, even though such changes reduce
the growth of the overall economy (Olson 1982). They may also be caused by
limitations in social science knowledge, where these entail both ignorance of
the possibility of better institutional arrangements and lack of the capacity to
implement them even if they are recognized.

It therefore appears that questions such as 'Should the strategy of reforms
be gradual or big bang?' and 'Should political reforms precede economic
reforms?' can be answered only with a good grasp of the delicate balance of
power between various groups, the legitimacy of the government, the political
skill of the ruler, the capacity of the bureaucracy, and other related aspects.
Research on the dynamic issue of reforms has started to appear only recently,

especially after the dramatic events in Eastern Europe and the former Soviet Union. However, the development of the link between theory in general and country-specific knowledge in particular has lagged far behind the demand. Institutional reform in a country has accordingly to proceed very often on a 'trial and error' basis, with success remaining heavily dependent on the luck and the ingenuity of political leaders.[10]

CONCLUSION

Individuals in any society, primitive and capitalist alike, face uncertainty and the possibility of disasters, in addition to the life cycle of their working abilities. They hope to survive and achieve a high level of satisfaction. Institutions can be defined as the behaviour rules commonly observed by the individuals of a society. They are human devices designed to cope with uncertainty and increase individual utility. Institutions, whether market or non-market, provide useful services in this regard.

Like other services, those of institutions are obtained with certain costs. Given the technology, transactions costs are the core in choosing competitive institutional arrangements in a society, and the arrangement which costs least to provide a given amount of service will be the most desirable. Replacing an existing institutional arrangement with another alternative is an expensive process, however, and unless the net gains to individuals outweigh the costs, voluntary institutional change will not occur.

Institutional changes often require collective action, and an institutional arrangement once innovated becomes a public good. Free-riders are thus an innate issue, and the voluntary supply of new institutional arrangements will be less than optimal. In addition, institutional arrangements are interrelated in society, where the efficiency of a particular arrangement cannot be assessed without first referring to others connected to it. It is true furthermore that, because of different cultural and other conditions, an institutional arrangement efficient in one society may not be efficient in another.

The state is the most important institutional arrangement in society and is able to take action to rectify the undersupply of institutions. However, a theory of the state is required to understand if the state has incentives to fulfil this role. Almost all less developed countries (LDCs) share the characteristic of tending to dominate civil society and of having substantial autonomy in policy-making. A useful framework for studying the behaviour of the state in LDCs is therefore the multiple-level, principal–agent framework. The state will innovate a new institution only to the extent that the benefits to it are higher than the costs, but for several reasons may also fail to institute the most efficient arrangements. These include the bounded rationality of the ruler, ideological aspects, group interest conflicts, and limited social science knowledge.

The theory of institutions and institutional change is one of the least developed spheres of modern economics. Research on institutions and institutional change in less developed countries may contribute not only to institutional reforms in those nations but to the development of economic theory in general.

NOTES

1. This chapter draws heavily on Lin (1989).
2. This is the definition given by Schultz (1968) in his celebrated paper. See also Field (1981) and North (1981, Chapter 15).
3. Becker's approach to the allocation of time, household production and social interactions is especially relevant for the study of institutions and institutional change. His papers about these subjects are collected in Becker (1976). The arguments that enter his utility function consist of senses, riches, address, friendship, good reputation, power, piety, benevolence, malevolence, knowledge, memory, imagination, hope, association and relief of pain (p.137).
4. Families, firms, hospitals, universities etc. are institutions not because of their physical buildings but because of the rules that organize the behaviour of individuals within them.
5. 'Free-riding' refers to the problem that occurs in a group when an individual automatically receives the service provided by the group even without contributing to the costs. To overcome the problem, a group needs to be able to provide selective incentives to members which encourage them to work for group goals (Olson 1965).
6. Moral hazard in the principal–agent literature refers to the case in which a worker contributes less effort than the value of his pay because of asymmetrical information or imperfect monitoring.
7. Although in the very long run institutional arrangements and structures of different societies may converge, in the short run the most efficient institutional arrangements will diverge among societies with distinct sociopolitical histories. Many journalists and politicians unfortunately fail to see this point, using the institutional arrangements of their own countries to judge the institutional arrangements of other societies.
8. Some institutional innovations are motivated purely by attempts to redistribute existing social income. In addition to some individuals losing out, society as a whole may also lose out because the innovation is a resource-consuming process. However, such an innovation will not generally be voluntary, and will usually be imposed by the government. This type of change is discussed in the next section.
9. In the modern Third World, the rewards given to bureaucrats by a ruler typically come not out of the latter's personal resources but from assigned jobs, import licences or contracts (Findlay 1990).
10. The sources of policy failures are treated in more detail by Lin (1989).

PART II

Institutions in Particular Markets

3. Institutions of Change in Rural Development: Mediating Markets for New Crop Technologies in Sumatra

Colin Barlow

This chapter is concerned with the process of developing the market for new rubber varieties, thus facilitating their introduction to Indonesian smallholdings in Sumatra. New technologies of this nature are basic to securing enhanced crop productivity and higher farm incomes, and learning to introduce them successfully is crucial for both Indonesia and the vast, smallholding, tree-crop sector of world agriculture. Reviewing the Indonesian experience in working towards such improvement and in establishing suitable facilitating organizations provides useful insights into institutional change in economic development.

The broad economic scenario of development in such rural contexts is already clear at a rather general level. Population growth acts to raise the scarcity and price of cultivable land, and Boserup (1965) describes how people are then stimulated to intensify their crop production and develop technologies enabling them to do so. Such people are encouraged to move to higher-yielding, land-saving methods which, at the same time, often require more capital. Pressures of this nature currently apply to the small Indonesian rubber growers whose case is examined here. However, adoption of new methods is usually constrained by 'incomplete markets', characterized by poor and inaccurate information, lack of active trading institutions and deficient infrastructures and services. Basically, steps must be taken to overcome such barriers and to encourage institutional arrangements within which economically desirable development can take place.

This chapter first reviews the general features of institutional change accompanying the economic transformation of societies. The particular instance of rubber smallholders in Sumatra is then examined, with a scrutiny both of traditional institutional structures and influences of change now impinging on them. Two contrasting types of new institutional arrangement helping to promote adoption of modern rubber varieties – planting material nurseries which have arisen as a response of the private sector and smallholder block development schemes which have been sponsored by government – are next analysed. Finally, the wider implications and conclusions from the Indonesian situation are drawn out.

GENERAL FEATURES OF INSTITUTIONAL CHANGE

In real life, markets do not have the frictionless transactions, perfect information and costlessly established property rights envisaged in much neoclassical economic theory. Even the French potato markets so carefully studied by Leon Walras in the 1860s did not approach his famous concept of a frictionless competitive economy, needing only certain institutional arrangements to underpin them. These arrangements paralleled those in other contexts in their 'economy' functions of internalizing gains from economies of scale and externalities, and 'security' functions of smoothing out production and consumption and limiting uncertainty (Lin 1989, p. 8, and Chapter 2, this volume).[1]

Economic and social activities in all situations are in fact featured by institutions undertaking economy and security functions, in a manner at least partially adapted to particular conditions. Thus Binswanger and Rosenzweig (1986) examine production relations in different types of agriculture, showing how various institutional arrangements arise to perform relevant economic tasks. The institution of paying piece rates in crop harvesting, for example, is only used where output is measurable in quantitative and qualitative terms, as applies to grains but not to apples, which are easily damaged (p. 520). The institution of large plantations has only emerged in the production of crops possessing technical-scale economies in processing and maintenance; these crops include sugar cane and bananas (p. 527), as well as oil palm and rubber. Many crops do not possess these economies, and are best produced in a small farm arrangement whose economic and social merits are discussed below.

Robertson and Langlois (1992) have explored this institutional adaptation theme with reference to manufacturing industries, showing how various organizational forms have arisen according to particular technological and other demands, as well as to stages of firms' life-cycles and historical conditions. They discuss the emergence in the nineteenth century of large, vertically-integrated companies to innovate and produce mass consumption items in an era when fragmented information and other facilities did not support this activity through small independent companies. In more modern times, however, with better communications technology, the large companies were partly replaced by networks of smaller agencies performing the generation of innovations and other basic economic tasks more efficiently.

It is likewise important to note, however, that determinants of institutional arrangements, adaptation and change are rarely straightforward, and frequently defy neat identification. Thus Field (1981) argued that a narrow focus on 'efficient economic organization' and an assumption that 'rules [as the basis of institutional structures] can be understood as resulting from the endogenous interaction of agents in an economic model which makes no appeal to some set of rules specified exogenously' needs to be questioned, if not rejected (p. 194). Field particularly directed his critique at the work of North and Thomas (1973), who attempted to demonstrate how the organization of European agriculture responded over 700 years to an endogenously induced institutional innovation impelled by price signals.

North and Thomas set out, for example, to explain the substitution in the thirteenth century of money payments or payments in kind for 'direct labour services' under the previous feudal system; they attributed this to the fact that transactions costs of the latter arrangement were much lower under the, then, monetizing economy (p. 60). Field offered trenchant criticisms of this and other similarly grounded interpretations, indicating their inconclusive nature as well as the fact that exogenously determined rules were often critical in determining actual outcomes. Thus Field (1981, p. 192) believed North and Thomas failed to explain a later widespread reversion to direct labour services despite the continuing advance of monetization, drawing attention to wider exogenous movements contained in various political events. He stressed the basic supposition of neoclassical theory that not only tastes, technologies and endowments but also rules (and accompanying institutional structures) are the variables which need to be regarded as exogenous in many economic and social circumstances.

Indeed, as Marx ([1858] 1972) showed in making institutions a focal point of his analyses, it is usually impossible to distinguish which variables are unambiguously endogenous and exogenous, or to clarify fully factors concerned in institutional change. In practice one is faced by complex situations where most economic and social factors are closely interlinked, where ideological and political elements in wider society are not independent of these factors, and where other institutions in the overall structure also influence what happens. The latter suggestion in particular is echoed by Justin Lin in Chapter 2. The comments of Marx, Field and others manifestly apply to the ideas cited above of Boserup (1965), Binswanger and Rosensweig (1986) and Robertson and Langlois (1992). But although Hayami and Kikuchi (1982, as quoted in Chapter 4, this volume) partly attribute alterations in labour-hiring institutions in Java to endogenous economic changes, they refer as well to the exogenous factor of differences between 'tightly knit' and 'loosely structured' villages. Chris Manning in his treatment of changes in labour-hiring institutions in Chapter 4 also recognizes the influence of 'interacting political and economic forces' (p. 53), thus bearing out Marx's prescription above. Analyses of institutional change should accordingly look carefully at the wide mix of factors involved, and that is the approach of the present chapter.

Despite the demonstrated adaptability of institutions in general, there are many constraints on institutional adjustment to change, with these notably including incomplete markets. Hence, entrepreneurs and other intending improvers are faced with devising institutional and other means of bridging the consequent gap between the traditional orbit of the village on the one hand, and the modern world of integrated markets and new technologies on the other. This segmented situation was characterized in extreme terms by Boeke (1930) who, after studying early twentieth century Indonesia, postulated a 'dualistic' two-sector society of minimal connections between the traditional orbit and the modern world. The former was almost completely shielded from new influences, while the latter was actively responsive to inducements to change. Although such extreme segmentation is rare in modern times, the division between the two sectors is still apparent both in Indonesia and other poorer countries. Thus although some linkages between sectors are substantial, it is frequently necessary to strengthen others so as to speed economic changes. This too is a theme in what follows.

SMALLHOLDER RUBBER IN SUMATRA

Smallholder rubber in Sumatra is a substantial sector, and in 1998 supported almost 3 million persons cultivating farms of a few hectares in a huge total area of over 2 million planted hectares (personal communication, Direktorat Jenderal Perkebunan, 1998). Such rubber is traditionally tilled on a cycle of 25–30 years, involving first the clearing of scrub or cutting down of old rubber, followed by the planting of new trees and intercropping of dry rice and other short-term items for one to two years. The young trees are then temporarily abandoned until tapping can begin about 10 years after initial planting. Such tapping subsequently continues for 15–20 years, after which the trees are exhausted and need to be replaced. Rubber trees planted under these conditions have been characteristically poor in quality, and even today most new plantings still comprise unimproved low-yielding seedlings of the same provenance as those introduced from Brazil in the early 1900s.

However, since the 1980s in particular, land for expansion has become scarce under pressures both from cultivation advances and from population increases, and land prices have risen markedly. There are growing pressures to intensify production in order to maintain incomes, while economic improvements elsewhere in the Indonesian economy have increased the desire of rural peoples to raise returns from their enterprises. These circumstances, as they apply to rubber smallholders in the province of South Sumatra, have been analysed by Gouyon (1991).

Limited progress in response to such pressures has been made over the past two decades, and by the late 1990s about 500 000 hectares of the total Sumatran rubber smallholding area had been planted with higher-yielding trees under the institutional auspices of government 'block' development schemes, all of which entailed the supervised improvement of groups of smallholdings on large blocks of land (personal communication, Direktorat Jenderal Perkebunan, 1998). Another 100 000 hectares of better trees were estimated as having been developed by individual smallholders in their little plots, employing materials purchased from the further new institution of small private tree nurseries.[2] Currently around 20 000 hectares per year of better trees are being established in Sumatra through a combination of smallholding block schemes and private nurseries, with a balance of 30 000 hectares still being planted under unimproved seedlings, using traditional methods.

Supplying higher-yielding rubber trees through private nurseries and smallholding block schemes are significant institutional innovations in response to economic and social change. The environment of this change and the mechanisms of underlying innovations are now explored for the particular cases of smallholders in the Sumatran provinces of North Sumatra and Riau.

The Pre-existing Structure[3]

The traditional structure of rural society in rubber smallholding areas of North Sumatra and Riau has close parallels elsewhere in the outer islands of Indonesia. The reigning institutions are broadly adjusted to local circumstances, performing pertinent economy and security functions. Hence property rights to what (until recently at least) has been plentiful land generally embody titles based on continued cultivation of particular crops, yet allow reallocation to other kinds of agricultural activity when land becomes idle. Thus farmers continue to possess cultivation rights as long as they tap their rubber, and may also switch to other items provided this too is farmed regularly. There are also barriers to land ownership by those coming from outside local society, which minimize disruptions through incursions of newcomers.

The dominant family smallholding in this structure is well attuned to cultivation of rubber and other traditional crops, all of which have few economies of scale in their production phases. Thus the governance arrangements of the family unit entail the economic advantages of low monitoring and supervision costs, while its workforce is well adapted to the many tasks that need to be performed (Pollak 1985). Its cohesiveness and sharing attributes, and its combination under one umbrella of production and consumption activities, provide important security to its members. Its difficulties over external transactions are overcome by the further traditional and more or less ubiquitous institution of an adjacent dealers' network, providing effective contact with the commercial world for limited wants as well as for sales of rubber and other items.

This institutional conjunction of smallholders and traders is actually quite responsive to economic change, as may be seen in the widespread and ultimately vast adoption of rubber-growing when seeds first appeared in Southeast Asia from Brazil early this century (Schrieke 1929). Similar dynamism and adaptability, albeit within limits, have been exhibited in other traditional structures of Indonesia and elsewhere. Hence Metzner (1982) reported on ways in which institutional flexibility assisted the quick uptake of new crops on the island of Flores in the southern part of eastern Indonesia, while Ruf and Siswoputantro (1995) covered such a phenomenon for cocoa in South and Central Sulawesi.

It is also important to note that village institutions in this traditional structure embody strong predilections for collective action, especially in activities with economies of scale. Thus Indonesian clan groups in particular often collaborate in small cooperatives or *kelompok* in such activities as land-clearing, planting, and constructing social facilities like roads and wells.[4] Clan groups also make collective decisions about land and other property rights adjustments, exercising these in conjunction with elected traditional leaders. These collective capacities once more appear to strengthen communities' abilities to respond to change, exhibiting strong economic advantages as well as important security roles through protection afforded by joint, as opposed to individual, endeavour.

Disequilibrium

As outlined by Justin Lin (this volume, Chapter 2,) a major force pushing towards institutional change springs from disequilibria that indicate the existence of profitable opportunities which could be realized given appropriate adjustments. Current sources of disequilibrium for both rubber and other traditional smallholders mostly arise in the modern world outside the village orbit, and may increasingly be seen as denoting needs for adjustment. The sources in the smallholder-rubber situation may be conveniently classed under the four headings indicated by Lin.

Thus Lin's first source of disequilibrium flows from 'changes in the institutional choice set', where increased knowledge arising from the introduction into smallholding areas of improved schooling, better lines of communication and altered government policies, including enhanced local health and extension services, acted to widen previous bounds on the rationality of local peoples; this subsequently enabled them to operate more complex institutional arrangements, as well as raising their demand for such structures. This first source was connected to an increasingly individualistic and commercialized outlook on the part of rural populations, making them more likely to want to move out of traditional arrangements. Lin's second source of disequilibrium is 'changes in technology' which, in the rubber case, involved the development by government and commercial agencies, essentially in response to population pressure along the lines posited by Boserup (1965), of trees giving yields two to three times those of traditional materials. Other technical changes in the wider Sumatran (and indeed Indonesian) rural context entailed improvements in automobile technologies, which resulted in the availability of trucks and motorcycles. Then, advances in infrastructure technologies permitted the construction of roads and other facilities, bringing down communications charges. The combined advent of automobile and infrastructure technologies enabled large reductions in transport costs

Lin's third source of disequilibrium is 'changes in relative factor and product prices', and notably concerned rises in land costs which stimulated more intensive cultivation including the adoption of higher-yielding rubber trees.[5] It additionally involved the lowering in transport costs just described, which increased relative returns from marketing rubber and other crops. Rubber prices themselves have been mainly in secular decline along with most international commodity prices, although recent major devaluations of the Indonesian rupiah have markedly raised returns from this crop. Finally, Lin's fourth source of disequilibrium in 'changes in other institutional arrangements' chiefly related to the alterations in wider society connected with the rapid economic growth in Indonesia (up to 1997) and an associated rapid spread of the cash economy. This change enhanced the penetration of modern-sector arrangements into the village orbit, providing more stimulus to linkages with the outside world.

All these disequilibria have acted to impel change as the actors concerned have been encouraged to search for new profitable opportunities. Until recently, however, traditional rubber smallholders have made only limited adjustments except in two significant respects: first, in offsetting the effects of land price rises in depressing financial returns by employing more labour in *traditional* techniques, hence securing moderate rises in yields (Barlow and Tomich 1991, p. 37); second, in using the new transport and communications facilities to move out to peripheral lands where further traditional development could be effected. Both adjustments were rational responses to new economic circumstances, and were made without greatly modifying traditional institutions. Such relatively sluggish responses contrasted sharply with those of the modern Sumatran sector of rubber 'estates',[6] where governance arrangements as well as factor and product markets were adapted vigorously and flexibly to handle revised technological and other needs. Hence high-yielding rubber trees and associated new cultivation methods were overwhelmingly taken up by these estates, which had virtually replaced all unimproved rubber areas by the early 1990s.

The slowness of smallholders was basically the result of limited information and skills, in circumstances of bounded rationality where possible fresh avenues of endeavour were not sufficiently evident. Thus, individual cultivators often did not know about improved rubber trees, or if they did know about them, were unable to produce them as a starting point to adopting new rubber technology. Even when such materials became available from external sources, the extra knowledge required to plant and grow them effectively was also frequently absent. To traditional farmers, the new technology was too sophisticated, difficult to master, and subject to uncertainty, and the dominant traditional structures did not assist in mediating it.[7]

It is pertinent to note that the new transport facilities in rural areas became available as a result of the profit-seeking activities of private transport-providing organizations set up in response to the improved automobile technology.[8] The government in turn reacted to the new infrastructure technologies by establishing public works agencies responsible for constructing new roads and other facilities. Both the improved transport and new roads then impinged on rubber smallholders as part of Lin's fourth source of disequilibrium; they comprised a penetration of modern-sector arrangements into the village orbit, encouraging rubber smallholders to move out to faraway lands as described.

However, the government's direct interventions to stimulate change amongst rubber smallholders were less successful. Efforts to bridge the knowledge and skills gap by establishing public planting materials nurseries generally entailed technology and institutional packages in a 'lumpy' form which involved cash expenditures well beyond the resources of individuals or local capital markets. It was only in the 1980s, after 70 years of using the old technology, that a combination of disequilibriating influences created the impetus for private nurseries and a certain kind of smallholding block scheme as substantial innovations, effectively encouraging the adoption of high-yielding trees. These initiatives, which essentially supplemented the traditional situation through new institutional linkages covering the production of better planting materials and their delivery to adopting farmers, are discussed in the following section.

PRIVATE PLANTING MATERIAL NURSERIES

The nurseries selected for case study are the hundreds of tiny commercial units, each covering up to half a hectare and most begun since the early 1980s. They are all in Labuhan Batu district, North Sumatra province, and are located in ethnic Javanese villages inhabited by some of the small Javanese minority amongst Sumatran indigenous peoples. This minority chiefly comprises descendants of migrants who came originally to North Sumatra as labourers on

Dutch estates (Thee 1977). The nurseries grow young high-yielding trees, which are made available in forms suitable for planting on a wide scale.

These trees are sold to both rubber smallholders and rubber estates in surrounding areas, as well as to cultivators in faraway regions including many in Riau province. While some trees are purchased directly from nurseries by demanding farmers, those for distant places are usually marketed through a chain of traders who collect them from producers, consign them in bulk and distribute them through town fairs in consuming areas. Detailed accounts and analyses of these developments have been given by both Zen et al. (1992) and Barlow (1997b). Similar nursery developments have occurred from clusters of Javanese villages elsewhere in North Sumatra, and also in the province of South Sumatra (Nancy et al. 1990).

It is noteworthy that amongst the disequilibriating influences promoting nursery development, the first source cited – 'changes in the institutional choice set' – was significantly enhanced through 'political entrepreneurs' like those described by Justin Lin (this volume, p. 17). Basically these people worked out new nursery production and marketing arrangements, and, in doing so, brought home to farmers and others the new possibilities springing up from the increased knowledge and techniques now available. They broadcast information vigorously and this acted to widen previous bounds on rationality, encouraging some villagers to produce the new planting materials technology and stimulating large numbers of others to purchase it. Such entrepreneurs were highly competent leaders, with previous experiences drawn from positions as nursery supervisors on big estates or smallholder development schemes. All were outstandingly enterprising individuals who benefited from advances in social science and technical knowledge; hence they were well placed both to encourage better cultivation and to organize efficient selling chains to sites of planting material consumption.

These entrepreneurs were assisted in promotion by the prior experience in nursery techniques of Javanese villagers becoming nursery operators, most of whom had knowledge passed on to them by fathers or grandfathers who once worked on estates. It is moreover interesting that even today only Javanese are involved in nursery-making operations, with virtually none of the large surrounding majority of indigenous Sumatrans being engaged in these enterprises. This lack of interest is due partly to comparatively limited family experiences of improved agriculture; but it may also have cultural underpinnings in that indigenous local peoples are less flexible than Javanese and other outsiders towards new ventures, especially those entailing the quite sophisticated materials production phase. For such peoples, entry into the latter may well await the emergence of commercially-motivated political entrepreneurs within their own indigenous group. Local Sumatrans are now heavily involved in buying the new planting materials, however, although even here they initially lagged behind the Javanese.

Another relevant observation is that planting-materials entrepreneurs often used the natural propensity of village groups to collaborate in *kelompok*, not only in the production of planting materials but also in their marketing and purchasing by consumers.[9] These entrepreneurs carefully employed pre-existing institutions and the associated inclinations of village people to build new effective and incentive-compatible arrangements which minimized the possibilities of free-riding. It is likewise noteworthy in looking at this process of institution formation that, although most private nurseries only started quite recently, a few did begin 20 to 30 years ago when new technologies first appeared and trees began to be provided to immediate neighbours. Like most human institutions, nurseries require prolonged learning and adaptation to develop effectively, but such extended preparation laid the foundations for the widespread burgeoning of many units in the 1980s, when both the institutional choice set and demand for better trees increased dramatically.

It is further relevant to note that enhanced demand for trees and nurseries was very significantly stimulated by Lin's fourth source of disequilibrium, in the form of 'changes in other institutional arrangements'. These entailed the establishment of smallholding development schemes and big estates on land near potential smallholder consumers of new tree technologies. The use by such enterprises of high-yielding trees spread knowledge about them amongst neighbouring smallholders. The latter observed from outside the benefits from planting such materials, and sometimes learned more by participating as workers in these modern ventures. Smallholding schemes in the case study area, for instance, are estimated to have encouraged already the further planting under improved trees of at least the hectarages of the schemes themselves.

Demand for trees and nurseries was also stimulated by many private nurseries effectively gearing their tree products to consumer preference, not only managing to produce them cheaply but also to fashion them in desired qualities and quantities. This compared with the expensive and almost entirely top-quality materials offered by the public planting material nurseries; the latter were essentially supply-driven, not only selling their products at prices beyond the cash resources of ordinary farmers, but also placing high limits on minimum purchasing levels.[10] The greater flexibility of private nurseries was based on organizational efficiency in responding to consumer requirements; again it reflected the crucial participation in the change process of entrepreneurs, who made it their business to be at hand giving relevant advice. Such flexibility clearly suited demanding farmers, who were thus able to make successive small purchases according to available cash resources.

It is, moreover, plain that by the 1990s information transfers chiefly engineered by entrepreneurs to consuming farmers were encouraging the latter to demand better-quality materials, and hence the requirement of adequately arranged nurseries to furnish them. This new demand again reflected an enlargement in the institutional choice set resulting from greater knowledge. It tested the capability of nursery operators to enhance their institutional arrangements, further improving the efficiency of units that managed to survive in what was actually a very competitive arena.

The growth of private nurseries in pursuit of good financial returns and induced by price signals is a different institutional innovation to that of smallholder block development schemes. These schemes were likewise linked to altered economic conditions, but were also imposed by government. They are reviewed and contrasted with the nurseries in the following section.

SMALLHOLDER BLOCK DEVELOPMENT SCHEMES

The chief schemes selected for review are the Smallholders' Rubber Development Projects (hereafter referred to as 'smallholders' projects') and Projects for the Rehabilitation of Export Crops ('projects for rehabilitation'). These schemes were prominent in North Sumatra and Riau provinces from the early 1980s to the early 1990s, and were in fact important in that period in all smallholder rubber areas of Indonesia (Barlow and Tomich 1991; Direktorat Jenderal Perkebunan 1992). The smallholders' projects were given important support by the World Bank, but both they and the projects for rehabilitation, as well as other kinds of development schemes in Indonesia, were significantly enabled by more plentiful government resources springing from the petroleum boom of the 1970s. The smallholders' projects have now been succeeded by similar institutional arrangements under another name, but the projects for rehabilitation have been dropped.

Both types of scheme were essentially designed as 'enclaves' within which problems of incomplete markets could be eliminated, making possible a direct move to a higher level of technical performance. By the early 1990s they jointly occupied 50 000 hectares in North Sumatra and Riau, with individual schemes covering up to thousands of hectares. A given scheme essentially comprised 100–300 hectare sub-blocks, where participating smallholders planted and developed their own individual plots of 1–2 hectares.

The schemes all entailed a centrally organized and hierarchical supervisory structure, with packages of assistance to participants including supplies of high-yielding trees from special nurseries, mechanical aids for clearing land, fertilizers and other material inputs, and sometimes wages for participants in their planting and maintenance work. Much of this help came as credit at a low and subsidized interest rate, with repayment expected once trees came into tapping (World Bank 1992).

It was thought that smallholders within this intensive cultivation system would achieve much higher technical standards, beginning to tap their rubber trees after six rather than the traditional ten years, and also securing much higher yields. The costs of such schemes in the early 1990s was high, however, running at over $ 2000 per hectare for the partly World Bank-financed smallholders' projects and $ 1300–$ 1500 per hectare for the projects for rehabilitation (ibid. 1992). These expenditures contrasted with the far more modest level of some $ 70 for purchasing the best materials from private nurseries and transporting them to one's farm (Zen et al. 1992). While most farmers participated freely in pursuit of higher incomes, there was sometimes a degree of compulsion and social pressure making it hard for minorities with different ideas not to take part.

The smallholders' projects in the case study area and elsewhere were quite successful in reaching targeted technical standards and participant incomes, and are still operating satisfactorily now that their rubber trees are well into maturity. It was noticeable in observing their progress through the 1980s that the quality of management improved markedly during the learning-by-doing process of implementation, with outstanding managers, comparable in activity and influence to political entrepreneurs, being encouraged to emerge and exercise positive influence at local levels. These attributes reflected a flexible central control which promoted a progressive honing of institutional arrangements towards greater operational efficiency and incentive compatibility.[11] The design of the projects again built cleverly on propensities to collective effort in the planting and maintenance phases, and likewise benefited from devolving responsibility to individual participants. A further crucial element of success was reliability of funding, which was enabled by World Bank support. This introduced important certainty into forward planning, and its combination with effective management meant targeted outcomes were reached in most instances.

In contrast, the projects for rehabilitation were far less successful, with poor management and underfunding resulting in nearly all plantings being so poorly established and maintained that they barely yielded any crop. Most participants did not secure the skills to inform proper planting nor the resources to allow it. What emerged in each sub-block was a patchwork of mostly unsuccessful plots, with a small 5–10 per cent of successful efforts by those farmers already having the necessary skills and resources. The majority of settlers later abandoned their plots, whose overgrown areas remained as testament to misdirected planning. The multiple problems of this unsuitable institutional arrangement produced ever greater uncertainty and disillusion, with settlers frequently engaging in free-riding in the use of their limited supplies. Original targets were not achieved and the projects were later classified by many supervising personnel as 'a complete failure'.[12]

It is also pertinent to note that neither kind of scheme was successful in credit repayments, with even the smallholders' projects recovering only a small fraction of their loans to farmers.[13] This is actually a common outcome in government projects in poor rural economies, where lack of incentive compatibility, owing to deficiencies in the original design of institutional arrangements, means that those engaged in projects find it personally advantageous to free-ride. The inadequate design with respect to credit was associated with the failure to engage broader community participation and responsibility, with the consequent absence of social sanctions against those participants not meeting repayment obligations.

One striking and positive aspect of both kinds of scheme, however, is in their substantial spread effects, over and above influences already mentioned on neighbouring farmers. Thus after lags that often extended over many years, original scheme participants with land elsewhere have been motivated to introduce into these places new rubber technologies, especially by purchasing high-yielding trees from the private nursery network. Another spread effect has occurred through the subsequent participation by staff of the schemes in the nursery trading networks discussed above. These secondary effects, which are frequently paralleled in other types of official venture and cover many technologies apart from rubber, once more illustrate the first source of disequilibrium springing from 'changes in the institutional choice set'. Hence, despite the immediate failure of the Projects for Rehabilitation, those who took part in them experienced a widening in their perceptions and bounded rationality with important long-term effects.

It is interesting as well to note international parallels with the Indonesian experience of block development schemes, where arrangements similar to the latter have been used as a significant institutional vehicle for tree-crop improvement in several other countries around the world, such as Malaysia, Nigeria, Colombia and the Philippines. Thus Barlow (1986) observed important differences between 'tightly' and 'loosely structured' oil palm development schemes in Malaysia, using a similar distinction as that used by Hayami and Kikuchi (1982). Barlow specifically compared the well-organized and broadly successful arrangements of the large Malaysian Federal Land Development Authority with a number of smaller, poorly-managed and poorly-financed schemes sponsored by other agencies, including state governments. The outcomes from the 1960s to the 1990s in this Malaysian instance were similar to those in the comparison between the smallholders' projects and projects for rehabilitation, again highlighting the key significance of adequate management and resources and careful and incentive-compatible designs to the success of such block endeavours.

IMPLICATIONS AND CONCLUSIONS

This exploration of institutional change shows how very different organizational arrangements can mediate a particular incomplete market, helping to bridge the gap between modern and traditional sectors and providing information, skills and other inputs through new linkages. The case of tree-crop improvement in Sumatra is a difficult one, and traditional arrangements have adapted only slowly to disequilibrium, but new institutions in the form both of private nurseries and smallholders' projects have given decisive impetus to change.

The organizational arrangements of the nurseries and the block schemes can be seen respectively as following designs that 'adapt institutions to people' and 'adapt people to institutions' in forms of social engineering (Goodwin and Brennan 1991, p. 7). The arrangement of nurseries evolved slowly over many years in the hands of political entrepreneurs, but responded quickly when economic opportunities grew in the 1980s. The arrangement also embodied nursery techniques which paid close attention to the preferences of consuming farmers, who were thus offered a tailored array of qualities and quantities. The nurseries did not have free-rider problems, partly because all participants in them and their associated networks were constrained to pay or be paid for services offered. They likewise operated in a highly competitive environment, where units that were not incentive-compatible were likely to collapse. They further appeared sustainable in the longer run, although seemingly limited to planting-material production by Javanese farmers. This constraint was not serious, however, in light of continuing infrastructure improvements with the consequent falling costs in transporting materials to consumers.

The organization of block schemes, on the other hand, embodied designs which essentially imposed the concepts of planners in Jakarta, albeit with adaptations to field conditions. The technology of both types of block scheme aimed for a high standard, including performances at the levels of good commercial estates. Such content reflected the common philosophy of official improvers that smallholders and other laggards in development should be moved to a higher technical plane in a large discrete jump. The basic hypothesis was that attaining this plane through an appropriate institutional arrangement, backed by investment of official resources, would generate take-off and sustained operation at that level. This appears to have been a reasonable assumption, given that the arrangement was suitably designed and backed by good management and adequate resources.

Thus both Sumatran and wider experiences indicate that the managerial and capital resources devoted to block schemes must be substantial, entailing expenditures of at least US$ 2000 per hectare at prices of the early 1990s. Less management- and capital-intensive scheme designs, as illustrated by the projects for rehabilitation, do not seem efficient or incentive-compatible and appear unlikely to produce good economic or social results. These latter institutional designs have now proved themselves through numerous trials around the world to be unsuitable, and have largely been rejected by policy-makers in Indonesia and other countries promoting tree crops.

It is noteworthy that both private nurseries and smallholders' rubber development projects were generally well adjusted to the tasks they performed. They did indeed have resemblances in this aspect, most notably in their basis in family smallholdings whose key economic and social functions were now supplemented by new linkages. It is interesting, in fact, that block schemes putting less stress on this basis, as was true of 'nucleus estates' which operated elsewhere in Indonesia, were generally not very successful despite involving costs well over the limit quoted above (Barlow and Tomich 1991). The nurseries and smallholders' projects were similar too in building on relevant collective tendencies in the communities involved. Apart from these similarities, the two new institutional arrangements each had linkages well adapted to particular needs, as where trading networks accessed by the nurseries mediated the planting material market for them and the credit provisions of the smallholders' projects obviated the capital market difficulties which would otherwise have faced participants.

It is tempting to estimate the extent to which particular factors have affected the emergence of the new institutions but, while the chief sources of disequilibrium and factors springing from them can be identified in general terms, apportioning weights in institutional inducement is much harder. These again are highly complex circumstances where both endogenous and exogenous factors act to promote institutional change, where much interaction occurs between these categories, and individual influences cannot always be measured. It seems clear that the widening of the institutional choice set coming from better social and scientific knowledge, profitable opportunities springing from new technology, rising land prices, transport cost reductions owing to infrastructure improvements, and changes in the institutional arrangements of wider society were key factors to which actors responded. The specific local factors arising from these causes are harder to pin down. It is clear as well that political entrepreneurs played a crucial role in the institutional change process, both for nurseries and for smallholders' projects.

Policy-makers and others are naturally interested in comparing the private nurseries and smallholders' projects as institutional vehicles for tree-crop smallholding improvement through new technology, and here there is no doubt the nurseries are superior in their much lower development costs per hectare. However, the key question also arises of the complementarity of institutional arrangements within the broad institutional structure, where Smallholders' Projects and other schemes like them seem despite their high costs to be crucial in establishing through their spread effects an example and consequent demand for higher-yielding trees. This in turn stimulates the growth of nurseries, which may well not have thrived previously in the absence of the block arrangements. It seems then that policies should provide for both new institutions, which will then interact within the array of other factors promoting moves to modernity.

The segmented markets of poor rural economies make it hard to build institutions effectively mediating new production technologies with their needs for diverse modern inputs. The Sumatran experience gives some indication of how this may be undertaken in the tricky situation of smallholding tree crops.

NOTES

1. Thus groups of traders banded together to perform central clearing (securing economies of scale in monitoring and other transactions costs), pool market intelligence (internalizing externalities to traders), and establish contingency funds (buffering adverse effects from unusually large price fluctuations).
2. This figure is estimated on the basis of data from surveys of Sumatran private nurseries (Nancy et al. 1990; Zen et al. 1992), which showed existing private nurseries were producing sufficient improved materials to plant about 30 000 hectares a year. Given that some 10 000 of these hectares were on smallholdings (with the rest of the materials going to estates or big corporate farms), and that such planting had continued at about that rate for 10 years to the present, a total of 100 000 hectares would have been established with improved materials on individual smallholding plots in 1998.
3. 'Pre-existing' in terms of what existed before the present incursions of new ideas and methods but, in fact, the traditional institutional structure is *itself dynamic*, and has altered progressively in response to economic and social changes.
4. Often there will be two or more such groups amongst the inhabitants of a given village, each with its own property and other arrangements and under the governance of traditional leaders.
5. Increasing land scarcity has already encouraged an addition to the traditional distributive arrangements described, wherein those cultivating land are now beginning to sell and buy it for cash.
6. These are much larger enterprises than smallholdings, and may involve up to several thousand hectares of rubber in a given unit. They are operated by paid managers and workers, and their chief motivation is profit-making. They adapted to changed economic conditions through vertical integration into both factor and product markets by groups of estates under single ownership, as well as through other devices enabling groups under different ownerships to come together. The size of estates also provided significant economies of scale in a number of key spheres, including access to new technologies and capital markets, and their existence in the modern sector enabled them to construct effective institutional linkages to exploit these.
7. Such difficulty of mastery has many parallels: one example being the trouble experienced by many older urban professionals in adopting computer-based work techniques. The broad principles of such techniques are easily understood, but their actual application requires considerable background and training. Yet at least these professionals work in a market which can mediate the skills to them.

8. These organizations were predominantly small family firms providing 'little bus' or *bimoh* transportation for 10–15 persons at a time.
9. Cooperating in *kelompok*(s) of around five to 30 persons is a ubiquitous practice in Indonesia, especially in rural areas, and is employed for any activity entailing economic or social advantages in collaboration. Thus in the planting materials sphere, nursery owners often join forces in the marketing phase, and groups of consuming farmers commonly dispatch one representative to purchase trees for all of them.
10. Hence government nurseries supplying planting materials offered them at too high a price for most smallholders, meaning they were usually either not purchased or were used only by estates.
11. 'Incentive compatibility' denotes an institutional mechanism which is informationally feasible and compatible with the 'natural' incentives of participants. Given these characteristics, individuals do not find it advantageous to free-ride or otherwise violate the rules of the relevant process, which works efficiently towards its economic or social ends. The conditions of compatibility (although not compatibility *per se*) are further discussed in Chapter 2 (p. 16).
12. Thus in 1992 more than 60 per cent of the area of the projects for rehabilitation in Indonesia as a whole were classed 'D' on the basis of expected performance, indicating a predominant lack of success (Direktorat Jenderal Perkebunan 1992, p. 4). Only 11 per cent of the total area of smallholders' projects was in this category, however.
13. 'Under current Indonesian tree crop projects, credit repayments are in the order of 10–20 per cent, although the implicit expectation ... at appraisal was for repayment rates near 100 per cent' (World Bank 1992, p. 4).

4. Labour Institutions: The Case of Indonesia

Chris Manning

The 1965 change of regime in Indonesia[1] resulted in major new directions in political structure and economic policy. New institutions were imposed, and rapid economic growth induced alterations in a range of existing institutional arrangements. In the field of labour, there were two spheres of particularly pronounced institutional transformation. First, controls were introduced over organized labour and especially over trade unions. Second, new rural labour institutions emerged. This chapter looks at the origins and functions of these controls and rural institutions, and their impact on economic efficiency and equity.

Both spheres provide useful insights for understanding the processes and consequences of institutional change in developing societies. With labour controls, changes were imposed directly by the state as much, if not more, for political as for economic reasons. With rural labour institutions, on the other hand, changes were a consequence of market forces arising from government policies to raise rice production. Economists gave some attention to the impact of rural institutional change on employment and welfare, but largely ignored the effect of modified approaches to industrial relations. However, many other social scientists viewed the emergence of both kinds of new institutions as symptomatic of the Suharto regime's emphasis on economic efficiency and capital accumulation, at the expense of labour rights and welfare. The consequent realignment of power relations, as well as the preference on the part of government and employers for 'exclusionary' arrangements towards labour and the removal of a pro-labour political voice within Indonesian society, were seen as fundamental causes of institutional alterations in both spheres.

The debates on the origins and consequences of rural institutional change relate primarily to the 1970s in Java, whereas those concerning controls over organized labour are relevant to a longer time period. Another look at both spheres is certainly relevant to applying institutional economics to issues of efficiency and distribution associated with economic policy and transformation in Third World settings. This chapter argues that neglect of the economic

42

functions of traditional and modern sector labour arrangements, as well as the intensity of labour market change, has contributed to a rather simplistic and deterministic interpretation of institutional change in Indonesia.[2]

The chapter begins with a brief discussion of economic and political structures and policies relevant to labour institutions before 1965 in Indonesia. It then examines the ways in which controls were extended over organized labour by Suharto and the military during their regime from 1965. It next deals with the economic functions of selected rural labour institutions and adjustments which have occurred in them, finally moving to some broad conclusions about the analyses made.

THE POLITICAL AND ECONOMIC CONTEXT OF INSTITUTIONAL CHANGE

The ideology underpinning the Suharto'New Order' regime emphasized from the outset the maintenance of political and economic stability, and promotion of economic development (*pembangunan*).[3] The contrast was drawn with the political uncertainty, conflict, economic instability and stagnation which characterized much of the first 20 years of government following independence in 1945 (Paauw 1963). On the political front, this led to the banning of the communist party and kindred organizations, including the All-Indonesia Workers Organization (SOBSI) and Indonesian Peasant Front (BTI). It also meant the assertion of tight state and military control over all political life, support for the ruling Functional Group Party (*Golongan Karya* or GOLKAR) (Crouch 1978), and creation of interest group bodies (such as a new trade union grouping) which were closely aligned to GOLKAR and controlled by state security agencies. The five principles of the Indonesian state philosophy, *Pancasila*, were affirmed as the major ideological principles guiding Indonesia's path of development, with special emphasis on cooperation and harmony within the tightly constrained political structure.[4]

In economic affairs, four major objectives of the regime were relevant to labour institutions.[5] The first two related to general economic policy: restoration of price and general macroeconomic stability; creation of conditions conducive to private sector investment and trade. In addition, the government promoted rural development, primarily through a rice self-sufficiency programme in the first decades of the regime, and extensions of physical and social infrastructure to reduce uncertainty and transactions costs and raise levels of human capital and welfare.

The New Order government was successful in achieving these political and economic objectives for nearly three decades and thus served the broad coalition of interest groups which brought Suharto to power. This 'success' goes a long way to explaining the longevity of the regime. Extraordinary political stability prior to the crisis of 1997–98 and the close of the regime was accompanied (and undoubtedly bolstered) by the well-documented economic success story. Economic growth was close to 7 per cent per annum, and gross domestic product per capita increased by just under 5 per cent between 1970 and 1995. Economic expansion was substantial in all major sectors and regions, and was accompanied by a more than halving of the agricultural share of gross domestic product and substantial rises in the shares of manufacturing and services. There was, too, a significant but much slower shift in employment structure away from agriculture, which accounted for less than half of employment for the first time in the mid-1990s. Initially the main gains in employment were made in services, and then from the mid-1980s in manufacturing and construction (Manning 1998).[6]

Yet rapid economic development did not produce the expected results in one area relevant to the discussion of institutions. Despite significant declines in poverty, real wage rates increased relatively little in agriculture, and gains in wages during the oil boom were not sustained in other sectors until the 1990s (ibid.). This was not inconsistent with the rapid labour force growth, and with extreme conditions of labour surplus existing in 1965. Indeed, even without labour force growth tighter labour market conditions depended on considerable mopping up and intersectoral transfer of underemployed and low-productivity workers initially remunerated at wage levels even below those in agriculture.[7]

Nevertheless, low wages and poor working conditions brought into question the system of labour controls established by the New Order. These controls were challenged by representatives from a variety of groups: the rapidly growing urban middle class, the now quite large, more educated and increasingly (geographically) concentrated manufacturing workforce, and both self-interested and concerned foreign parties. Two aspects are addressed in the discussion below.

CONTROLS OVER INDUSTRIAL LABOUR

The discussion of labour market institutions in microeconomics has given most attention to the adverse effects of government interventions to raise wages above market clearing rates. The discussion has focused mainly on the impact of public sector and minimum wage policies, although the monopoly (and political) power of union organizations has also been examined.[8] The negative influence of government intervention has been highlighted in relation to two specific issues. One involves the high rates of urban unemployment and associated rapid rural–urban migration. The other issue is the failure of countries to take advantage of the low opportunity cost of labour to expand labour-intensive manufacturing exports. Fields and Wan (1989) have suggested, for example, that one factor underlying the earlier successes of some East Asian newly-industrializing countries were policies enabling labour-cost advantages to be exploited.[9] Other researchers have proposed that minimum wages recommended by many governments are less favourable to workers, on efficiency and equity grounds, than collective bargaining through company unions in countries like Indonesia (Devarajan, Ghanem and Thierfelder 1997, pp. 165–8).

Labour Market Controls in Indonesia

During the New Order period, controls over organized labour and industrial relations processes were one of the most important elements of direct government intervention in labour markets. For most of the period they overshadowed policies to improve labour welfare or minimum wages, although in the 1990s the latter were promoted more vigorously. Until 1990, there were no sanctions for non-compliance with government rules, and in most provinces official minimum wages were at the lower end of the wage distribution range. As in most developing countries, quite ambitious labour protection legislation was introduced shortly after Independence. But there was little genuine attempt to implement major articles of the labour law outside the relatively small modern sector.[10]

What was the nature of labour controls and their rationale, and how did they affect economic efficiency and welfare? The guiding principles were set out in the *Pancasila* Industrial Relations Framework adopted by the government in 1974 (Murtopo 1975). This stressed the common interests of business and workers, and in line with state ideology emphasized cooperation and conciliation based on 'family' principles.[11] 'Tripartite' cooperation between government, business and labour representatives, and representation of each on a range of bodies such as wage and dispute councils was the principal mechanism for executing industrial relations in this context.

In practice, however, there was a large gap between government ideology and the practice of industrial relations. Labour interests were heavily circumscribed by both formal and informal methods of labour control, with the formal approaches entailing three main mechanisms. First, rights to organize and form independent trade unions were heavily curbed for much of the New Order period, with all non-communist unions being merged in 1974 into one national organization which remained the only active trade union until 1990.[12] Most union leaders were selected from the ruling *Golongan Karya* party, and this became increasingly so after 1980. Both leaders and other union office bearers were also carefully vetted by security officials.

Second, the right to strike, although officially permitted, was severely curtailed.[13] Third, the government maintained the system of compulsory arbitration through regional and national disputes settlement bodies, which had been established in the previous Sukarno era (Hawkins 1963). Although these bodies had representatives from government, labour and the employers, they were convened by the Ministry of Manpower which in practice tended to have the major say in their decisions (Manning 1998).

However, informal methods of labour control were of equal, if not greater, significance in governing labour relations processes and institutions.[14] Most important among these was the *de facto* government control over the appointment of national, provincial and local trade union officials. At national and provincial levels, pro-government GOLKAR and ex-military representatives with little direct experience in union affairs emerged as the key union leaders, partly as a result of the indirect involvement of government in election processes. Informal control was also exercised through the frequent intervention of local police and military officials at the request of factory managers, both in settling disputes and detaining strike and other labour leaders unlawfully. One might also mention the bribery of government labour protection and disputes council officers by private business; this, although widely acknowledged to exist, is less easy to document.

Why was there such a huge gap between the official ideology of labour relations with its emphasis on harmony and cooperation, and the reality of institutional forms and processes governing employee–employer relationships? Three major reasons can be suggested. First, several goals of the industrial relations institutions established by the government conflicted with the ideology. These goals placed high priority on the political control of organized labour and industrial peace, especially given the history of labour unrest under the previous regime and the government's eagerness to promote investment and growth. While collective bargaining and tripartite negotiation were key principles in the basic laws, institutions were established to ensure that government determined the nature of industrial processes and their outcomes. The political influence of the military, and overriding concern with security and stability, meant these objectives rather than the key principles dominated the practice of labour relations.

A second reason for the ideology–reality divide related to the dynamics of the political economy of the New Order. The involvement of government and military officials in business (Robison 1986) meant that many persons entrusted with implementing industrial relations policy were interested in outcomes favourable to employers. A third reason was that conditions of excess labour supply obtained for much of the period under examination, making it relatively easy for employers to recruit new workers and giving the latter an ever-present threat of unemployment. Such circumstances undermined effective trade union organization,[15] while the capacity of unions to deliver significant improvements in wages and working conditions was also heavily constrained.

Labour controls, efficiency and equity

Despite the obvious curtailment of labour rights, it can be argued that labour controls may well have contributed to a more efficient and more equitable labour market than might have emerged if trade unions had the same freedom as before 1965. As in other countries, Indonesian trade unions have always been more active in the modern sector and especially in foreign firms. The tight official restrictions over dismissals in these firms tended, moreover, to give trade unions a degree of monopoly power in dealing with management.[16]

If unions had been more effective, wages and labour standards in general would almost certainly have been higher in some modern-sector firms, and this would especially have been so if the unions had been backed by more powerful industry-wide and national union organizations. Given the sharply-differentiated Indonesian industrial structure ranging from a myriad of small operators to a smaller number of large organizations, this would have contributed to a wider disparity in wages and working conditions across firms and industries.[17] It can be argued too that employment growth might well have been slower in the modern sector as a consequence.

One can still argue for greater union freedom on other than human rights grounds, maintaining that unions might have helped overcome monopsony power, imperfect information or labour immobility in a large and fragmented labour market. The argument is compelling in the case of monopsony, provided it is assumed that unions would help enforce a minimum set of standards in modern-sector firms which have access to a pool of low-wage workers from agriculture and the informal sector. The monopsony argument is less acceptable, however, if one believes that wages should be market-determined, regardless of national or international standards. Claims that unions can assist in reducing imperfect labour market information are, moreover, not generally persuasive in the Indonesian case. Most research suggests employees have relatively good information on job opportunities, and tend to be mobile across regions in response to wage differentials (Hugo 1978; Hugo et al. 1987).

To what extent did labour controls contribute to lower-than-market clearing wages, as a result of discrimination against or targeting of vulnerable employee groups in export-oriented, manufacturing industries? Many investors in these industries, who were mainly Korean and Taiwanese, paid lower wages than firms with similar characteristics in industries producing for the domestic market, and employed a high proportion of female, child and migrant workers (Manning 1998). Wages in such industries were nevertheless higher on average than in agriculture or traditional sectors, particularly in food and beverages.

The presence of such firms did not appear to have had a general wage-depressing effect, but it did contribute to discrimination in favour of employing more vulnerable and lower-wage workers. The willingness of such persons to put in long hours and their lower propensity to join unions and become involved in labour action was critical to the success of some highly-competitive export activities. However, wage discrimination between classes of employed persons was less obvious, since few prime-age male workers, the relevant reference group, were employed in similar jobs.

Finally, did labour controls contribute to lower labour productivity than might have prevailed if there had been fewer restrictions on union activity? Here the answer is most likely 'yes'. In particular, it seems that freer enterprise unions could have promoted better work standards and a more committed work force, and hence contributed to higher productivity. 'Exclusionary' labour relations, combined with state paternalism as two key features of industrial relations in Indonesia, were an unfortunate combination for greater worker initiative, effort and participation (World Bank 1995).

To sum up, the new institutions of labour control introduced by the New Order government in Indonesia severely curtailed labour rights and reduced the bargaining power of labour *vis-à-vis* management. The concept of *Pancasila* industrial relations did not further workplace harmony or cooperation, although the level of labour disputation was not high by international standards. Nevertheless, there is little evidence that labour policies adversely affected the efficiency of labour markets, and the reverse may well have been true, but a freer trade union movement and less intervention in the labour market in favour of employers would probably have helped secure better labour standards and higher labour productivity in modern-sector firms.

LABOUR CONTRACTS IN RICE FARMING IN JAVA

Two major factors encouraged economists to focus on the institutional structure of rural labour markets in heavily-populated Java during the New Order period. First, there was increased interest in economic rather than social explanations for the persistence of so-called 'traditional' rural institutions.[18] Second, researchers sought explanations for changes in labour-sharing institutions that accompanied the technological change associated with the green revolution, which saw a near doubling of rice yields in many parts of Asia.

Rural labour institutions were given a central place in the more general economic development literature as a result of Lewis's (1954) emphasis on average product pricing of labour and disguised unemployment as a fundamental characteristic of a labour surplus economy. Subsequent interest in the efficiency of labour market institutions was partly stimulated by the research on tenancy contracts, transactions costs and the persistence of sharecropping as a viable system of land tenure.[19] Transactions costs were also singled out as important in determining preferences for more permanent rather than casual labour contracts, and in choices made between time, piece-work and contract systems of remuneration (Binswanger and Rosenzweig 1981). A major issue related to labour market institutional arrangements and structure has been the downward rigidity of wage rates, despite the existence of rural unemployment and underemployment. There have been various explanations for this phenomenon: custom in setting subsistence wages, efficiency wage theories (especially with regard to minimum nutritional requirements), and the payment of above-market clearing wages by monopsonistic employers concerned with costs in labour recruitment.[20] Although there is much debate over these ideas, all help to explain the persistence of surplus labour and wage gaps in rural labour markets. Pincus (1996), for example, emphasized the influence of the strength of social ties on wages, related to the distribution of resource endowments, as well as access to non-farm employment. However, it is also broadly agreed that rural wages tend to be flexible on a seasonal basis across regions, in accordance with changes in labour market conditions (Bardhan 1984; Hart 1986).

Related to this literature, a variety of explanations have been advanced for the demise (or adaptation) of traditional labour-sharing institutions associated with the 'green'-revolution in Asia. Sociologists and some economists have stressed the weakening of patron–client ties and traditional income-sharing relationships. Others have attributed changes principally to stronger profit maximization motives related to more intensive use of purchased inputs and greater reliance on markets (Scott 1976; Booth and Sundrum 1985). Several writers on Southeast Asia have also drawn attention to increasing inequality and political support for the rural elite, as factors contributing to rationalization in production relations (Hart, Turton and White 1989).

An alternative explanation for changes in worker-hiring arrangements has been suggested by Hayami and Kikuchi (1982), in terms of adjustments to customary contracts as labour-force growth and technological change influenced relative factor prices and returns. This explanation is explored further in discussing harvesting institutions below.

Induced Institutional Change on Java

There is a marked contrast between the casual and personalized labour contracts and employment relationships in rural areas of much of Java, and most formal-sector jobs in modern manufacturing. Most workers have characteristically been employed as family workers or wage labourers on small farms. Despite long exposure to market relationships from colonial times, intensity of market participation rose when the dominant rice crop in Java experienced the introduction of new inputs and technology during the green revolution in the

1970s and 1980s (Collier 1981; Manning 1988). A higher proportion of rice output was marketed, wage employment expanded and a much bigger share of rural households became involved in non-farm employment.

Developments in rural Java have played a prominent part in debates regarding institutional change induced by the green revolution in Asia. The discussion focused on changing institutions governing the so-called 'traditional' unrestricted right of villagers to participate in any landowner's rice harvest and share in rewards from the harvest. It was noted that two institutions, *tebasan* and *kedokan*, were more widely adopted as the green revolution spread on Java. *Tebasan* involves selling the harvest to a contractor, who usually employs his own team to undertake the harvest. *Kedokan* (sometimes termed *ceblokan*) refers to the interlinking of harvest and pre-harvest labour contracts: labourers undertake unpaid pre-harvest tasks in return for exclusive rights to participate in the harvest.

Both *tebasan* and *kedokan* limited villagers' rights to participate in harvest work. Village surveys suggested that numbers engaged in the harvest had increased substantially over time, mainly as a result of population growth. This resulted in output losses and imposed considerable transactions costs in the supervision and distribution of harvest shares. Three interrelated yet fundamentally different explanations were advanced for the adoption of the new contracts.

First, the spread of new arrangements was viewed as part of a more general trend towards profit-maximizing behaviour. It was contended that farmers were no longer prepared to honour customary obligations to the village poor, in particular the landless, who constituted a sizeable fraction of the population in many villages of Java.[21] A second explanation related to the markedly increased incomes which harvesters – rewarded in terms of output shares – secured as a result of yield increases associated with the new rice technology. Thus Hayami and Kikuchi (1982) suggested the adoption of *kedokan* contracts was a socially acceptable adaptation of village institutions to bring returns from the harvest into line with wage rates in other rice operations.[22]

The third explanation introduced broader considerations of political economy and the allocation of labour between agricultural and non-agricultural activities. Hart (1986) suggested the spread of *kedokan* and *tebasan* arrangements in Java needed to be viewed in the perspective of heightening class divisions in rural society, attributed to New Order economic policies which included support for the rural elite. She argued (pp. 189–91) that removal of all political support for the landless and other poorer sections of the community after 1965 allowed landowners to introduce new contracts and onerous conditions of credit, while cultivating a small group of dependent clients.[23]

The maintenance of these 'exclusionary' contracts depended on a pool of surplus labour forced to seek out lower paid wage work for most of the year. Hart thus suggested the emergence of a dualistic labour market, consisting of a small minority of protected workers and a secondary labour market in which most of the village poor operated.[24] One advantage to the employer from creating a group of attached workers is the reduction in transactions costs of recruiting and supervising labour, for more intensive rice cultivation.

An important aspect of the spread of new and modification of old institutions in Java was the diversity of contracts prevailing, even in harvest operations. Hayami and Kikuchi (1982) attributed this to differences in social obligations across villages. They contrasted outcomes in a tightly-knit village where *kedokan* was acceptable with those in a more loosely-structured and recently-established community, where the more radical *tebasan* arrangement was adopted.

Lessons from the Java case

Intensive debate arose on the causes and consequences of new institutional forms related to the spread of the green revolution on Java. It raised important issues relevant to the general literature on institutional change.

One issue entailed a re-examination of the so-called traditional values and social functions of traditional institutions, where such values and functions had previously been seen as the chief causal factors. Economic efficiency was now found to be an important factor sustaining institutions in several cases. For example, research suggested that using the pre-green-revolution approach of harvesting paddy with the highly labour-intensive *ani-ani* or finger knife had important technical and economic functions. Individual panicles were cut separately, and this was done in association with open harvest technical and economic functions (Alexander and Alexander 1982). The finger knife facilitated handling longer-stem varieties, while the participation of large numbers of harvesters and the *bawon* (harvest) system of payment connected with use of the knife encouraged quick and high quality work and minimized supervision costs. This challenged the argument implied in the shared poverty notion of Geertz (1963) that the finger knife and open harvest persisted primarily as labour-sharing arrangements.

Another issue was the evidence that the same institutions could coexist in different locations for different reasons and perform different functions. Several labour institutions likewise underwent subtle change, disappeared and re-emerged, primarily in accordance with changing labour-market conditions. Hence *kedokan* was found in one region of Java in the early part of the twentieth century, but disappeared from there again during the depression years. It predated the green revolution in many upland areas of Java, partly as a means of giving family and close neighbours preferential (and often reciprocal) rights to engage in the harvest (Wiradi 1978). In contrast, it spread in other regions primarily as a device to reduce transactions and other costs associated with increasing numbers of persons participating in the open harvest. There is evidence of similar variations in the incidence and functions of the closed harvest and other labour institutions (Manning 1988).

A further issue arising from experiences with labour institutions was the insight that their distributive roles were also significant but not always predictable. The structure of control over assets – and in particular land – played an important part in determining the distribution of benefits of particular institutions. In situations where landlessness was widespread, the *kedokan*, tenancy and other exclusionary labour arrangements helped to worsen income distribution by providing preferential access to income for a small, protected group of labourers. However, the same institutions were actually a reflection of labour-sharing arrangements in more egalitarian environments where land was more evenly distributed (Pincus 1996).

Some researchers also emphasized the changed political relationships in Indonesia after 1965 as being necessary for the spread of exclusionary labour arrangements, whereas others placed greater emphasis on population growth. However, both explanations tended to ignore the immense changes in communications and infrastructure, and the more intensive linkages with growing towns and cities. These factors enabled much greater intra-rural labour mobility between villages and regions, and contributed to an uneven impact of rural–urban migration on rural labour markets (Hugo 1978; Breman 1992; Pincus 1996).

For example, on the one hand, greater mobility helped explain the pressure which workers from outside the village placed on existing labour contracts (such as the open harvest), and transactions costs associated with augmented labour supply. On the other hand, a more mobile population helped elucidate the diversity of labour contract systems which emerged in the 1970s in Java. In some villages, for example, intensive chain-migration links were established with urban centres, and contributed to a shortage of labour at peak periods in the agricultural cycle. Thus contract labour systems such as *tebasan* were a response to rising transactions costs associated with relative labour scarcity rather than population pressure or changed political relationships.

CONCLUSION

This chapter has addressed two quite different cases of institutional arrangements associated with modified political and economic circumstances: those imposed by the state through controls extended over organized labour, and those induced by alterations in rural labour markets associated with the green revolution. Both cases were related to the restrictive political environment and pro-business and pro-capital policies of the Suharto regime. It has been argued in regard to each that the impact of institutional changes on the welfare of wage workers was ambiguous, and that one can too easily jump to conclusions regarding the impacts of institutional developments. This is especially true where inferences are based on preconceived theories which ignore political, economic and social interactions, or place too much emphasis on developments at a particular point in time, or in specific locations.

In the case of labour controls, the pervasive influences of informal as well as formal institutional arrangements have hardly been consistent with the principles of *Pancasila* industrial relations. It has been argued too, however, that modern-sector labour controls had only a marginal effect on the welfare of wage workers in general. Nevertheless, as the Indonesian government began to take the protection of wage workers more seriously – at least in the modern sector – the largely political objective of restricting the rights of organized labour began to conflict more sharply with the goal of improving labour welfare. Enhanced labour standards were partly dependent on giving greater reign to union activities, at least at the enterprise level.

The discussion of rural institutions emphasized the role of transactions costs. However, institutional changes were an outcome of interacting political and economic forces, and adversely affected the employment and incomes of some groups of wage labourers, but not others. As in the case of modern manufacturing, constant wage rates were accompanied by continued employment growth in agriculture and non-farm jobs, and welfare gains on Java (Manning 1998). It seems also that, while the notion of institutional change induced by the green revolution is attractive, technology was only one element which encouraged such institutional change in a period when rural income growth was supported by a variety of external stimuli.

NOTES

1. The 'New Order' government of President Suharto (1966–98) effectively assumed power from the previous administration of President Sukarno (1945–67) in late 1965, although there was a period extending up to early 1967 when Sukarno still retained the title of 'President'.
2. The author follows Justin Lin's (1989) distinction between imposed and induced institutional change.
3. The successive Suharto cabinets have all been given the prefix 'development', being termed '*kabinet pembangunan* I, II', and so on.
4. Thus the New Order regime explicitly rejected 'western' democracy, capitalism and socialism as guiding principles, aiming rather to accept elements of all and mould them in accordance with Indonesian (Javanese) values and institutions.
5. See especially Booth and McCawley (1971) and Hill (1996). Not all objectives have received the same emphasis at all times during the past 25 years, but all have remained major elements of the development programme.
6. These two sectors accounted for less than 20 per cent of all jobs in 1985, but contributed to almost half total employment growth from 1985–95.
7. Higher than market clearing wages in agriculture can in part be explained by seasonality in labour demand. They can also be attributed to an institutional floor to rice sector wages (especially in the off-peak season) and efficiency-wage considerations and monitoring costs. The latter apply especially where timeliness is critical and there is a tight time constraint on the completion of specific operations.

8. See especially Turner (1965), Squire (1981) and Mazumdar (1989) for general surveys of these issues.
9. Fields and Wan did not argue, however, that governments of newly-industrializing countries were not involved in wage-setting. Singapore in particular was an obvious example of government intervention, but that intervention did not significantly distort relative factor prices.
10. This especially applied to hours of work, overtime rates and menstruation and maternity leave for women (Manning 1979; White et al. 1992).
11. The heavy emphasis on non-confrontational labour relations contrasted with the situation before 1965 when the major union, the All-Indonesia Workers Organization, followed an aggressive strategy to win concessions from employers and the government.
12. Although initially set up as a federation of industry-based unions, the new organization operated in practice as a unitary body and was formally constituted as such in 1985. Although two small independent unions were formed in 1990 and 1992, they were neither officially registered as trade union organizations nor encouraged or financially supported by the government.
13. Dispute reconciliation procedures required that written permission to initiate strike action be granted to worker organizations by the dispute settlement committees. In addition, strikes in public and 'vital' enterprises were banned before 1990 – another legacy of the Sukarno period of government.
14. For detailed accounts of these informal methods, see especially Indonesian Documentation and Information Centre (1981 and 1982–87/8), Yayasan Lembaga Bantuan Hukum Indonesia (1992) and Hadiz (1997).
15. Olson (1965) makes a similar argument regarding the growth of union membership in the United States, which he argues tended to be much more rapid during periods of tighter labour markets.
16. Retrenchment of workers had to gain approval from the provincial disputes reconciliation committees, and 'mass' dismissals of ten or more employees from the central disputes committee. The law was often circumvented by employment of workers on short-term contracts, however, and by policies which encouraged employees to accept voluntary quitting. The procedure was rarely applied in small-scale enterprises.
17. Although given higher remuneration, chiefly on efficiency-wage grounds, in many modern firms, the impact on wage differentials may not have been large.
18. This was a natural extension of earlier research which rejected the notion of Third World peasants as irrational and constrained in their response to economic stimuli by limited wants, traditional values and institutions (Stiglitz 1986).
19. Tenancy contracts play a central part in the literature (see Binswanger and Rosenzweig 1981 and Bardhan 1989 for a summary) because of their interest in involving transactions in both land and labour. Risk, monitoring costs, interlinked factor markets (including credit) and variations in labour quality have all been identified as factors contributing to the prevalence of sharecropping in a variety of economic environments.
20. See Binswanger and Rosenzwieg (1981) and Booth and Sundrum (1985) for summaries of the literature, and Rodgers (1975), Stiglitz (1976) and Bardhan (1984, Chapter 4) for studies of agricultural wages. Efficiency wage theories focus on the relationship between the level and composition of wages, and labour productivity,
21. See especially Collier (1981). The prevalence of labour-sharing arrangements had been seen as a classic example of the way in which villages in Java adapted to continued population growth by absorbing more labour in rice cultivation. Geertz (1963) coined the well-known term 'shared poverty' to describe this process.
22. A parallel was drawn by Hayami and Kikuchi with the spread of similar *gama* harvesting contracts in the Philippines. These responded to similar economic changes.
23. Hart (1986, p. 175) reports interest rates of 100–150 per cent per cropping season for production credit, and suggests that small farmers had no alternative sources of credit available to them outside loans which they could acquire from larger landowners.
24. No analogy can be drawn with labour markets in the industrial sector where enterprises often depend on employees because of firm-specific skills. In Hart's model landlords could replace tied labour at no cost to the farm enterprise.

5. Industrial Institutions: The Case of Malaysia

Tham Siew-Yean
Mahani Zainal-Abidin

After achieving independence in 1957, the Malaysian economy has in four decades shifted from primary commodity production to the production of manufactured goods. Manufacturing has raised its share in gross domestic product from 13.9 per cent in 1970 to 35.4 per cent in 1997, and its contribution to total employment has accelerated from 8.7 to 27.5 per cent during the same period. This transformation has also changed the export structure, with manufacturing exports increasing their proportion of total exports from 11.9 per cent to 80.4 per cent in the same period. In sharp contrast to the 1960s when Malaysia was the leading world exporter of natural rubber, it is now a leading exporter of electronic components.

This structural change in Malaysia has attracted policy-makers as well as researchers, who have sought to analyse aspects of the industrialization process involved. However, little attention has been paid to the institutional perspective, despite growing evidence of the importance of institutions to economic development. This chapter attempts to fill the gap by considering the impact of industrial institutions on cluster development in manufacturing. It first reviews changes in the institutional structure of Malaysian manufacturing from 1970 to 1997, proceeding to look in detail at cluster development in three manufacturing sub-sectors. It finally draws conclusions, especially considering the role of the state in attempting to further promote such development in Malaysia.

THE INSTITUTIONAL STRUCTURE OF MALAYSIAN MANUFACTURING

Malaysia started industrializing through import substitution before Independence. This was continued in the 1960s, with tariff protection and fiscal incentives as the main instruments for drawing foreign direct investment into manufacturing.[1]

However, the government realized towards the end of the 1960s that import substitution was not sustainable due to limited domestic market size, with the additional factor of persistent unemployment. Consequently there was a switch to developing manufacturing through export promotion.

The ethnic riots in 1969 resulted in the New Economic Policy, aimed both at eradicating poverty and restructuring society to correct imbalances including, especially, the identification of race with economic function. An important target of this policy was 30 per cent ownership of all commercial and industrial activities by the Bumiputera[2] or original inhabitants. Introducing the policy changed the rules for industrial development from the relatively *laissez-faire* system of the 1960s to a considerably expanded role for the state (Jesudason 1990). This development related especially to policy goals from 1970 to 1985, but then the economy was liberalized owing to the mid-1980s recession. The periods from 1970 to 1985 and from 1986 to 1997 are now examined in turn.

New-Economic-Policy-led Industrialization, 1970–85

In 1970 the economy faced the relatively high unemployment rate of 8 per cent, and the government courted multinationals in attempting to generate the employment needed to eradicate poverty (ibid.). Free-trade zones were used to attract foreign investment in export-oriented industries. These were exempted from Bumiputera equity requirements so long as they exported all outputs; they were also not liable to customs duties, had fiscal incentives including tax holidays, and imposed restrictions on union formation.

These efforts coincided with globalized production in electronics and textiles industries, where American semiconductor firms relocated labour-intensive operations to Southeast Asia. Total foreign equity in Malaysia grew almost thirteen-fold from $201 in 1971 to $3162 million in 1985, while the share of foreign direct investment in manufacturing rose 44.4 per cent. Foreign investment in the free-trade zones was concentrated primarily on electronics and textiles, so that by 1980 electrical machinery, appliances and parts accounted for 47.7 per cent of total manufacturing exports, while textiles, clothing and footwear contributed to another 12.8 per cent (Fong et al. 1985).

However, the promotion of zones created a dualistic industrial structure. On one side were multinationals in electronics and textiles producing primarily for export, using cheap labour and importing duty-free inputs. On the other side were firms with less than 100 employees comprising 78 per cent of total manufacturing establishments in 1985 but contributing only 30 per cent of total manufacturing employment, 20 per cent of value added and 19 per cent of fixed assets (World Bank 1989). These smaller firms were concentrated in areas more amenable to small-scale production, like food processing, wood products and light engineering, requiring less capital and mainly catering for local demand.

This dichotomy did little to enhance linkages between the zones and the domestic economy.

Despite New Economic Policy exemptions for foreign capital in the free-trade zones, domestic capital became governed progressively more by policy requirements. New regulations and organizations were instituted to ensure that the economic participation of the Bumiputera conformed with policy goals. State control over industrial development increased in 1980 with the heavy industries programme, which was soon headed by the Heavy Industry Corporation of Malaysia. This programme was formulated to develop linkages to deepen the industrial structure and improve the economic position of the Bumiputeras (Bowie 1991). Tariff protection that had been reduced in the late 1970s was reinvoked to promote second-round import-substitution for state-led investments in developing the Proton national car as well as cement, steel and motorcycles. Subsidies and other measures were also used to hasten expansion of a strong, Bumiputera-driven, capital-goods industry (Rasiah 1997a).

Unhappily, the Heavy Industry Corporation's ventures incurred large initial losses despite scale economies (ibid.), and more general difficulties flowed from global recession and falls in commodity prices in the early 1980s. The fiscal and external deficits accumulated to finance the overall goals of the New Economic Policy and import-intensive heavy industries exerted negative pressures on the troubled economy, with the share of manufacturing in gross domestic product actually falling from 19.6 per cent in 1980 to 19.1 per cent in 1985. There was an obvious need to reconsider the industrialization strategy, especially when the economy slipped into recession in 1985.

Foreign-Direct-Investment-led Industrialization, 1986–97

Efforts to strengthen the industrial structure led to the formulation of the First Industrial Master Plan, 1986–95, with export promotion, foreign direct investment and fiscal incentives again being used to encourage growth in the manufacturing sector. The 30-per-cent foreign equity restriction on foreign investment was removed subject to the fulfilment of export conditions, while generous incentives were provided and licensing procedures liberalized. These liberalization efforts were complemented by favourable external conditions, with appreciation of East Asian currencies leading to inflows of Japanese and other regional direct investment. Production sites were also relocated from home countries to counter rising production costs and because privileges under the Generalized System of Preferences were withdrawn from the Asian Newly Industrialized Economies (NIEs).

The influx of foreign capital meant foreign direct investment in manufacturing grew almost fourfold, from $1778 million in 1986 to $6561 million in 1995. This capital was highly concentrated in electrical and electronics goods, with some also going into textiles and textile products, food manufacturing, chemical and chemical products and non-metallic mineral items; its share in these sub-sectors amounted to 61.5 per cent in 1995, and, since most of the investment was export-oriented, it accounted for a large proportion of manufactured exports.

The dominance of multinationals in export-oriented manufacturing once more contrasted with the other 84 per cent of manufacturing establishments having less than 75 full-time workers in 1992 (Malaysia 1996a). A national study of small and medium-scale industries[3] in 1994 found that these were concentrated in food, beverages and tobacco, fabricated metal products, machinery and equipment, wood and wood products, textile and wearing apparel and leather (ibid.); although the majority of such industries were geared to the domestic market, some also exported their products. Significantly, 26 per cent of small and medium firms were foreign-owned, having been established to service the input needs of the multinationals. This was especially true of Japanese companies affiliated to enterprises that had shifted their production to Malaysia (Aoki 1992).

The improved economic conditions after the recession raised domestic income and demand for items produced by import-substitution heavy industries, with restructuring, rationalization and the injection of new technologies improving the performance of most enterprises except Perwaja Steel (Rasiah 1997a). Thus the Proton car was able to capture the protected domestic market and thereby sustain necessary economies of scale, but, although it could be seen that industrial development had produced commendable growth, the industrial structure created was hollow and dichotomous in nature.

The New Economic Policy was replaced in 1990 with the National Development Policy, emphasizing the private sector and private investment. The Second Industrial Master Plan, 1996–2005, was later launched, proposing an industrial structure paradigm to overcome weaknesses, including technological dependence, lack of indigenous technological capability and poor linkages, and also to raise industrialization to a higher phase of development. The Plan adopted a cluster industrial-development approach, attempting to nurture intermediate goods producers as well as firms acting as cores of high value-added industries.

The Cluster Approach

This was popularized by Porter (1990), who modified the concept of geographical clusters[4] and applied it to an integrated industrial structure. Clusters are not location-based, but take the form of vertical integration within an industry or among industries; they attempt to develop a chain from research and development

(R&D) through production of critical components to assembly, distribution and marketing. R&D centres are established to serve the needs of firms within an industry, while groups of small and medium-scale firms supply critical components to larger firms doing assembly. For manufacturing, individual industry clusters comprise a network of core industries, supporting firms, infrastructures and institutions that are interlinked and interdependent (Figure 5.1).

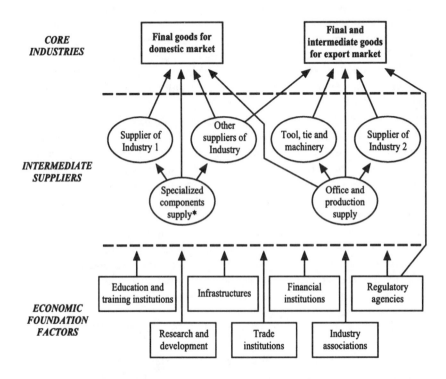

Note: *This sub-sector also links with other suppliers and with export industries, but the arrow is not drawn in.

Source: Malaysian Institute of Economic Research and DRI/McGraw-Hill (1995).

Figure 5.1 Clusters in Malaysian Manufacturing

Core industries are leading producers, both of final goods for the domestic market and of final and intermediate goods for export. They often enjoy initial advantages like favourable domestic factor endowments, strong technological bases, large capital and solid export networks. Supporting firms are producers of intermediate goods, either from within the industry or related industries. Infrastructures and institutions are the economic foundation factors, including skilled human resources, accessible and advanced technologies, financing facilities, specialized physical infrastructures and conducive regulatory environments to improve efficiency. Depending on circumstances, the cluster concept supports the growth in the core of vertically integrated firms, with networks of small and medium-scale supplier firms. In the electrical and electronics industry, large firms are best in the core as most benefits derive from economies of scale. In the rubber products industry, however, small firms are more flexible towards changes in consumer preference; even here, however, suppliers of intermediate goods will gain by expanding scales of production while also broadening product ranges to meet the demands of other industries.

The cluster concept was adopted to develop a more interlinked structure for Malaysian manufacturing, where this was regarded as necessary to generate higher value added. The latter can come from owning technology, developing products and producing intermediate goods. Innovation can be attained through the cluster's flexible network structure, ensuring the maintenance of international competitiveness as the sector adapts to its own changing requirements and the vagaries of international circumstances. Promoting intermediate suppliers also helps remove long-standing dependence on imported components.

The main problem with clusters lies in implementation, for the policies to create them are indirect in nature. Hence skills programmes are broad-based, and it is hard to forecast specific skills needs. In addition, improving economic foundation factors entails a long gestation, which means rapidly changing industrial requirements are difficult to satisfy. Introducing interventionist policies to foster intermediate suppliers may be crucial, but such policies may at the same time hinder their flexibility and innovativeness.

INSTITUTIONAL ISSUES IN INDUSTRIAL CLUSTER DEVELOPMENT

Malaysian manufacturing sub-sectors or industries can be categorized as 'internationally linked', 'resource-based' and 'policy-driven' clusters, according to evolutionary processes and institutional characteristics. The internationally linked cluster containing electrical and electronics items, chemicals, and textiles and apparel is primarily driven by multinational corporations, with output being geared mainly to global markets. Its growth and sustainability are dependent on global factors. On the other hand, the resource-based cluster comprising wood, rubber, palm oil and oleochemicals, cocoa and fruits and vegetables is highly dependent on local factors, including inputs, ownership and technology. The policy-driven cluster including transportation, materials and machinery is created by specific policy interventions, being almost totally dependent on foreign technology and not utilizing domestic factors. The industries in these three clusters were estimated to account for 76 per cent of total manufacturing value added in 1995 (Malaysia 1996b).

One industry is now taken in each type of cluster, and attention given to the different ways in which the state intervened in its development. The electrical and electronics industry is chosen in the internationally linked cluster, where the state utilized multinationals to promote development. Rubber products are selected in the resource-based cluster where, although the state again used multinationals, it also led research in natural rubber production and downstream processing. The automotive industry and specifically the Proton car are picked in the policy-driven cluster, which was characterized by direct state investment and protection. In each case the vital issues in cluster development of human resources, technology and linkages are considered.

The Electrical and Electronics Industry

This very significant sub-sector which in 1994 contributed 27.6 per cent of manufacturing value added has since free-trade-zone days been dominated by multinationals, particularly in the case of electronics firms. While Japanese and American investments prevailed in earlier years, the Japanese segment is now dominant and Taiwanese and Korean investments have also emerged.

Human resources

Electronics production in the 1970s was mainly labour-intensive, with assembly lines utilizing female unskilled workers. The latter were given on-the-job training, and foreign companies did not offer more training than Malaysian establishments (Fong et al. 1985). Foreign technical personnel such as engineers were utilized and labour turnover was high. This reflected poor working conditions, including the practice of adjusting labour forces according to electronics demand; another case was the tightening labour market in the late 1970s.

However, the introduction in the 1980s of flexible production systems and automation changed the skill requirements of workers. Consequently, Rasiah (1995) reported training to enhance skill levels in various new production procedures such as statistical process control, quality-control circles, and materials-requirement planning. Later in the decade firms automated increasingly as the economy moved towards full employment and labour shortages emerged. While large multinationals such as Acer Technologies, Intel and Motorola had their own training facilities, organizations such as the Skills Development Centre set up by the Penang state government were utilized by both foreign and domestic firms to instruct workers in modern production procedures. The vendors of machines also contributed to training staff from firms that bought their equipment. With such activity Malaysia developed one of the richest pools of expertise in semiconductor assembly and test automation in the world. Trained engineers and technicians from multinationals also carried their experience with them when they left to join other firms or to start their own enterprises, thereby creating positive spillovers.

The acute labour shortage continued in the 1990s, particularly involving skilled and semi-skilled workers and exerting pressures on firms to continue automation and intensify training. Moreover, increasing global competition and rapidly changing technologies further accelerated the need for instruction, with automation through robots to ensure consistency in product quality and speed in production.

Technology

Technologies can be those of production and those of products (Narayanan and Lai 1996), with multinationals being the source of both in the sub-sector. For production technology, parent companies either provided technical advice to local subsidiaries or decided its sourcing. In early years 'used' equipment from other affiliate operations of the multinationals was utilized in Malaysian subsidiaries, although these machines were 'new' in Malaysia. Such labour-intensive production technology then evolved to the fully automated processes utilized currently. Thus Narayanan and Lai (ibid.) reported firms acquiring expertise in operating, maintaining and repairing or modifying machinery used, with further incremental innovations. However, full maturity in production technology has yet to be achieved, since local sourcing of inputs has not been developed fully.

For product technology substantial R&D capability is involved, with the need to innovate continuously to keep product current and competitive and, if necessary, to replace it by something new. Hence, it is not surprising that the R&D activities of multinationals are located in their home countries, given scale economies and the need to safeguard trade secrets. There is little evidence that product technology was transferred from multinationals through relocating R&D to Malaysia or teaching related skills to local personnel.

Because of unavoidable costs and levels of expertise, very few local firms can afford R&D. Instead, they generally attempt to acquire production and product technology via licensing arrangements, joint ventures or equipment suppliers (Fong et al. 1985). Of late, local companies have sought to secure the relevant technology either through using foreign workers with specific skills not available in Malaysia or opening subsidiaries in developed countries. Technology can also be obtained through technology-transfer agreements, with the electrical and electronics industry being most prominent in this. However, lack of proficient bureaucrats has hindered the governance of transfer agreements, while 90 per cent of agreements in the manufacturing sector have involved intra-foreign transfers (Rasiah 1997b).

Linkages

Foreign firms in the free-trade zones in the early 1970s imported most intermediate inputs mainly because of the lack of domestic supply, and local content in electrical and electronics goods was only 2 per cent (Aoki 1992). These firms had almost no procurement linkages with Malaysian companies, and were sometimes referred to as 'tenant industries' or 'export enclaves'.

This pattern changed, however, when utilization of just-in-time and point-of-sale production technologies focused on zero-inventory production and required proximate suppliers. Some local engineering firms acquired expertise to act as suppliers through hiring former multinational-trained employees, especially engineers and technicians, while other supplying companies were established by former multinational employees themselves. Certain parts and materials procured by the multinationals also came from small and medium industries in countries other than their own.

Another emerging linkage pattern was the formation of international networks, whereby Asian affiliates of Japanese firms set up factories in other Asian countries. Thus Aoki (1992) noted a horizontal intra-firm division of labour among Asian affiliates operating in Malaysia, Thailand and Singapore, with inputs increasingly sourced from a number of places within a region rather than a particular country. Hence local sourcing can vary substantially, from zero in the case of Syquest Technologies to 90 per cent in the case of Acer Technologies. Yet despite increasing domestic sourcing, the electrical and electronics industry is still characterized by exceptionally high import content, with parts and components for it comprising 44.3 per cent of total intermediate goods imports in 1995.

It appears that the purchase of local inputs depends both on the policy of a company and the availability and capability of local suppliers as well as their competitive positions. Thus, inputs are procured from local producers if transactions costs are lower, but otherwise sourcing is from alternatives including subsidiaries in neighbouring countries. Given the borderless integrated production systems of multinationals, they and not national objectives determine the location of procurement. Increasing functional specialization by different subsidiaries of multinationals has produced an internationally rather than nationally based industrialization process (Morris-Suzuki 1992).

The Rubber Products Industry

This benefited from availability of high quality natural rubber in a country drawing on more than 100 years' experience in rubber cultivation, as well as government-led research institutions which were world leaders in their field.

The potential of rubber products was recognized in the early 1970s, drawing on Malaysia's comparative advantage in manufacturing latex goods made from abundant local latex. However, because production and product technology as well as markets were at that time in the hands of multinationals, in trying to develop this industry the state pursued the route of joint ventures. The industry was also targeted as a priority in the First Industrial Master Plan, on the basis of its potential to increase rubber consumption, employment and export earnings. The industry grew rapidly, fuelled mainly by latex products, including especially rubber gloves and catheters for which demand had increased as a result of the HIV/AIDS scare in the late 1980s. Malaysia became the sixth largest global producer of rubber products in 1993, contributing 4.6 per cent of world output, but the sub-sector was still small in the Malaysian industrial picture, constituting 6.3 per cent of manufacturing value added and 2.2 per cent of gross manufacturing exports in 1995.

By the 1990s a diverse range of products including tyres and tyre-related items, latex goods, footwear, industrial rubber goods and general rubber articles was produced by this industry, which was dominated by domestic firms in terms of the number of establishments and paid-up capital. These firms coexisted with multinationals, which were foremost in all exports except tyres. Rubber products were small in exports due to the strong performance in this sphere of electrical and electronics goods and the emergence of new export-oriented industries such as transport equipment, chemical and chemical products and furniture (Malaysia 1996a).

Human resources
The government investment in developing the Rubber Research Institute of Malaysia as a premier research centre included large expenditures in training, and senior staff who later moved into industry became an important source of experienced and highly qualified professionals (Ong 1996).

However, although formal training at supervisory level was conducted by both the Rubber Research Institute and the Plastics and Rubber Institute of Malaysia, it was inadequate for the needs of the industry (ibid.). Again at firm level, there was little evidence of private-sector, long-term investment in training, and the skills acquired by workers were thus very much honed on the job. Such training depends critically on the level of technology utilized by the firm, which in turn depends on the ownership pattern as well as the type of product produced. In this regard, multinationals in more capital-intensive sub-sectors like tyre manufacturing could provide better opportunities for the development of workers' skills through their utilization of more sophisticated technology.

The significant rubber gloves sector of the rubber products industry is labour-intensive, operating on matured technologies. Compared to the electrical and electronics industry, the option of using automation as a means of overcoming labour shortages has been hindered by lack of available technology, especially in labour-intensive areas such as stripping and packing gloves. Thus labour shortages from the late 1980s have been met with imports of foreign workers. In this context, training labour to raise its productivity is perhaps more pertinent to enhancing human resources in the cluster development of this industry.

Technology
Although the Rubber Research Institute was initially set up for research on producing natural rubber, its functions were later expanded to cover consumption and end-use aspects. The maintenance by government of a research body working on end-use in England and establishment in 1976 of a technology centre in Kuala Lumpur helped spearhead the early development of the rubber products industry.

The Institute provided invaluable technical support for manufacturers in four specific ways (ibid.). First, its basic work in latex technology established an extensive technical base for supporting dipped-goods manufacture. Second, it did specific research on problems encountered by the industry. Third, its laboratory testing services helped maintain as well as improve the quality of both rubber and rubber products. Fourth, its consultancy and contract research services were geared to address the needs of individual firms. However, the Institute's technical support was more beneficial with latex goods, where the main input was natural rubber latex.

With tyres, which also depended on other inputs such as synthetic rubber and tyre cords, the cost-advantage from investments in public-led research was smaller. Unfortunately, in the late 1990s the Institute was facing increasing financial constraints, which would restrict its ability to assist downstream rubber manufacturing.

The technology utilized by rubber products firms depends on the ownership and size of operations (Lim 1989). Wholly foreign-owned or joint-venture companies, which are usually larger, tend to use more sophisticated technology sourced from parent companies. With local entrepreneurs, technology other than that provided by the Rubber Research Institute has been transferred through experiences in joint ventures as well as through licensing agreements, technical support from machinery suppliers and the imitation of foreign-produced goods via trial and error. Although private local R&D efforts in Malaysia remain limited, they are expected to improve following the establishment by the big local company, Sime Darby, of a technology centre.

Linkages
A study of input–output tables for the early 1980s denotes rubber products as ranking third among six industries found to have high net-total linkage effects. This is not surprising, given the industry's backward linkage with natural rubber and especially its consumption of latex concentrates which have latterly been imported with the rapid growth of latex goods. This backward linkage was

promoted through subsidies from natural rubber producers, who paid export duties together with R&D and replanting cesses from which rubber manufacturers were exempted. The latter also bought local rubber at a discount to internationally traded prices. The export duty exemption and discount were, however, rescinded in 1991, while withdrawal of cesses in 1998 will remove the final cost advantages of using Malaysian input.

The use by rubber products manufacturers of locally made machinery depended on the type of output. Thus domestic industry was able to supply equipment and related services for latex goods, where mature technology was used and experience in making machines had grown over many years. However, the complex plant required in the technologically more sophisticated tyre-making was imported from countries with greater scale economies in its production. Again, precision mould and die facilities were mostly imported, due to the limited abilities of local industry. Furthermore, local engineering and technical support services were inadequate to back up complex machinery and precision laboratories, and only limited rubber chemicals were produced to meet industry needs. Yet backward linkages in all these spheres were being created over time.

The forward linkages in rubber products were mainly between the tyre sub-sector and local car manufacturers and assemblers. Hence more than 80 per cent of the output of major tyre factories was utilized either as original equipment tyres for Malaysian car makers and assemblers or as replacement tyres. This linkage was encouraged by tariff protection for both tyres and automobiles, with the protection of tyres being higher than that of rubber footwear and other rubber products (Tham 1994).

The Automotive Industry

Despite its small contribution of 4.8 per cent to total manufacturing output in 1995, the automotive industry was important in domestic industrial growth. Prior to 1983 the industry was fragmented, with assemblers producing various foreign models at uneconomic scales in the limited domestic market. In 1983, the government rationalized and upgraded the industry by promoting a single manufacturer, Proton, which was launched through the Heavy Industry Corporation of Malaysia. Proton was given higher protection than other assemblers, many of whom ceased their operations or diversified into related activities such as the production of component parts.

Proton was viewed by government as a strategic project, and its role extended to developing domestic component parts manufacturing by providing a sufficient scale of production. It had the further function as a technology and skills leader to its suppliers, helping them to attain a high level of competency. Thus by 1996 it was sourcing 60 per cent of its components domestically. Proton has grown fast since 1985, with annual production increasing from 60 000 units in

1984 to 180 000 in 1996 when 14 per cent of its output was exported. It has also ventured into car design, establishing an R&D centre and acquiring foreign technology. The automotive industry can be regarded as one of the most developed clusters in Malaysian manufacturing.

Human resources

Compared to the latex goods sub-sector, Proton employed more highly skilled labour thanks to the more capital-intensive production process. The latter required high precision, and this was reflected by the extensive use of robots in certain stages of production, including body assembly. The tight labour market from the late 1980s also encouraged automation. In 1983 there was a pool of trained workers previously employed by assemblers, and this spared Proton the high cost of initial training while allowing it to quickly achieve high production. However, for key tasks Proton still relies today on expertise from its foreign technology partner, Mitsubishi, since skills have not been successfully transferred.

Proton also sourced semi-skilled production workers from local technical and vocational training institutes sponsored by government, itself providing higher training to supplement basic skills imparted by the institutes. This link with institutes allowed it to achieve its further goal of upgrading the skills capabilities of Bumiputera workers. That goal was also secured among parts suppliers,[5] who attained reasonable skills levels with help from Proton and foreign technology partners who were themselves suppliers of Mitsubishi.

Although Proton was quite successful in skills development, its competency was low in critical spheres including product and mechanical design, engineering and computer-aided manufacturing, with progress towards becoming a global automotive producer and owner of technology depending on strengthening these skills. This lack of skills impeded the transfer of technology, which was also delayed by reluctance on the part of the technology partner, Mitsubishi.

Technology

When Malaysia embarked on the path to producing its own car, it did not possess the required technology. Its only route was to bring in foreign technology through a joint venture, on condition that there would be transfer of expertise. While Mitsubishi's share was small in terms of equity, its ownership of technology gave it a strategic position. The Malaysian government's equity in Proton was subsequently sold to the public, although it retains control through indirect ownership.

The technology arrangement with Mitsubishi has implications both for Proton and its parts suppliers. First, the Japanese partner chooses products to be made and inputs to be used. Such choice of products has restricted Proton's ability to produce new models meeting market demand, as any changes require the partner's agreement. This constraint may have affected Proton's export performance, although its domestic market share was less influenced, thanks to the price advantage. Second, the partner's decision on types and quality of inputs has restricted Proton's control over production costs, which have been high, with sourcing of most items from Japan. Non-Japanese inputs were not feasible, being judged unlikely to meet strict specifications. Such foreign-sourcing of inputs likewise exposed Proton to currency fluctuations.

Third, the technology arrangement also controlled the development programme for parts suppliers. The latter were closely linked with Mitsubishi's Japanese suppliers through tight technical link-ups (Mahani 1996), with raw materials coming largely from Japan. These link-ups determined the standard of component parts, involving high royalty and technical agreement costs. Each vendor had a partner to help in maintaining a certain level of efficiency and quality. Yet, although this third aspect limited Proton's ability to manoeuvre, it was a key factor ensuring cluster development, for in copying the Japanese production system Malaysia generated a similar cluster network.

Under these conditions, however, growth could only proceed to a certain stage, and the next level of cluster development to full technology competency and product design may be difficult to achieve owing to unwillingness on the part of the technology partner to transfer the required expertise. This issue has a political economy aspect, since the mostly Bumiputera-owned parts suppliers were supposed to provide a base for further industrialization. In its quest to own technology, Proton has sought other partners, and even bought a specialized automotive company with advanced technological capability. These new moves have yet to prove as successful as the partnership with Mitsubishi, however.

Linkages

Proton's linkages are among the most extensive in Malaysian manufacturing. Its parts suppliers are well established and it has its own marketing, distribution and services networks. These linkages can partly be attributed to the protection afforded to Proton, comprising very high tariffs of 200 to 300 per cent, quantitative restrictions on importing complete cars and preferentially low duties on imported parts. This protection guaranteed sufficient production to make parts-supplying and related services activities profitable.

Proton likewise tried to ensure the viability of suppliers through a single sourcing policy, absorbing all output of one supplier assigned a specific part. Further assistance was extended in technical aid, quality control and support, financial assistance and capital for technology improvement. Proton also extended these benefits to parts manufacturers other than those with whom it had long relations; it secured components from these so as to meet the mandatory local content programme whereby 60 per cent of parts should be sourced locally by the year 2000, against threatened higher import duties. These policies encouraged the production of component parts to expand substantially, including exports to global automotive producers. Yet this success in establishing backward linkages was not without its weaknesses, where protection of Proton parts suppliers allowed these to operate below an internationally efficient level with high production costs.[6.]

The single sourcing policy, although vital for viability, aggravated the situation, since it did not encourage increases in productivity and competitiveness. Furthermore, the local content programme did not solve the problem of high import content, because most sub-components were still imported.

CONCLUSION

Malaysia paved the way to industrial development through export promotion and import substitution strategies, entailing extensive intervention through subsidies and protection. Its export promotion depended on multinationals to generate employment, growth and exports, while its import substitution involved retaining control so as to fulfil national policies of redistribution. This chapter has considered the aspect of cluster development, and the way this has affected economic progress within Malaysian industries.

The dependence on multinationals constrained the state's ability to promote cluster development, since these companies had global strategies and optimized global rather than national resource use and profit. The clusters they form in each host economy depend on the types of product, production technologies, the size of the host and regional markets; they also hinge especially on human resources in the host economy, as well as host policies affecting transactions costs. Thus, in Malaysia with the electrical and electronics industry, backward linkages were developed with the host economy based on the use of new production technologies. With rubber products, linkages were forged through the availability of raw material and use of matured technologies. However, linkages were limited where scale economies were important and the size of domestic market small, as in tyre production.

In contrast, the cluster formed by the state in an import-substitution industry like Proton was cultivated, with specific policy measures besides provision of protection and subsidies. These measures enabled the domestic market to be captured by Proton, guaranteeing scale economies necessary for developing domestic suppliers. But it remains uncertain as to whether networks formed in this sub-sector can survive international competition with removal of tariffs and subsidies.

It may be concluded on the basis of experiences recounted that, despite limitations, state intervention has facilitated the formation of economically useful clusters in Malaysian manufacturing. At the same time, limitations were encountered with different interventions. The issue that needs addressing is whether forms of intervention should be modified as objectives of industrialization change over time. Thus, the drive to develop more integrated manufacturing envisioned by current national planning requires careful rethinking, especially concerning how intervention can assist the development of higher value-added and technology-intensive industries.

First, tariffs, subsidies and specific interventions regarding the import-substituting sector and exemplified by Proton need an explicit time-frame for withdrawal. There should be a concurrent and complementary plan for improving the competitiveness of protected firms, in terms not only of quality of exports but of wider technological and skills capacities. Second, interventions focusing on economic foundations are very useful, offering scope for firms to develop organizational forms best suited to individual environments (Robertson and Langlois 1992). In particular, developing indigenous technological capabilities as well as innovative abilities requires state intervention in R&D and education given the long gestation period and the economies of scale involved. Strengthening future cluster development will, accordingly, require a shift in focus from promoting exports and import-substitution to promoting technology and human resources.

Promoting technology as an industrialization strategy needs alternative modes of technology-acquisition and development besides the traditional dependence on transfer from multinationals or technology partners. One option is the 'bottom-up' approach to technology acquisition suggested by Morris-Suzuki (1992); here state aid is used to set up research organizations like the Rubber Research Institute, helping local producers by providing basic scientific and technical support as well as testing facilities. Another alternative is to use state investment in acquiring appropriate technology subsequently licensed to independent local firms to enhance their technological capabilities, but the question arises whether the state can identify the appropriate technology, and this would require close collaboration with industries, perhaps through consultative meetings between industry associations and technically trained bureaucrats.

Technology promotion may be seen as going hand-in-hand with human resource promotion, with the latter comprising not only the provision of scientists and engineers for the state but also the furnishing of the skilled labour necessary to adapt and improve acquired technology and develop new indigenous technologies. Technology and human resource promotion represent the new twin prongs of industrial development that crucially accompany cluster formation in deepening industrial growth in Malaysia.

NOTES

1. Jesudason (1990) suggested that the government's partiality towards foreign direct investment could possibly be due to Malay insecurity with Chinese economic power.
2. Bumiputera means 'sons of the soil'. This group includes the Malays, Iban and other earlier inhabitants of Peninsular Malaysia, Sabah and Sarawak.
3. SMIs were defined as manufacturing establishments with less than 2.5 million ringgit in paid-up capital and 5–75 full-time workers.
4. In economic geography, a cluster is a spatial concept, where firms locate in a regional centre close to markets to derive mutual agglomeration benefits including economies of scale and lower transportation and transactions costs.
5. The parts suppliers involved are known in Malaysia as 'vendors', being nurtured by automotive manufacturers through special programmes and incentives.
6. Under the ASEAN Free Trade Area programme, products traded in the region will face a tariff rate of 5 per cent or less. This rate is much lower than the level presently enjoyed by the Malaysian automotive industry.

6. Entrepreneurship and Institutions: The Southeast Asian Experience

Jamie Mackie

Where does a chapter on 'entrepreneurship' belong in a set of essays on institutional approaches to economic development? And what light can we expect it to throw on such a topic? There are no easy answers to either question, although some of the ideas explored here may point towards fruitful ways to think about them. The primary purpose of this paper is to examine the notion of 'entrepreneurship' within the institutional rather than the more usual 'cultural', or values-oriented, frame of reference. This is done with particular regard to one distinctive feature of Southeast Asian economic development – the overwhelming dominance of Overseas Chinese commercial and industrial enterprise at the levels both of small and medium enterprises and of large-scale enterprises in most parts of the region (Mackie 1992, 1998). Which factors, be they institutional, structural or cultural, are most important in explanations of why so many Southeast Asian Chinese seem to have been better endowed with commercial and entrepreneurial skills than indigenous people?

The answers most frequently given to those questions have tended to stress most heavily certain well-known values of the Overseas Chinese, such as their hard work, frugality, diligence, high savings rates, persistence and so on. These values have been so widely observed all over Southeast Asia throughout many decades that it would be absurd to suggest they are not directly relevant to any interpretation that might be offered for the highly entrepreneurial character of Chinese commercial enterprise in much of the region. Hence the legacy of traditional Chinese values and Chinese culture is often said to be the key to their success. But that alone is not a sufficient explanation, for innumerable hard-working and diligent Overseas Chinese have remained poor while those same values and their cultural traditions have not generated the same success in China itself in recent centuries; thus there must also be other elements to take into account in the equation.

In this chapter the stress will be put mainly on several institutional factors which are relevant – the nature of Chinese family firms, the benefits or costs of distinctively Chinese business practices, the importance of the almost legendary Overseas Chinese networks at different points of time, and the significance to

72

be attached to the large Chinese conglomerate corporations which have emerged as one of the most striking features of Southeast Asian capitalism in recent decades. The latter are often taken to be emblematic of Chinese entrepreneurial dynamism, but it is necessary to look more deeply into all these things – and also into the concept of entrepreneurship itself – before jumping to simplistic conclusions about the connections between them.

Various definitions and explanations of entrepreneurship have been put forward by economists and other social scientists over the years, yet the mystery of just what the secret ingredient is which may be found at its core (if any) remains as elusive as ever. As Kilby (1971, p. 1) has put it:

> The search for the sources of dynamic entrepreneurial performance has much in common with hunting the Heffalump ... a large and very important animal [who appears in A.A. Milne's *Winnie the Pooh* children's stories]. He has been hunted by many individuals using various ingenious devices, but no one has yet succeeded in capturing him. All who claim to have sighted him report that he is enormous, but they disagree on his particularities.

For that reason, it is preferable to talk about entrepreneurial qualities (plural) which may be of diverse kinds, rather than to assume that entrepreneurship (singular) consists of some unique distinguishing characteristic or inner quality of an almost Platonic 'essentialist' type. By taking a more flexible approach to the subject instead of being confined to narrow definitions of the entrepreneur as being, for instance, a creator of 'new combinations' of factors of production along Schumpeterian lines, it is possible to extend the concept beyond a special kind of individual to also embrace large corporations or even government instrumentalities of an especially dynamic nature. Conversely, while many entrepreneurs are of the Horatio Alger, rags-to-riches type, by no means all are of that ilk, so that kind of stereotyped notion should not be allowed to dominate thinking about who can or cannot be classed as an entrepreneur.

It is noteworthy that after 20 years of pioneering work – under Schumpeter's auspices at the Harvard Center for Entrepreneurial Studies – on entrepreneurship and the life histories of leading entrepreneurs, as well as the publication of the useful *Explorations in Entrepreneurial History*, the end result turned out to be a bewildering diversity of approaches and endless definitional debates about who could properly be labelled as 'an entrepreneur' (Aitken 1963). There was not much point, observed Aitken, in scanning the historical record in search of entrepreneurs as if they alone were the primary agents of growth. For the kind of behaviour to which the term 'entrepreneurial' could be attached was just as characteristic of large business firms as of individual capitalists of a Schumpeterian or Weberian stamp. To explain why a particular firm or particular country or period of time had proved more enterprising or productive of entrepreneurship than another, it was often better to investigate the structures of the society or firm itself rather than the motivations, personalities, social origins or education of particular capitalists.

When this kind of approach of looking not for some single quality common to all but to a range of qualities is applied to the question of why the Southeast Asian Chinese have been so much more lavishly endowed with entrepreneurial drive and business acumen than their indigenous counterparts, it becomes easier to identify reasons why the former have done better, on the whole, than the latter. One reason, which could in one sense be described as institutional, is that many of them have been able to gain an early start in the race to climb higher up the ladder of socioeconomic advancement towards the commanding heights, thereby effectively excluding rivals from the most desirable positions in the hierarchy (Mackie 1998, pp. 137–8). Their success in this has certainly not been due to any ingrained capacities or attributes, nor simply to a unique set of inherited values or mental characteristics; but it does seem to have its roots in a complex tangle of factors like Chinese family structures, childhood socialization patterns, and aspirations, value systems, clan solidarity and various distinctive features of Chinese family firms and business practices. All these factors have been called upon as partial explanations for the higher degrees of business success of the Chinese, or for the lesser inclination towards business careers among indigenous groups. It is more fruitful, therefore, to examine the inner dynamics and interconnections of these factors for the light they throw on central problems here, than simply to search for some secret essence of entrepreneurship as such. Yet it is equally important to discover in what circumstances entrepreneurial qualities flourish abundantly, and when they do not.

ENTREPRENEURSHIP AND ECONOMIC DEVELOPMENT

Many development economists in the 1950s and 1960s took the view that there could be no real development in Southeast Asian, less-developed countries until a class of indigenous entrepreneurs or capitalists had emerged to carry out the pioneering tasks of capital accumulation, risk-taking investment and technological innovation that European capitalists had performed with such great success and profit during the 60 years or so prior to World War II (Allen and Donnithorne 1957). Hence there was a spate of studies of the Heffalump-hunting type, directed towards either finding embryonic entrepreneurial groups who might serve those functions, or at least identifying value systems that would be most favourable to nurturing such a class (Geertz 1956; Ayal 1969; Carroll 1966), assuming that this was a necessary condition for capitalist development. In the eyes of researchers influenced by Weberian ideas of the role of value systems as main determinants of motivations among the more dynamic businessmen, as in the case of the Puritan ethic and rise of capitalism, it was thought that in less-developed countries a profound shift in values away from those of traditional cultures towards those of the modern world was essential before a new capitalist class could emerge to pioneer economic development.

By the late 1960s, however, it was becoming apparent that the rise of a capitalist class was not a necessary condition for the development of dynamic capitalist economies in the Third World, since rapid growth was taking place in several countries where relatively few highly entrepreneurial capitalists had yet appeared. As Benjamin Higgins (1989, p. 33) later pointed out, it is essentially 'the sudden opening up of opportunities to make money through a different kind of economic activity [in Libya, in his case] that triggered the explosion of indigenous entrepreneurial effort. ... [There was] no apparent evidence of long, slow but fundamental cultural change before the appearance of indigenous entrepreneurship ...'.

Leff (1979) has also commented that, whereas a lack of entrepreneurship had earlier seemed to constitute a serious problem for less-developed countries, the situation had subsequently changed, for 'the actual experience of most less-developed countries in the postwar period has belied expectations that lack of entrepreneurship would prove a constraint on economic development. And since the early 1970s the subject has virtually disappeared from the literature, suggesting that in some sense the problem has been resolved.' In short, where and when opportunities are plentiful, lots of business persons with entrepreneurial qualities are likely to emerge, whereas in situations where trade is severely restricted or funds are scarce they will rarely do so. That still leaves us with a chicken-and-egg question about how development gets started in situations where few entrepreneurs or capitalist are in evidence, unless we assume some exogenous source of rising incomes and demand (as in the Libyan case of Higgins, where an oil boom made the difference). The latter does seem to have been the situation in the Southeast Asian 'Economic Miracle' of the 1970s to 1990s, although local capitalists soon emerged as entrepreneurs.

CHINESE COMMERCIAL PRACTICES AS AN INSTITUTIONAL FACTOR

A fine account of Overseas Chinese commercial culture and institutions in Southeast Asia is given in Omohondro's 1981 study, *Chinese Merchant Families in Iloilo: Commerce and Kin in a Philippine City*. It is especially good on the complex interplay of ethnicity and economic roles in the context of Iloilo, a long-established and relatively small trading community of about 5000 ethnic Chinese in the western Visayas. 'Chinese ethnicity owes much to the fact that almost all Chinese are merchants in Iloilo', he observes. In discussing 'the economic advantages of the social structure', he sees the socio-cultural traits associated with Chineseness as beneficial in the Iloilo situation, where business life and family life are still so closely interwoven as to be almost inseparable. 'Chinese are better businessmen than Filipinos because of the advantages in their social structure ... Chinese cultural features relating to business success are most likely to be preserved. Thus the merchant niche and Chinese immigrant culture are interacting in several ways ...'. The Chinese are a very homogeneous group, 'a closed ethnic community under a tight rein' with the powerful sanction of ostracism available to punish deviant members, by making use of extensive commercial networks which reach far across the country. A businessman who gets a bad name for lack of trustworthiness will soon find doors closed to him far and wide.

> Many of the mercantile practices used ... are cultural forms which developed in China and were adapted by them to colonial and immigrant situations. The banking system, apprenticeship cycle, high reliance on *sin-ion* [trust], certain forms of partnerships, loans, and ... various types of merchant organizations, were social structural features of Chinese society which provide a competitive advantage when doing business among Filipinos, who are without similarly developed institutions.

Omohondro goes on to describe the 'merchant culture' that preserves and transmits those business values and institutions in other, more subtle ways – the organizational complexity, the 'intangible and unstable nature of wealth' in relation to social prestige within the community as well as the distinctive socialization of children, all of which give them 'stronger and more positive attitudes toward work ... business and businessmen ... practicality and materialism, and more negative attitudes towards government regulation and profit-sharing' (pp. 83–7).

A study of business strategies and management practices among Southeast Asian Chinese by Limlingan (1986) supplements Omohondro's account in this respect. It seeks to show that their commercial success is primarily due to the characteristic Chinese business strategy of working with low profit margins and high turnover in order to build up market share, a practice reported from many other sources also. It has to be questioned here, of course, whether the Chinese always keep profit margins low once they have achieved a strong market share or a near-monopoly position – and if they do, why? Omohondro gives a useful account of the Chinese 'cash-flow system' of accounting, which he claims has the advantage of simplicity over double-entry although it also has disadvantages, and of the related custom of issuing postdated cheques and settling all accounts prior to Chinese New Year as a device for clearing books and clarifying profits or losses. It is easy to imagine that under circumstances of small-scale trade and rudimentary financial control systems these devices may have served the Chinese well, but whether they suit more complex large-scale enterprises is more questionable.

Another attempt to provide clues about ways in which the Overseas Chinese combine the methods of the family firm with the requirements of larger forms of corporate enterprise was given in a much-quoted but distinctly problematic account by Henny Sender (1991) of what she calls the 'maddeningly impenetrable' Hong Kong–Southeast Asia network. It seems indeed that the latter should surely be visualized as plural, not singular, and hence as a tangle of often unrelated or loosely connected networks, and by no means simply one. Sender explains that the international outflows of Chinese capital associated with those networks are due to the fact that they are 'too large and too conspicuously in control of sectors of the local market ... [hence they must] snap up similar assets outside the region' (p. 30). This seems to be a highly dubious inference in most cases. In other cases it is a matter of diversification, she says, or defensive acquisitions of secure markets abroad, or of hedging against political risks by keeping a nest-egg off-shore. Yet none of those strategies except perhaps the latter is distinctively Chinese.

Sender further comments that in their corporate structures 'many of the great Chinese families in the region array their holdings as a squat pyramid: the public companies form a broad base, while the most lucrative assets – the ones that command the attention of the head of the enterprise – are reserved for the private holding company at the apex ...'. Many transactions take place between companies in the pyramid, at low prices going up and high prices on the way down. Some of Hong Kong's *taipans* (leading business persons) are 'notorious for raising money from shareholders at lower levels of ... the pyramid, then infusing the capital at the top' – at the expense of other shareholders whose assets are thereby diluted in value. 'What is profit is 100% mine, and what is loss is mostly not mine', she asserts.

How far these allegedly Chinese commercial practices really are characteristic of the more successful Southeast Asian Chinese business persons and their firms is a factual question which no one has yet investigated in detail. They could be most relevant, if verified, to any explanation of the causes of their entrepreneurial success, but until more work similar to Omohondro's has been done towards sorting out realities from mythology regarding these matters, it is unwise to draw more than carefully qualified conclusions.

CHINESE FAMILY FIRMS: ANALYTICAL AND INSTITUTIONAL ISSUES

It is impossible to probe very far into the entrepreneurial drives of Southeast Asian Chinese without looking closely into the character of their small family firms, which have so often pioneered the commercial development of the region over the past century. These firms appear to be utterly different from the business organizations of the various indigenous peoples, despite some similarities in kinship structures and a shared belief in strong family solidarity. However, the Chinese family firm is predominant not just at the rudimentary small and medium enterprise level, but also among the large corporate conglomerates found at a later stage of development in all parts of Southeast Asia. So any inquiry into these family firms leads into a tangle of issues about how the values and socialization patterns inculcated within the family have influenced the actual behaviour of family firms, both small and large.

It used to be thought that 'familism and economic development are antipathetic [in the Chinese socio-cultural milieu] ... individual saving is discouraged ... the extended family tends to dilute individual incentives to work, save and invest' (Wong Siu-lun 1988, p. 134). That was a belief which led Max Weber to write of 'the sib fetters on the economy', but since the great economic successes of the Neo-Confucian or Post-Confucian newly industrializing countries (and of the Southeast Asian Chinese) that view is no longer tenable. Writers searching for explanations of those countries' successes have been looking closely at Chinese values, family structures and family firms as key variables.

Those variables were undoubtedly very important in the early years of Chinese emigration to Southeast Asia, when family firms were the classic form of Chinese economic organization and family labour (along with the discipline fathers could exert over their sons and daughters through control over the family patrimony) was crucial to their success. It is less clear how relevant these variables are today, as more and more small Chinese family firms have grown into larger, more complex corporate enterprises utilizing modern managerial techniques and employing graduates and masters of business administration from overseas. Nearly all the largest Chinese conglomerates in Southeast Asia are still family-owned firms, as well as the innumerable smaller enterprises. But questions arise about the extent to which traditional Chinese business practices or attitudes deriving from the small family firm still persist in larger organizations. Is there an inevitable trend towards a global 'modernity' and homogeneity in outlook, or will the old, distinctively Chinese characteristics persist among the Overseas Chinese, just as distinctively Japanese ones have done in Japan? The latter seems most likely.

Accounts of the economic behaviour of Overseas Chinese nearly all emphasize the versatility and entrepreneurial flair of their family firms, along with the particular characteristics of Chinese family structure, as the primary sources of socialization and transmission of values conducive to business success. Surprisingly little has been written about Chinese family firms as such in Southeast Asia, however, excepting Omohondro (1981) and parts of the older ethnographic literature on the region's Chinese. Some clues can be found in the growing literature on the subject in Northeast Asia, and especially in the illuminating works of Wong Siu-lun (1985 and 1988) which may suggest parallels elsewhere. One would expect to find both similarities and differences, although the former may be less marked among those Southeast Asian Chinese communities which have experienced substantial modification of their older Chinese values. Where some acculturation towards local customs and values is occurring, the firms may already differ significantly from those of mainland China, Taiwan or Hong Kong, but until more empirical research is done on this subject, it is only possible to make guesses on that point.

'The essence of Chinese economic organization is familism', observed Wong Siu-lun (1985, p. 58). By familism he meant any one or all of three things: nepotism, or preferential recruitment, employment or promotion of kin; a paternalistic ideal of how superiors and subordinates should interact; and an emphasis on maintaining family ownership and control of business assets rather than on subdividing them among siblings. These characteristics were not inherently related to each other, he noted, although they often went together, but he also observed more significantly that 'what is relevant is not the dichotomy between kin and non-kin, but between "personal and impersonal"', for the Chinese have a strong antipathy to impersonal institutions and contracts as a basis for business dealings. Wong Siu-lun postulated a stylized cycle of development of the family firm entailing emergent, centralized, segmented and disintegrating stages, which is a more sophisticated version of the old Chinese saying about a three-generation cycle from rags to riches to ruin. He also found that the chief executive role was not often rotated among family members. Chinese enterprise tends to be 'strong in entrepreneurialism but weak in management' (ibid., p. 197).

It must be remembered, however, that family enterprises still play an important part in business in other parts of the world; they are not a uniquely Chinese phenomenon, nor dependent solely on the value systems or tight family structures of the Chinese. There is a substantial literature to be found in other countries on the strengths and weaknesses of large family firms, which are numerous in France and still significant even in the United States and Britain (Mackie 1992, pp. 54–5). The more that is learned about the general structural characteristics or morphology of such firms, the better for an understanding of what is distinctive about the Chinese variety.

Any inquiry into the dynamics of entrepreneurship among family firms leads also into a consideration of the links, if any, between small and medium enterprises and large corporate structures, and the patterns of growth of the firm from the one to the other in Southeast Asia, about which little is yet known. The Northeast Asian economies reveal a variety of patterns which have emerged. In Japan, the big *keiretsu* conglomerates have played a dominant part in shaping the economic development of the country, with small and medium enterprises serving mainly as sub-contractors to them. Only a few of Japan's large corporations started out in the small enterprise category, with Sony and Toyota being the most notable among these. By contrast, Taiwan's rapid growth until the 1980s at least was due mainly to the efforts of myriad small and medium enterprises, constantly rising to the top and many then collapsing like a 'bubbling cauldron'. South Korea has had nothing like the plethora of such enterprises that Taiwan has had, because of the dominance of the dozen or so great *chaebol* since the 1950s and 1960s. While Taiwan has also begun to generate a few large-scale conglomerates since the 1970s, they appear very different types of organization from the Korean *chaebol*, the Japanese *keiretsu* or the Southeast Asian conglomerates.

Hong Kong has had both small- and large-scale enterprises, but is closer to the Taiwan pattern than the Korean. Yet nearly all enterprises in the countries mentioned here are still essentially family firms, except in Japan which is quite a different story having had a much longer history of large-scale business houses which were originally family firms but are no longer so in most instances. A few of the Japanese houses like Mitsui and Sumitomo have also lasted well beyond the three generations normally attributed to the life cycle of Chinese firms. The reasons why each of these countries has had its own distinctive pattern in this respect cannot be reduced to any one or two structural or institutional determinants. They have to be traced out in historical and socio-cultural detail, involving family types, family enterprises and the kinds of 'structure and strategy' issues that are explored in other contexts by Chandler (1962).

GROUPS, CONGLOMERATES AND NETWORKS

To understand the economic rationale – as distinct from the political connections so often invoked to explain them – behind the emergence in Southeast Asia over the last 20 years of large-scale conglomerates mostly owned by local ethnic Chinese, there is no better starting point than the work of Nathaniel Leff (1976, 1978) on 'economic groups' as he discerned them in Latin America. He sees these groups as contributing significantly to economic development in less-developed countries by helping to 'relax the entrepreneurial constraint' on the pace of economic change there (ibid., p. 670). The groups in those countries have their origins in the prior existence of market imperfections. Leff also writes that:

> In an ideal-type market system, without uncertainty, factor-market imperfections, and externalities, entrepreneurship would not be necessary. But those conditions clearly are not likely to be found in most less developed countries, and government interventionism and the big business groups (which can internalize the costs arising from uncertainty, inadequate information, and capricious factor-market flows) have accordingly emerged to substitute both for a perfect market and for pure entrepreneurship. Indeed, the very success of robber barons in less developed countries in dealing

with difficulties of entrepreneurship has led to 'a redefinition of the difficulty'; the problem has now become the new economic distortions, social imbalances, and political dissension engendered by successful economic performance (Leff 1979, p. 60).

In Leff's theory, the economic group performs several of the economic functions formerly attributed to entrepreneurs. It generates growth and reduces transactions costs by internalizing them within the group; it integrates imperfect markets, permits economies of scale and gains ready access to credit thereby performing the capital accumulation function which used to be regarded as the major constraint to growth in poor countries. The group, he says,

> can be conceptualized as an organizational structure for appropriating quasi-rents which accrue from access to scarce and imperfectly marketed inputs. Some of these inputs, such as capital, might be marketed more efficiently, but in the conditions of LDCs they are not. Some ... are inherently difficult to market efficiently; for example, honesty and trustworthy competence on the part of high-level managers. ... The absence of markets for risk and uncertainty also helps explain another feature of the groups' pattern of expansion – their entry into diversified product lines ... diversification has an obvious appeal in economies subject to the risks and uncertainties of instability and rapid structural change (Leff 1978, p. 667).

Leff goes on to propose that the group pattern of industrial organization conforms well with Leibenstein's (1968) theory of entrepreneurship and development, which suggests that

> entrepreneurship in LDCs involves the opening of channels for input supply and for marketing of output in situations where a routinized market mechanism does not exist. In the absence of such 'intermarket operators' some input and/or output quantities, qualities, and costs would be so clouded by risk and uncertainty that investment and production in these activities would not take place. The groups create a channel both for mobilizing and for allocating such inputs and outputs. In fact, the group can perhaps best be understood as an institutional innovation for internalizing the returns which accrue from interactivity operations in the imperfect market conditions of the LDCs.

These perceptions are useful contributions to the understanding both of entrepreneurship and of the growth of conglomerates in developing countries, particularly as they underline the point that entrepreneurial dynamism is not just a quality to be sought in the motivations of individuals with drive, foresight or frugality, but something that may inhere in the institutional structures of large-scale, impersonal corporate enterprises, regardless of the individual qualities of the chief executive (Chandler 1990). It can now be seen that the earlier focus on rags-to-riches entrepreneurs as the potential pioneers of capitalism was wrongly directed. This is illustrated, for example, by Geertz's ill-fated 'shop-keeper revolution' in Indonesia, which he sought among petty traders in subsistence markets but which never happened. In fact, it could even be argued that the free-wheeling, entrepreneurial character of the large Indonesian state oil company, Pertamina, under its first director, Ibnu Sutowo, made a more important contribution to the growth of Indonesian capitalism in the early 1970s before it crashed under a mountain of debt in 1974. This was because it raised the confidence of Indonesians and gave them the experience to play in that kind of big league.

Contrary to Leff's hypothesis, however, Ramon Myers (1989, p. 288) has argued that Chinese firms in mainland China prior to 1949, and in Taiwan and Hong Kong, 'have traditionally handled their transactions costs in the marketplace rather than trying to internalize those costs within the firm, an action requiring more impersonal interactions and a more complex assignment of tasks. This avoidance of impersonal ties and strong preference for personal ties to handle transactions costs is not only a salient feature of Chinese firm behaviour but flows well from specific Confucian values and behaviour.' It remains to be seen whether Southeast Asian Chinese firms try to externalize their transactions costs, as Myers suggests, or internalize them à la Leff. In short, is it culture or structure and institutions that plays the greater part here?

One limitation of the group approach at this stage is that it does not in itself give much information about how or why large groups have emerged; it is merely a theory purporting to conceptualize their significance as agents of development in terms that fit comfortably within neoclassical economic theory. Yet it is still important to know whether they emerged because of some particular entrepreneurial qualities in their founders (or the men and women who pulled various firms together to critical-mass size), and if so what those qualities were. It is further significant to ascertain the institutional circumstances and policy regimes within which they were able to prosper.

Finally, the significance of Chinese commercial and financial 'networks' originally based on *pang* or speech-group ties deserves attention as an associated phenomenon for reducing transactions costs, ensuring 'trust' and reliable information about the reputation and creditworthiness of individuals among traders scattered across a wide area, and providing access to market information and an easily accessible source of commercial funds in communities with rudimentary banking and credit facilities. These networks also functioned initially as a form of sanction against bad debtors. Recently they have attracted more attention as a means of gaining access to large sums of capital on the basis of personal contacts and *guangxi*. Both the early and modern types of network imply great reliance on personal contacts in the marketplace and a consequent low degree of internalization or institutionalization of transactions costs; this aspect seems to conform more closely to the Myers paradigm than to that of Leff.

CONCLUSION: ENTREPRENEURSHIP AND THE INSTITUTIONAL APPROACH

The old notion that development cannot occur until a class of entrepreneurs has emerged (or that a dynamic and efficient state sector has taken on the kinds of role they normally perform, as seen in Singapore) was apparently based on a misconception. Entrepreneurial drive and business skills are likely to emerge quickly once sufficient momentum of growth has been generated, no matter whether exogenously or endogenously, so that ample opportunities present themselves for what Higgins has termed 'making a buck'. The Indonesian Chinese had been displaying entrepreneurial qualities in abundance for decades (or centuries) before Suharto's New Order economic miracle began to open up wider horizons for them following his assumption of power in the late 1960s. There was little sign prior to 1965 that those qualities would enable them to spearhead the process of economic development in Indonesia, mainly because the momentum of growth was too sluggish and policy environment too adverse for them to invest confidently in anything but short-term projects. Chinese capital was until then directed mainly towards fast-turnover import-export trading activities or commodity dealing. The situation in present-day Vietnam, where a pool of Chinese talents also exists, shows that the momentum of growth is too feeble to generate much entrepreneurial activity since the economic environment is too unfavourable.

The contribution made by both Chinese and European entrepreneurs through institutional innovations integrating markets and reducing transactions costs in early Southeast Asian development may well have been as important as the technological improvements they also introduced. The conglomerates also performed the very significant economic function at later and more advanced stages of development of integrating markets across wider regions. They facilitated provision of finance, information flows, political contacts and necessary approvals for new projects, as well as access to credits, contracts and other benefits from government.

If the economic roles throughout the early twentieth century of the Southeast Asian Chinese are examined, the market integrating functions of the commodity traders and small *warung* (shop) owners who played a major part in the commodities collection process must have constituted one of their most valuable contributions to the development of the regions where they settled and traded. For example, the many small Chinese traders who handled smallholder rubber in South Sumatra and the innumerable Chinese coastal shipping firms throughout the archipelago certainly made a huge contribution towards stimulating cash crop production by Indonesian farmers in areas concerned. This contribution was probably far more than that of the great *towkays* (merchants) like the Indonesian Chinese Oei Tiong Ham, whose sugar plantations and ancillary services were only marginally different from those of the Dutch, or of the big Chinese *kretek* (cigarette) and batik merchants in Java who made big profits – thereby attracting most attention - in industries already set up by indigenous entrepreneurs.

Many questions remain to be answered about the ways in which the Southeast Asian Chinese have made their greatest contributions to development of the region. Has it been through their innumerable small-scale activities as petty traders opening up new areas and new product lines before World War II, or as pioneers since the 1960s of modern large-scale enterprises with big economies of scale and reduced transactions costs helping to generate large profits and overall national productivity gains? The answer must probably again be 'a bit of both – depending on the circumstances of every case, on the cost and price structures, and the level of development prevailing'.

The Chinese family firm was well adapted to the needs of small-scale enterprise in the earlier decades of the twentieth century, when the labour of family members could be utilized and trust was at a premium. That kind of firm has been adapted very successfully to the needs of quite different large-scale, diversified enterprises in the period since the early 1980s. So too have the networks which played such a crucial part in early decades when commercial institutions were rudimentary and trust was at a premium. They still have a role to play in the modern period, although of a very different kind to their earlier functions. Family firms and networks as well as the new conglomerates seem to be responding well to changes brought by modernization, corporatization and globalization in its early stages, although it remains to be seen how they will adapt in the long term to the dramatically-changing circumstances.

A radically different institutional environment now confronts even the most entrepreneurial Southeast Asian Chinese business persons in the late twentieth century, in the form of new organizations such as the stock market, modern accountancy rules and procedures, company laws requiring full disclosure of relevant financial data (even from politically-favoured corporations), and more open access to relevant business information in public companies. The family firm's secrecy must gradually, albeit reluctantly, give way to greater transparency in its new form as the public company. The progress towards more fully corporatized company structures will inevitably occur, however slowly. In the meantime, Chinese family firms will no doubt continue to offer advantages as a source of security and strength for the most dynamic and adaptable entrepreneurs.

7. The Economics of Institutional Change: Making Economic Policy in Thailand

Medhi Krongkaew

A major area of concern in studying economic development is the role of state or government in making or deciding public policy. The issues involved include the legitimacy of government, which is important for the acceptance and compliance of the people toward that policy. There are rules that government must satisfy or follow for its legitimacy to be accepted. Here the institutional aspect is significant, where institutions are defined as 'rules of the game in a society ... that shape human interaction' (North 1990, p. 3). It is important in this framework to look at agents who influence and direct public policy-making, and at the separate benefits from policy changes that accrue to different groups of people.

Thailand was an absolute monarchy until 1932. Theoretically, therefore, all public policies were made by the king or his officials. However, a group of military and civilian officers staged a coup, and successfully changed the country from an absolute to a constitutional monarchy. The power to make public policies was now in the hands of a government composed mainly of these military and civilian elements. From then until the early 1970s, the political system of Thailand could be rightly called a 'bureaucratic polity' (Riggs 1966).

Since the 1970s, however, the private or business sector in various guises and forms has played an increasing role in making public policies, so that now traditional military and civilian bureaucrats may be said to have lost their earlier sole power to make public and, especially, economic policies. This institutional change could be interpreted as both the cause and effect of economic development in Thailand in the last half of century or so, and is the subject of analysis and discussion in this chapter.

The approach that follows is to first describe economic policy-making under bureaucratic polity, especially during the 1960s and 1970s. The change in roles of the private business sector *vis-à-vis* the public and still largely bureaucratic public sector in designing and implementing economic policies is then addressed, with case studies being presented to illustrate this. It is finally argued that despite important alterations in the private sector's role, the bureaucracy is still very important, having adapted its form and substance to accommodate alterations in Thai economic development.

THE BUREAUCRATIC POLITY AS A POLITICO-ECONOMIC MODEL?

It is useful to start analysing the economics of change in economic policy-making by looking at the political structure of Thailand, and by seeing who holds the power over policy decisions. This is an area well covered by the studies of Thai and non-Thai scholars, most of whom supported Riggs's 'bureaucratic polity' description from 1932 to 1973, when the military government was toppled by the student-led uprising. Riggs also portrayed Thailand as having had an uninterrupted absolute monarchy for hundreds of years, only changing to Western-style democracy in 1932, with the king as the head of state under a new constitution.

Yet, although the new political system had the appearance of a democracy, with a system of general elections, legislative processes through representative parliament and executive processes through representative government, real political power still lay with a small group of military leaders and civilian bureaucrats. It was the dominant, 'official' class of bureaucrats, defined to cover both top decision-makers and the policy implementers just below them, that constituted the bureaucratic polity.

In this political context, the private business sector was seen as subservient to the power and direction of the public sector. As most private businesses in Thailand were run by ethnic Chinese business persons, the social discrimination against Chinese by the government at the time made the political role of these persons even weaker. However, the commercial class survived partly by acting as trade brokers or compradors to influential Western businesses in Thailand, or by 'continually buying protection from the Thai elite' (ibid., p. 251). They had become what Riggs called 'pariah entrepreneurs', whose wealth and income were used to purchase help. The post-World War II government attempted to counter the economic influences of 'foreign' business firms (Western as well as ethnic Chinese) by setting up numerous state enterprises. Yet, when this attempt largely failed because of the inefficiency of the enterprises, the government began trying to assimilate rather than discriminate against Chinese business persons.

The toppling of the military government in 1973 showed the vulnerability of this bureaucratic form of governance, and many scholars began to question the ongoing relevance and applicability of this political model. Thus Hewison (1989) considered that Thailand in the latter part of the 1970s had changed politically, socially and economically, with the power of the state no longer remaining monolithic. The rise of the Sino-Thai capitalist class from the postwar period onwards had shown that they were not merely compradors depending on foreign capital but an independent and autonomous capitalist class of their own. The state–business relationship had now been redefined so that the state now 'has developed policies, strategies, and rules beneficial to the capitalist class (or particular fractions of it), and has protected the property interests of this class' (ibid, p. 2). The pariah entrepreneurship was gone.

Several other analysts rejected the idea of bureaucratic polity as the relevant model for Thailand from the 1970s, with perhaps the strongest criticism coming from Anek Laothamatas (1992). He contended that the dramatic economic development of the last three decades had spawned extra-bureaucratic forces impinging on the stranglehold of the military–civilian bureaucracy. A chief force were the business associations, both in Bangkok and the provinces, which had been successful in proposing an export-oriented strategy, tax and tariff reductions, removal of bureaucratic delays and inefficiency, and a number of other key measures. Anek Laothamatas argued that in the economic realm, major decision-making had ceased to be the monopoly of the bureaucracy, being influenced significantly by organized business. The latter now influenced public policy through its strategic position in the capitalist economy, through clientelistic ties with high officials or simply through organized pressure groups.[1]

Despite these well-reasoned criticisms, however, the true picture of the Thai state and its economic ramifications is too complicated to lend itself to simple elucidation. Most criticisms of the bureaucratic policy were founded on political structure rather than on the real mechanisms of economic policy-making or the economic implications of power structure changes. It would indeed be erroneous to conclude that in this more recent period Thai bureaucrats no longer maintained their influence over making economic policy. Thus the well-known economist Rangsun Thanapornpan (1989) recognized the changes in the role and influence of the capitalist class in economic policy-making after 1973, but believed that pointing to the end of the bureaucratic polity would be too hasty (ibid., p. 146). Although democratic forces had a larger role in making economic policy, the power elite, drawn from the bureaucracy and groups of technocrats, still played a principal part in what occurred.

A further analysis of the above institutional change will now be made, against this background of an apparent contradiction in the way some economists and political scientists look at changed power structure in Thailand.

THE PROCESS OF ECONOMIC POLICY-MAKING

Drawing on the pioneering approach by Rangsun (1989), the formulation of economic policies may be looked on as an outcome of interactions between supply and demand in the economic policy market. Economic policy also has the characteristic of a public good as its availability provides joint consumption for all and, as a rule, no one can be excluded from enjoying it.

The Supply Side of Economic Policy

Rangsun suggests four groups of actors in the supply of economic policies in Thailand, these being (a) the power elite, (b) the technocrats, (c) the political parties and (d) the parliament. The system under which the first two groups operate constitute a 'bureaucratic polity', although some members of the elite might not be bureaucrats in the commonly understood sense.

The power elite in the present author's small modification of Rangsun's formulation consists of cabinet members who are political office-holders at the highest level, including the prime minister and ministers. The technocrats embrace 'executive-level officials' (ELOs), including civilians ranked as permanent secretaries and directors-general, and military officers of equivalent status. They also include bureaucrats and others who are publicly-appointed policy advisers to the power elite. These technocrats constituting the political bureaucracy[2] are supplemented by further persons from the permanent bureaucracy of 'middle-level executive officers' (MLEOs), who execute economic policies, monitor economic changes, analyse economic problems, project future economic scenarios and suggest new actions. While the power elite comes and goes through changes of government by democratic means or otherwise, these technocrats representing key state agencies are a permanent bureaucracy with a life of its own which, in a certain way, is quite independent from the political organization at the top.

The third group on the supply side of political parties is involved in making public policies through initiating and introducing bills to the fourth group, the parliament. A bill is deliberated and voted on by members of parliament before becoming law, but despite the importance of these further groups in a democracy, their roles in determining public policies in Thailand are neither effective nor impressive, as is shown below.

The Demand Side of Economic Policy

Rangsun identifies four groups of actors likely to be involved in the demand for economic policies. They are (a) the general public, (b) economic pressure groups or interest groups, (c) mass media and (d) academicians. The general public is a large group of people whose demand for economic policies is not revealed,[3] meaning that policies must be provided by the state as public goods to this target group. Economic pressure groups are smaller entities than the general public, and have clearly identifiable areas of interest or concern. The famed business associations which are the main subject of the analysis of Anek Laothamatas (1992) are included in this group, along with trade unions, professional associations and consumers' associations. The mass media, and especially daily newspapers and other magazines, function as the sounding board for their readers' demand for public policy and as the demanders of certain public policies in their own right. Finally, the academicians in Thailand are at times quite effective in suggesting or pressuring for the establishment or changing of certain policies, although their records of success are uneven and unpredictable.

STRENGTHS AND WEAKNESSES OF THAI BUREAUCRATIC AND POLITICAL SYSTEMS

The determination of an economic policy comes about as a result of interactions amongst the actors just identified. In real policy-making, however, the interactions are a complex matter, with the final outcome being complicated by additional institutional factors such as the role of external capital, outside policy influences and other political considerations. Analyses are now made of the impacts in shaping Thai economic policy of the legal foundation of bureaucratic power, of the parliament and the involvement of external forces.

The Legal Foundation of Bureaucratic Power

Because Thailand has never been a colony of any Western country, it has been able to adopt a mixture of Western legal and administrative systems to suit its needs. It has adopted essentially the French civil law code emphasizing strong, autonomous and centralized bureaucracy, and the British system of government where executive power is drawn from the legislature and must be accountable to it. However, in reality the legislature is weak and incompetent, so the executive branch usually dominates it. Recently Thailand even experimented with the American system, having stronger executive power and a system of checks and balances in political decision-making. With these mixed systems it is not surprising that the nature of Thai political, administrative and legal arrangements is difficult to understand.

One reason the Thai bureaucracy has been so strong can be found in the legal framework within which it operates. Thus Rangsun (1989) and Christensen et al. (1992) point out that Thailand's administrative law code makes the bureaucracy resistant to legal challenges and other extra-bureaucratic pressures. This code gives enormous power to ministers and permanent officials to subordinate or selectively utilize legislation under their control. Normally acts of parliament grant general authority to appropriate agencies, whose officials with a great deal of discretion and leverage then issue a hierarchy of regulations and notifications. Christensen et al. (1992, p. 42) were right in stating that parliament as an institution had little power of scrutiny over the bureaucracy, and that it acted as a vehicle to the cabinet rather than as a strong, autonomous policy-making institution.

Even when there are conflicts between ministers and permanent bureaucrats, the existing administrative code still provides the latter with protection against punitive action. A minister can appoint, transfer or remove from office the permanent secretary of the ministry, but not lower-ranked officials, whose promotions or demotions are decided by the secretary. Thus, a minister wishing to transfer a lower-ranked official must ask the permanent secretary to do this, and if the secretary refuses, the latter is the one who receives punishment.[4] This is a way of protecting bureaucrats from the use (or abuse) of power by those in the political elite.

Technocrats foreseeing a possible danger of economic excesses by politicians have also been able to write limits into economic laws to prevent these. A good case in point is the *Budget Procedure Act, B.E. 2502* which specifies, among other things, that public debts incurred by the government each year must not exceed a certain proportion of the annual budget. This stipulation helps stop politicians from overspending and incurring high debt levels, and at the same time gives bureaucrats a greater role in economic management.

The usual practice of appointing only internal staff members to leading positions in an organization has also meant that outside appointees can hardly get cooperation from insiders. This institutional rigidity has worked – for good or ill – to strengthen the position and power of each bureaucracy.[5] Hence it appears that the legal foundations of bureaucratic power in Thailand are still forces to be reckoned with.

The Weakness of the Present Parliamentary System

There are many reasons why the parliamentary system cannot function effectively in supplying economic or other public policies. First, the power of the elected House of Representatives is often countered by the power of the appointive Senate. Although the constitution upholds the eventual power of the lower house, an uncooperative Senate can delay policy-making. Second, members of the House of Representatives are often prohibited from individually proposing bills,[6] with the latter having to be put forward by a group of members or by the cabinet, especially in financial cases. Third, members of parliament have only the power to cut budget appropriations and not to increase them. Fourth, it is the tradition of the Thai parliament to send important bills to *ad hoc* parliamentary subcommittees rather than to existing standing committees. The executive branch can accordingly bypass ordinary legislative committee systems in screening important bills. Fifth, the legislative branch has little ability to control the activities of executive government. Normally it has no power to reject the policy of the new government when it is announced in parliament. It does not need to approve the actions of executive government in negotiating and entering into agreements with foreign governments or organizations. Examples of this include the international Multi-Fibre Agreements, and the application for membership in the General Agreements on Tariff and Trade. The legislature does not have to give consent to, or even be informed about, the executive government's borrowings overseas or guarantees of overseas loans. Finally, it often does not have power even to audit the public spending of the executive, as the Office of the Auditor-General is attached to the Office of the Prime Minister rather than to the Office of the Parliament.[7]

When all these aspects are coupled with the traditionally unfavourable image of members of the House of Representatives (who are often accused of getting into offices through vote-buying, and of unscrupulous voting behaviour in the parliament and other personal misbehaviour), the House does not appear as a key actor in the supply of public policies.

External Forces in Policy-making

There have been numerous occasions when external organizations are said to have influenced the making of domestic policies. Indeed, Petcharee (1985) cited the involvement by foreign companies as a reason to question the bureaucratic model. This section discusses one episode in making early 1980s macroeconomic policy, wherein Thailand was seen as pressured by the International Monetary Fund (hereafter referred to as 'the Fund') and World Bank.

As the Thai economy was hit by the second oil shock in 1979–80, its external position became very weak and a severe balance of payments problem occurred. In 1981 the Thai government was forced to borrow over 800 million special drawing rights from the Fund on stand-by arrangements. The conditions 'imposed' by the Fund were such that the government was constrained to improve its revenue collection and reduce its fiscal deficit. There was an implicit pressure by the Fund on the government to devalue the Thai baht, and this the government did in 1984.

Yet, despite such apparent external influence, it can be argued that the most crucial role in actually formulating these and other economic policies is still played by the executive-level officials or ELOs who may be seen as the true representatives of the Thai bureaucracy. Hence Rangsun (1989) showed that the success of the macroeconomic policy of Thailand in the early 1980s was not strictly attributed to conditions set up by the Fund and World Bank, but to provisos made by Thai technocrats themselves, in agreement with the personnel of the two organizations.

Even when Thai technocrats from the Ministry of Finance and the Bank of Thailand disagreed with the Fund or the World Bank, they appeaared to fall in with these organizations on points of dispute. They implemented, in the meantime, other aspects with which they had no problem, while securing later quiet adjustments on points they disliked. The cordial relationship between the Thai and foreign personnel throughout their active interactions during the 1980s was unusual, considering the experiences of the global financial bodies in other countries. It may be explained by the high respect accorded to the Thai technocrats as professionals, and the realization that they were crucial forces in actual policy-making, If agreement could be secured with them, implementation was likely to be successful, but if there was disagreement, the technocrats would ignore conditions imposed on them. The positive outcomes of interactions led to successful macroeconomic adjustments.

THE RISE OF THE BUSINESS SECTOR AND ITS ROLE IN ECONOMIC POLICY-MAKING

The postwar change in policy regarding ethnic Chinese meant that Chinese entrepreneurs quickly assimilated themselves into Thai society and began to prosper. These entrepreneurs became Thai or Sino-Thais, and were very much in control of the private business sector by the time of the First Economic Plan in 1961. They organized trade groups and associations to protect their business interests, and the government enacted the Trade Association and Chamber of Commerce Acts in 1966 to promote and control these fast-growing trade groups. The Thailand Board of Trade (BOT) was set up to represent Thailand's private business sector in dealing with government agencies and in international forums and negotiations.

While the BOT is mainly concerned with trade, the industrial and manufacturing issues of private companies are looked after by the Federation of Thai Industries established in 1967. This clearly represents major industrialists, and has recently been elevated to the same status as the BOT. Its activities include the investigation and solution of particular industrial complaints, and the protection and promotion of members' general interests. It, like the BOT, has a strong secretariat, and has been represented on various committees and subcommittees of government.

The Thai Bankers' Association is another important business group which, although only a basic trade association, represents what until recently was the fastest-growing and richest subsector in the economy. However, its activities are often circumscribed, because some operations of commercial bank members must be regulated by the Bank of Thailand. It does not have a large secretariat, and is not as active as the two business groups.

These three groups together were involved in forming the much-analysed Joint Public–Private Sector Consultative Committee. This Joint Committee is seen, more than any other group, as indicating the successful penetration into public policy-making by the Thai business sector.

The Joint Public–Private Sector Consultative Committee

When General Prem Tinsulanon became prime minister of Thailand early in 1980, the country was encountering the great economic difficulties already outlined. Prem was not an elected politician, and his support came from an agreement amongst government coalition parties and the army. He needed to stabilize and adjust the economy, and doing this in difficult times required the assistance and cooperation of private business. He agreed with the recommendation of his advisers and technocrats of the National Economic and Social Development Board (NESDB) – the planning agency of the Thai government – on the desirability of close economic association with the business sector, involving active participation in joint economic decision-making.

While some members of the association that preceded the Federation of Thai Industries wanted closer relations with the government, their major objectives were to secure incentives and protection for their own industrial activities. They succeeded in setting up regular dialogues with the government, especially the prime minister. However, the key person instrumental in forming the Joint Committee was the secretary-general of the NESDB, Dr Snoh Unakul, a trusted technocrat working with prime minister. Snoh and his staff realized the significance of collaborating with the private sector in times of economic difficulty, making a detailed format for a Joint Public–Private Sector Consultative Committee (hereafter referred to as the 'Joint Committee'), chaired by the prime minister and comprising all economic ministers and representatives from the three business groups referred to above, with the prime minister as chairperson. The NESDB provided the secretariat, with Dr Snoh himself as secretary.

The Joint Comittee was established in 1981, and up to 1988, when General Prem decided to leave office, had more than 60 meetings which he chaired himself (Sunetra 1991, p. 60). Its objectives, which did not alter, were:

1. To coordinate the making of cooperative plans and projects between the public and private sectors in important economic areas, for the welfare and benefit of the population at large.
2. To consider problems concerning the operation of the public and private sectors, and find ways of solving them quickly.
3. To discuss a bigger role for the private sector in supporting national development.
4. To follow up on works assigned to related agencies.
5. To appoint subcommittees and task forces to work on certain assignments.

The monthly meetings of the Joint Committee in General Prem's period were quite formal, with Dr Snoh specifying that agenda issues must be well prepared and of common interest to the economy. The secretariat could screen and reorder issues discussed at the meetings. When resolutions were reached on issues involving action by appropriate government agencies, the secretariat facilitated transmisssion and instituted follow-up procedures. As might be expected, Joint Committee meetings mainly concerned measures to improve industrial production, trade and services, including tax reductions and simplifications and other business incentives. Issues involving benefits to the general public, such as income distribution, poverty alleviation and full employment, were negligible.

The activities of the Joint Committee continued when General Chartichai was prime minister (1988–90), but were given less emphasis and attention. Yet, when the general was succeeded by Mr Anand Panyarachun (1991–2), the activities of the Joint Committee were revived. Then, however, the political situation was such that joint action between public and private sectors was less critical, since the government could decide and implement policies quickly through authoritarian support of the military or through special legal powers.

Although the formation of the Joint Committee can be seen as a recognition by government of the importance of private business, it would be misleading to conclude that the latter sector forced this organization on government. The initiative and impetus for it came from technocrats who planned and then operated it for many years, also maintaining its image as a body pursuing overall economic benefits rather than primarily helping powerful business groups. Without the government's positive attitude, the Joint Committee would not have existed.

Rangsun (1989, p. 126) interestingly quoted a remark made by a former member of the Joint Committee representing the Thai Bankers' Association that what could be considered the Joint Committee's performance credits were already within the government's capability to implement on its own. Indeed, numerous issues proposed by private-sector representatives on the Joint Committee and subsequently agreed upon were those on which the government was already prepared to act. It is also interesting that many business persons complained about the long queue of submissions to the Joint Committee, in a setting where the secretariat prepared the agenda. The Joint Committee thus appears as a safety valve for business to release its complaints, enabling their 'cooling down' while government receives much-needed private-sector cooperation and support in return.

Although rules governing the making of economic policy have certainly changed, the triangular relationship between business, the power elite and the senior technocrats is too complex to permit a simple conclusion. The following policy case studies might be helpful before attempting some judgement about the relationship.

CASE STUDIES

The cases of public enterprise privatization, automobiles and sugar trade illustrate the ways in which the Thai bureaucracy has interacted with private organizations in formulating policy.

Public Enterprise Privatization

Public enterprises in Thailand had their heyday after World War II, when the government set up numerous public enterprises in a nationalistic attempt to counter the economic influence of foreign and Chinese companies. At the launching of the First Plan in 1961, however, it became obvious that state capitalism would be abandoned in favour of a greater role for the private sector. The government started reducing the number of public enterprises from what were then 100 entities, but progress was slow. Most enterprises that remained were still plagued with inefficiencies in production and management, and depended on government subsidies and protection. It became clear during the early 1980s crisis that reforms in and privatization of some public enterprises would have to be carried out quickly.

The public enterprise sector at that time was almost a 'second government', with revenues and expenditures often larger than those of the central government. Its continued subsidization and support, through domestic financing or foreign borrowing, could potentially get the government into financial trouble. In 1983, the cabinet adopted a new privatization policy to improve public enterprise performance. This policy contained five strategies: (a) changes in enterprise executives; (b) changes in management techniques; (c) improvements in marketing techniques; (d) joint ventures with the private sector or private management of enterprises; and (e) sales of public enterprises to the private sector.

Understandably, the policy ran into difficulties, with frequent and strong resistance from management and public enterprise workers' unions. Not until the latter part of 1980s, when the economy was growing rapidly and the fiscal position of government improved, did it feel confident enough to pursue privatization rigorously. Ironically, the military coup in early 1991 helped accelerate privatization, as the powerful unions were disbanded and the civilian government protected by the military junta could quickly implement its plans. In 1991 and 1992 rights were granted to private companies to provide and operate several public utilities including telephones, telecommunications and electricity supplies. Many large and successful public enterprises, such as the Thai

International Airways and Petroleum Authority of Thailand, floated their shares to the general public, and numerous private professionals were invited to manage troubled public enterprises. When the military's position weakened in the public outcry against their brutal crackdown on demonstrators in May 1992, the new civilian government could dislodge military officers from the boards of many public enterprises and replace them with private professionals.

Public-enterprise privatization may be seen as an achievement of government technocrats, especially those in the Prime Minister's Office and the Ministry of Finance. There is now less opposition to privatization from management and workers; the government has shown the benefits to management resulting from the relaxing of controls over price-setting in most public enterprises, while worker welfare has not been hurt when productivity is maintained. Expected increases in efficiency and revenue to the enterprises concerned should make this important institutional change worthwhile for national development.

Automobiles

The automobile industry began in 1962 as part of an import substitution policy, with assembly of cars being given investment promotion privileges and other protection. By 1970 there were ten assembly plants for 20 makes and 100 models of passenger and commercial cars, but locally-assembled cars still comprised less than a quarter of total domestic demand with the rest being imported (Petcharee 1985). Assembly plants mainly survived thanks to tax subsidies, an obviously untenable situation for a small economy like that of Thailand. When the government decided to raise import tax on car parts as well as on other imports to help reduce balance-of-trade deficits, the local assemblers protested. The government then attempted to come up with a long-term automobile policy.

The 1962 automobile policy was one of the first major events in Thai economic history in which business influenced the power elite and industrial policy bureaucrats, even though the latter initially invited the private sector to participate. As cooperation progressed, the position of bureaucrats *vis-à-vis* the business representatives and power elites with personal automobile industry interests became weakened, forcing them to compromise (ibid., Chapter 4). The 1971 automobile policy, stipulating for the first time 25 per cent local content and continuing other incentives previously offered, could be considered a victory for the business sector. Despite probable inefficiencies in local content provision, this policy was presented as almost a preordained way of stimulating local automobile parts industries, not only saving foreign exchange but also satisfying public demand for industrial self-reliance. The government had decided to provide further protection in the hope of stronger future industrial development.

However, prices of locally-manufactured cars started to rise, with competition from imports of completely-built-up automobiles being kept low by high import and other taxes. In 1978 the local content requirement was raised to 35 per cent, and the import of complete cars banned. This was somehow anticipated by automotive investors, with noticeable increases in the mid-1970s in new automobile plants and expansions in automotive parts production. Local consumers had now become captive buyers of expensive local automobiles, and the mandatory local content was lifted again to 50 per cent in 1982. With pressures from the worsened economic situation of the early 1980s, a group of bureaucrats proposed rolling back the local content provision, removing the ban on complete car imports and eliminating incentives on low-volume models. But this attempt to increase the efficiency of the automobile industry was unsuccessful, and there was merely a slight reduction of local content to 45 per cent.

Throughout the 1980s, the automobile industry was one of the most distorted industries in Thailand. Normally the very high prices of local cars should reduce the buyers' demand, but paradoxically the demand for cars in Thailand kept growing throughout the latter half of the 1980s. This was because the economic boom which started in 1987 had increased the real income and purchasing power of large groups of the population; it was also because Bangkok householders in particular needed to have their own vehicles, as an alternative to the inadequate public transport system.

The bureaucrats of the Ministry of Industry were in no position to challenge the power of political leaders trying to protect their own interests in the automobile industry. However, an opportunity arose when Mr Anand came to power in 1991 with autocratic military support. Though a businessman himself, he took the role of a technocratic public servant, directing his economic policy along the path of economic efficiency, competitiveness and transparency in policy determination and implementation. He supported the bureaucrats in cutting import and other taxes on car parts and lifting the ban on car imports, which resulted in an immediate fall in new car prices. However, after 18 months the automobile manufacturers regained their positions, and again began raising the prices of new models.[8]

This case history of automobile policy denotes the continuing struggle between politicians, business interest groups and bureaucrats. The latter could re-exert their power if they could realign themselves with the power élite, convincing them of the need for change even in the face of strong challenges from the business sector.

Sugar Trade

Sugar became a major upland crop of Thailand in the early 1970s; its production subsequently doubled every ten years or so to reach 47.5 million tonnes in 1991 (Prayong 1992, p. 3).

Unlike many upland cash crops, sugar cane production and trade have had some government involvement since the late 1940s, when the sugar industry was still small. The government then supported the formation by sugar millers of a limited company to promote increased sugar cane cultivation and refining, and had responded to its lobbying for sugar protection. It also maintained relations with a federation of sugar cane farmers formed in the 1970s by producers in the Eastern Region.

The Ministry of Industry was always keen on intervening with sugar to ensure there was sufficient domestic supply, to stabilize the price, to increase productivity and to promote orderly exports. The Ministry's policy measures over time included successively encouraging and discouraging the establishment and expansion of sugar mills, stipulating the opening and closing times of milling seasons, specifying sugar outputs from mills, overseeing the movement and storage of sugar, banning sugar imports, controlling sugar exports as well as premiums and subsidies, and intervening in sugar price-setting. Such extensive engagement with one crop was unusual.

In 1972 there was a world sugar shortage which helped Thai sugar exports. The domestic price of sugar also increased, but was not as high as the export price. A domestic sugar shortage thus developed, forcing government to intervene strongly in sugar storage and movement to ensure adequate supplies for domestic demand. The windfall gains by exporters from high sugar prices enabled the government to extract premiums from sugar exports and put them into the Farmers' Aid Funds for future use. The overall effects of this event were expanded sugar-growing and a deeper involvement of the government in the sugar industry.

Two years later, when the international price fell, the sugar cane farmers and sugar millers could not agree on the domestic sugar price. This was when the government first decided to participate fully in the negotiations and setting up of the sugar price between farmers and millers. The government agreed to use the money from the Farmers' Aid Fund when necessary to subsidize sugar millers in buying sugar cane from farmers at an agreed minimum price. Thereafter it was always difficult for the farmers and millers to agree on the sugar price, and the government was always pulled in to mediate. This made a lot of sense and the government-aided policy packages almost always benefited both farmers and millers.

In 1981 there was a glut in the world sugar market, and sugar prices fell drastically with consequent difficulty for farmers and millers. The government, on the recommendations of bureaucrats in the Ministry of Industry, then decided to replace the annual price negotiations between farmers and millers with an arrangement in which farmers and millers together joined in sugar cane production and manufacturing, sharing the returns from export and domestic sales. The government, through adept manœuvring, overcame the initial resistance from the millers, securing an agreement between them and the farmers' groups. It set up a public company to handle domestic distribution of sugar and exports, with the net proceeds from sales being shared between the farmers and millers on a 70:30 basis. It guaranteed the floor price of domestic sugar to ensure local sugar cane farmers could survive. This agreement, which was put to use experimentally in 1982, satisfied both sides and was still operating in 1994.

The sugar policy experience is often referred to as an instance of private sector influences successfully bringing to bear on the policy-making of bureaucrats. To a certain extent this is true, and may be explained by the smallness of the farmers' group, enabling it to organize itself effectively with little risk of free-rider problems.[9] However, it should be noted that the government entered the bargaining between farmers and millers not as a neutral mediator but as an interested partner. Hence, it is natural that the farmers and millers should form an alliance to extract benefits and concessions from a government already willing to cooperate.

The government could have continued to allow farmers and millers to negotiate sugar-pricing among themselves, yet chose of its own account *not* to do this. The politicians leading the government may have acted to secure political favour from the farmers, and the bureaucracy may have sympathized with less advantaged farmers in their negotiations with powerful millers. The short-term gains from the adopted policy (showing the government as actively pursuing the welfare of the farmers, preserving peace and order in agricultural markets and so on) must have been judged to outweigh the long-term loss to consumers (having to pay a high domestic price for sugar) and to the economy as a whole (encouraging cane growers to expand production in response to an uneconomically high domestic sugar price). The case demonstrates the key role that bureaucrats took in formulating sugar policy.

CONCLUSION: THE ECONOMICS OF BUSINESS-ORIENTED BUREAUCRACY

Despite changes with rapid development, the power of Thai bureaucrats in making economic policies is seen to remain strong. While the newly-prominent private business class in manufacturing, trade and services sectors has made significant inroads into economic policy-making, the public sector technocrats retain the crucial key in most policy formulation and implemention.

Clearly the rise of business people as the new 'middle class' in Thai society challenges the bureaucrats of the traditional middle class. The income and wealth of the new class have pressured bureaucrats to re-examine the goals of development and the means of achieving them, and to assess whether to adopt more socially or business-oriented policies. On a personal level, the erosion of traditional welfare associated with public-sector work has seriously depleted the quantity and quality of the human resource pool available to the Thai bureaucracy. A weakened bureaucracy is also prone to influence and dominance by business and other societal interest groups. Yet the administrative structure of the Thai state has deep roots in a stable society undisturbed by foreign colonization, meaning the environment of the Thai bureaucracy retains significant power.

Three concluding observations are pertinent to the economics of the important institutional change in decision-making caused by the rise of the business class. First, Thai bureaucrats are not a homogeneous group with a common orientation and outlook; they may be bound by the same administrative duties to work for the state and protect its interests, but the specific objectives of their bureaus could cause them to conflict with one another. Christensen et al. (1992) pointed out one such feature of Thai bureaucracy in the bifurcation of macroeconomic and microeconomic policies. On the one hand, technocrats specializing in broader macroeconomic issues, such as those in the Bank of Thailand, the National Economic and Social Development Board, or Ministry of Finance, often preferred conservative macro policies based on stability and growth. On the other hand, bureaucrats in line ministries with more restricted objectives are chiefly concerned with microeconomic or sectoral policies.

Christensen claimed that typically, the macroeconomic technocrats distrusted line ministries (ibid. p. 50–51), believing these were dominated by narrow bureaucratic interests, including the promotion of private firms to generate rent-seeking rather than socially-optimal objectives. The tensions in relations between formulators of macro and micro policies exceeded any coordination and complementarity. The bifurcation of policy areas allowed the management of a stable macroeconomic policy regime, while overall performance was less effective when systematic attention to a given problem was required. These adversarial arrangements and the lack of formal linkage mechanisms between macro and sectoral policy officials often limited the state's ability to formulate and coordinate overall development policy (ibid., p. 52).

Second, the experience of economic policy-making during Anand Panyarachun's prime ministership was unique, and against the general trend. Mr Anand himself and most of his cabinet were not members of the conventional power elite, since they were neither elected politicians nor coup leaders. They were technocrats given additional power to act as this elite. The Anand government was a bureaucratic/technocratic administration rather than one of business persons, because with few exceptions it and its economic policies aimed to benefit the general public instead of the limited interests of certain business groups or companies.

Third, the business-oriented bureaucracy in cooperation with other non-bureaucratic sectors in the economy succeeded in fostering an open, competitive, growth-oriented economy. Gross domestic product in the two decades up to 1997 grew at about 7 per cent per annum in real terms, which was high by international standards and resulted in per-capita gross national product rising from around $ 435 in 1970 to $ 2410 in 1994. The apparent trickle-down effects of growth had helped reduce the national incidence of poverty from 32 per cent in 1975 to 22 per cent in 1988 (Medhi et al. 1992). However, the growth-oriented policy also increased income inequality, with the Gini coefficient rising from 0.426 in 1975–6 to 0.479 in 1988 (ibid.). As long as the economy kept growing with general rises in absolute real income, income disparities were not a big issue. However, with the current economic downturn those at the bottom rung of income distribution are suffering first and most, and such income inequality can lead to social unrest.

The Thai bureaucracy has the obligation of initiating changes in economic policies that address the dilemma of inequality. Other problems also need the attention of a strong public sector, including those of the environment, education and health, and public safety and order. These are spheres which the present business-oriented bureaucracy is ill-equipped to handle, both quantitatively and qualitatively. Contrary to many opinions, the economic development of Thailand is judged by this author to need a stronger and more capable bureaucracy that can attract personnel of the same high calibre as those joining the private sector. The relevant question is not whether bureaucratic polity is dead (it is not), but how to equip it to operate in constantly changing economic situations without losing sight of the proper role of the state.

NOTES

1. Anek (1992) also pointed out that the relationship between the state and organized business in Thailand was not without weakness, one major aspect being the exclusion of the popular sector from economic policy-making. Despite intermittent calls for including farmer and worker groups in the Joint Public–Private Sector Consultative Committee discussed below, senior officials of the National Economic and Social Development Board insisted that such inclusion was undesirable.
2. If bureaucracy refers to rules governing the activities of personnel in the public sector, then ministers or political office-holders fall under a category of bureaucracy where the exercise of their political power is subject to established, publicly-recognized rules governing the scope of and limitations on their power, their obligation to follow certain legal procedures, their accountability in duties and so on.
3. This is a classic case of non-revealed preference of public good demand by the people, who are more inclined to be free-riders to avoid paying for its supply either through taxes or user charges.
4. The Minister of Industry under Chuan Leekpai's government (1993–5), for example, asked the permanent secretary of his ministry to remove the director-general of the Department of Natural Resources, whom he thought unsuitable for the job. When the permanent secretary refused, he was transferred instead to an inactive post in another ministry.
5. The appointment early in 1992 of an official from the Minister of Finance to become the new Director of the Budget Bureau, an organization in the Prime Minister's Office, ended with the official requesting to be transferred back within a year. This was because as an 'outsider', he had received little cooperation from Bureau staff.
6. This is mainly to prevent the proliferation of bill proposals from MPs who merely act for the record to impress their own constituents.

7. But during the government of Prime Minister Chuan Leekpai, the Office of the Auditor-General was transferred back to the Office of the Parliament.

8. They were able to do this owing both to their oligarchic power over new car markets in Thailand and to buoyant consumers' demand. Private importers who imported cars of the same makes and models from abroad were met by the refusal of these car manufacturers and dealers to service outside imports.

9. Olson (1965) stipulates that a smaller pressure group will be more effective than a larger one in pursuing its activities. The expected benefits from collective action are more clearly defined within the smaller group, with little leakage of benefits to free-riders not contributing to its efforts.

PART III

Institutions in National and International Economic Change

8. Government and Deregulation in Indonesia

Hadi Soesastro

Immediately after assuming power in the mid-1960s, the New Order government[1] began liberalizing the economy, with the aim of restoring stability and promoting growth. It inherited an economy in shambles. The measures it took were based on pragmatic considerations, but guided by a conscious decision to steer the economy away from statism towards market-oriented measures and deregulation, and to promote private-sector activities. This 'total correction' away from a state-led economy was based on a decision by the Provisional People's Consultative Assembly (*Majlis Perwakilan Rakyat Sementara*) in 1968. Implementation of the correction was fully entrusted to the government, with President Suharto assisted by a team of economists – the 'technocrats' – being given the full mandate to take necessary measures.

Following the successful restoration of economic and political stability, the country embarked in 1969 on its first Five-Year Development Plan (*Repelita*). This plan was indicative, containing broad guidelines, and not an elaborate, centrally-managed type of instrument. The government outlined the general directions of economic development and structural change, defining areas where it would involve itself directly through annual budgetary outlays. Its role was dominant in earlier years, with a share of 75 to 80 per cent in total capital outlays. The private sector was free to fill in the gaps between the overall agenda of the plan and areas of activity reserved for government. This broad structure of economic management has remained largely intact over the past 30 years, but latterly the share of the private sector has risen to about 75 per cent of total capital outlays. What is remarkable is that throughout this period the development of the economy was overseen, supervised and largely directed by one person, President Suharto, who was unofficially called the 'Father of Development' (*Bapak Pembangunan*).

Given the dominance of the state, the strong role of government and the central position of the president, the economic and political environment has been largely shaped by changes in government policy. These changes have modified the role of government in the economy, but by and large that role continues to be dominant. Structural changes from an agrarian, traditional economy into an industrializing, modern one have posed a host of new institutional challenges, yet after so many years of development, the institutional setting remains largely underdeveloped. This fundamental deficiency, however, has not been sufficiently appreciated in Indonesia nor perhaps elsewhere, as long as the economy has continued to perform well. It is only recently, and particularly in relation to the deep economic and financial crisis that has befallen Indonesia since mid-1997, that attention has been given to issues of institutional arrangement and development. Some persons believe the underdeveloped institutional setting has been partly responsible for the crisis.

Examination of the processes of deregulation and economic liberalization in general in Indonesia over the past 30 years helps in understanding the evolution of the institutional setting. The study by Battacharya and Pangestu (1996) is thus far the only comprehensive one on institutional aspects of the process of deregulation over the whole of this period. Analyses cove ing a shorter interval in the 1980s, when sweeping reforms were undertaken iı. a number of areas, can be found in Soesastro (1989) and Sjahrir and Brown (1992). These studies have shown that deregulation has brought about new institutional challenges, and that its advance will be seriously hampered if insufficient attention is given to institutional development in both the narrower and broader senses discussed in this book.

A study of the circumstances suggests there was progress in institutional development in the earlier years of deregulation and economic development. Those times saw a qualitative shift from the use of informal, *ad hoc* and irregular mechanisms of economic policy-making and implementation to the establishment, strengthening and exercise of more formal, structured and coherent arrangements. It needs to be remembered that the, then, new government had to undertake the task of economic stabilization and rehabilitation without having the necessary institutions in place, since the bureaucracy was no longer functioning owing to ideological and political conflicts during the Old Order.[2] The government subsequently began rehabilitating the bureaucratic structure and building new institutions around it. Institutional development also took place in other fields, including that of politics. The establishment of more normal and regular processes of government and 'governance' with accompanying institutional arrangements resulted in the emergence of a 'corporatist' state system, characterized by a strong role for the bureaucracy in directing the economy.

Later phases, however, saw clear stagnation in the process of institutional development, and perhaps even 'institutional involution'[3] as institutions progressively lost their independence and became part of a system of government and governance that became increasingly more patrimonial or paternalistic in nature. While the economy grew more liberalized and open to the world over the years, much economic activity came to be conducted under a patrimonial system centring on the president. This change did not occur abruptly, however, and perhaps this explains why it was not promptly recognized and did not have an immediate, negative impact on the economy.

This chapter is organized around three consecutive phases of deregulation and liberalization that appear to have been driven by distinct events. It is possible that these events also influenced the direction of institutional development. The first phase, from 1966 to 1982, began with the change in government and the introduction of new policies as a total correction to those of the previous administration. The latter half of this phase saw a reversal of those policies. The second phase, from 1983 to 1993, was one in which deregulation and liberalization of the economy were driven by the need to reform the economy as oil prices continued to drop. The third phase from 1994 onwards was one in which liberalization measures appear to have been introduced in response to a regional environment characterized by heightened competitive liberalization.

THE FIRST PHASE

Inheriting an economy on the verge of collapse, the new government moved swiftly and decisively from 1966 to restore macroeconomic stability and introduce market-oriented reforms. A first measure was to bring about discipline in the budget, since state expenditures were way out of control as a result of the heavy burden of military manoeuvres in the struggle for the return of West Irian and the adventurous policy of *konfrontasi* towards immediate neighbours.[4] In 1967 the government adopted a balanced budget policy, which became one of the important cornerstones of the New Order's economic management. This policy prohibited the domestic financing of the budget in the form either of debt or money creation. In order to bring down inflation, the government also adopted a stringent monetary programme, and the exchange rate was adjusted to realistic levels through a series of large devaluations. The multiple exchange rate system was unified in 1970, and following a further devaluation in 1971, the capital account was fully liberalized. This was a daring step, since the capital account in most developing countries is usually the last to be treated in this way. Yet the open capital account has become another significant cornerstone of the New Order economy.

The early years of the New Order government were marked by a style of economic management resembling the operations of an army unit given the task of mobilizing resources and then controlling them in order to achieve a particular objective. Suharto, himself an army commander, was at the helm and immediately began organizing groups to undertake specific tasks in mobilizing resources. He himself retained full control of these mobilized resources. In addition to macroeconomic stabilization, the technocrats were assigned to mobilize foreign aid with the help of the World Bank and International Monetary

Fund. Various persons were dispatched as Suharto's personal envoys to lobby foreign governments for increased aid, and to develop links with foreign companies with a view to attracting investments. The president made a few of his army colleagues heads of important state enterprises, not only to restore their functioning and economic health but also to mobilize resources for various non-budgetary expenditures. Thus the head of the state oil company (Pertamina), General Ibnu Sutowo, was also given the task of providing supplementary resources for the armed forces whose receipts from the budget had been drastically reduced.

Suharto himself formally chaired the Economic Stabilization Council, formed in 1968 to oversee the economic rehabilitation programme. However, the main forum for economic policy coordination under more normal conditions in later years was the regular cabinet meeting on economic affairs. The extent to which policies were discussed and debated among cabinet members and the president in these meetings has been questioned. It is believed that, as time passed, matters were increasingly decided during bilateral meetings between the president and the relevant minister or ministers, with policies only being subsequently reported to the cabinet meeting prior to a public announcement.

This structure of centralized economic policy-making seems to have worked well. The key to success lay with the organization of policy inputs to the president, who made the final decisions. The technocrats who were initially recruited as economic advisers to Suharto when he was acting president became ministers in the cabinet, and were given the most important portfolios. Working as a group under the leadership of Professor Widjojo Nitisastro, they were able to propose coherent policies that received the full backing of the president. Being in charge of the most important economic ministries and with good cohesion, they could implement policies despite a weak bureaucracy. The wide recognition of the enormous challenge of stabilizing and rehabilitating the economy allowed the technocrats to formulate policies without having to face political pressures and interference, even from the military. As noted earlier, the latter received, through the offices of the president, supplementary resources from non-budgetary origins to meet their financial needs. This helped guarantee that economic policy-making was largely 'insulated', an important factor for achieving success in economic development that Indonesia had in common with other East Asian economies (Campos and Root 1996).

Another factor ensuring such insulation was the visible and swift results that reform programmes delivered. The economy grew rapidly, initially as a result of increased efficiency in utilizing existing production facilities, and subsequently due to the increased inflows of aid and foreign investment. Inflation was controlled and food production increased. No other groups could compete with such a record, nor provide an alternative input superior to that of the president. The development agenda of the technocrats did not remain unchallenged for long, however.

Within a few years the country was seen to have opened its doors too widely to foreign investment, particularly from Japan, arousing nationalist sentiments that culminated in riots during the visit of the Japanese Prime Minister, Mr Tanaka, to Indonesia in January 1974. The extent of the riots, which were compounded by internal political struggles among competing factions of the political elite, came as a shock to the leadership. A series of economic and other policies were introduced in response to demands strongly expressed by the public over foreign investment in particular. The regulations concerning such investment were amended, and became more restrictive.

The direction of development was further altered as a result of the oil bonanza in 1973–4. With increased availability of resources, public enterprises began assuming a dominant role in a number of sectors, and public investments were increasingly directed into heavy industries, petrochemicals and mining. The civil service also expanded rapidly, and bureaucratic intervention became rampant. To promote import substitution in government-initiated upstream industries, the incentive regime was made progressively more inward-oriented. Investment licensing and credit allocation at subsidized interest rates reinforced distortions in the trade regime. The oil boom directly increased the amounts of resources at the disposal of Pertamina, and these were used to finance the development of heavy industries (Krakatau Steel), air transport (Pelita Air), a rice estate in Sumatra, hotels throughout Indonesia and other major projects. In addition, a new division of advanced technology headed and developed by Professor B.J. Habibie was set up within Pertamina, and was the embryo of what later became the Agency for Research and Application of Technology (*Badan Pengkajian dan Penerapan Teknologi*).

It was believed that over time Pertamina retained an increasing portion of the central government's oil revenues, and with these augmented resources, its head, Ibnu Sutowo, began challenging the technocrats with an alternative vision of development. However, Pertamina's rapid expansion, including the development of its own fleet of tankers, led to a severe financial crisis when oil prices began weakening in 1975. Apparently the president was not informed about the tanker deal, and dismissed Ibnu Sutowo as head of Pertamina while calling upon the technocrats to resolve the situation. A supervisory board that included several technocrats as members was instituted to oversee Pertamina's operations.

For a while, the structure of economic policy-making was back to what it had been, but then new challenges arose. The economy became heavily dependent on oil revenues and suffered from the 'Dutch disease' problem, entailing an erosion of competitiveness in the non-oil economy due to appreciation in the real exchange rate associated with emergence of a booming sector. The government devalued the currency in September 1978 by about 30 per cent, but another even larger oil boom followed in 1979–80. The appreciation in the real exchange rate led to pressures to protect the newly-developed industries and a host of non-tariff barriers were introduced. These barriers included an import licensing system, import bans and quotas, and various informal quantitative restrictions.

The import licensing system was introduced with the intention of promoting import substitution in such basic goods as cement, fertilizers, chemicals, synthetic fibres, and iron and steel. The number of products requiring an 'approved-importer' licence was continuously increased, but the number of approved traders reduced to as few as two or three companies. Initially, approved trader status was mainly given to state enterprises, but as years went by it was increasingly handed to private companies with strong links to the centres of political power. Import bans and quotas were used as instruments to raise the local content of various domestic assembly activities. These initially involved motor vehicles, tractors, diesel engines, and motorcycles, but were subsequently extended to construction equipment, diesel engines, home appliances and electronic goods.

An attempt by the Department of Industry to establish a system of administrative guidance failed, and it now appeared that fair deals could not be reached as more and more import monopolies became related to the powers-that-be. The bureaucracy was powerless to facilitate a process in which powerful business groups were involved, and fair rules of the game could not be formulated under such circumstances. The import licensing system created a high-cost economy, however, and gradually some exporters who were seriously damaged by the import protection scheme began to promote its dismantling. As observed by MacIntyre (1992), these exporters later became valuable allies of the technocrats in undertaking reform of such high-cost conditions, which was the main objective of the second phase of deregulation.

In the late 1980s, the Minister of Trade, Mr Arifin Siregar, proposed the creation of a formal mechanism for government–business relations, but unfortunately he did so in terms of the idea of 'Indonesia Incorporated'. The mechanism was strongly opposed in many quarters, since it was seen to give legitimacy to the practice of government–business collusion which by then had become very visible (Soesastro 1989).

THE SECOND PHASE

The technocrats in the latter half of the first phase were not only trying to deal with excessive rent-seeking activities, but also to limit the damage caused by the policy of inward-oriented industrialization. They made maximum use of three important disciplining devices to deal with government colleagues who favoured large, capital-intensive upstream projects and high technology ventures. These devices were the balanced budget, the open capital account and a rule-of-thumb limitation in the use of foreign capital, which were aimed at maintaining a maximum debt-service ratio of 20 per cent of the value of exports. The devices enabled the technocrats to maintain sound macroeconomic policies, and to prevent financial disasters like those experienced by other large oil exporting countries (Nigeria, Venezuela). The Pertamina financial crisis in 1975 stood as a powerful reminder of such dangers.

However, the technocrats also felt the high-cost economy resulting from rampant rent-seeking activities would make it increasingly difficult for them to hold the fort, and in this context the weakening oil prices in 1982 came as a blessing in disguise. The severe effect of these on an economy that had become so dependent on oil created a sense of crisis sufficient to set in motion a new round of reforms. Dr Ali Wardhana, a member of the technocratic team and a long-serving finance minister behind Indonesia's deregulation drive, offered 'a simple chain of economic reasoning', arguing the necessity of undertaking structural reform. He reasoned that:

1. Economic growth and development need export growth to pay for imports and to service debt.
2. Reliable export growth requires non-oil exports from agriculture and manufacturing.
3. Non-oil exports depend on an efficient, productive economy, which hinges on a competitive domestic market.
4. Protectionist policies and government controls are inimical to this competitive domestic market, creating a high cost economy.
5. The policies and controls must therefore be dismantled, leading to a liberalized and deregulated economy.

Dr Wardhana further asserted that government must develop non-oil revenues to be able to play a constructive role in development. That role would involve ensuring the benefits of liberalization and resulting economic growth were widely and evenly spread, with continued emphasis given to rural development (Wardhana 1989).

The increased pressures on the country's balance of payments in 1982 led to a few measures on the trade front, including a relaxation of export taxes and restrictions on trade with the Socialist Bloc. A scheme of counter-trade was also introduced. However, the government was more concerned with the import side, where earlier attempts to curb imports had resulted in the creation of an import licensing system that, over time, had become entrenched. This system was also misused to promote industrialization through a combination of import-substitution policies, regulation of investment and state ownership. The vested interests behind this industrialization drive likewise became very strong.

The technocrats encountering strong resistance to the deregulation of trade and industry were left with the financial sector in which to launch this process. They could begin with this sector where they felt reform was long overdue because they were in charge of the central bank and the Ministry of Finance. However, the decision to liberalize the financial sector was a daring move, and as with the shift to the open capital account in 1971 went against the conventional wisdom that financial-sector liberalization should not precede that of the real sector. Interestingly, it was the threat of capital flight that helped induce deregulation of trade and industry at that time.

The continuing low oil prices helped keep up the pressures for reform, also allowing the technocrats to adopt a gradual approach to liberalization with the planning and execution of reforms within their capacity (ibid.). Gradualism was chosen over the 'big bang' approach, because it had the advantage of progressively winning over a new constituency for further reform. More substantial deregulation was introduced in 1985, with the announcement of an across-the-board reduction of import tariffs and the issuing of a presidential decree that the Indonesian customs service would be subcontracted to a Swiss-based private surveying company, SGS. The latter was a radical step which ran counter to Indonesia's strong nationalist instinct. Even so, observers felt that the measures did not go far enough, with the assault failing to be directed at the core of the problem, which was the rampant rent-seeking activities of import monopolies.

The government introduced its first package of trade and industrial deregulation in May 1986. This measure allowed major exporters to procure foreign-sourced inputs directly, without going through licensed importers. It also replaced an export subsidy programme with a duty drawback, but the import monopolies remained untouched. Then a first step to the dismantling of the complex import licensing system was taken in October 1986 – by abolishing import licences. This was followed by an announcement in January 1987 of a further round of tariff reductions and the removal of non-tariff barriers to imports, including the dismantling of the monopoly on steel and plastic imports which was seen to symbolize the then emerging cronyism.

The technocrats might have realized they had reached the limits of what could be achieved, for it became clear that any further major surgery to trade and industrial measures would face great resistance from the president himself. Accordingly they turned their attention again to the financial system, with its deregulation in October 1988 being heralded as the most sweeping initiative in that sector. The deregulation removed most entry barriers, with state enterprises that hitherto had only been able to use state banks now being permitted to deposit up to 50 per cent of their funds in private banks. New foreign (joint venture) banks and domestic banks were allowed, and foreign banks could open branches outside Jakarta. These liberalization measures resulted in a dramatic growth in the financial sector, and the number of banks increased from 61 in 1988 to close to 120 in 1991, and to 230 in the mid-1990s. The growth of assets and credits of private banks expanded rapidly, resulting especially in a big increase in the role of private domestic banks at the expense of their state counterparts.

Concerns were expressed that the rapid expansion of bank credits could lead to financial distress and financial instability in view of the growth of problem loans and bank failures. In 1990 some banks had a run on their deposits, following rumours of their difficulties. In August 1990, it became public knowledge that one of the largest domestic foreign exchange banks, Bank Duta, had incurred losses of US$ 400 million in foreign exchange dealings. It was also revealed that the losses had already been realized when the bank went public in early 1990, but this was not evident from the bank's financial statement. In this case, the open capital account was not at issue, since it had been in place for a long time. The concern was rather with the ability of the authorities to supervise adequately the rapidly expanding banking sector. Although efforts were made to strengthen prudential regulations in 1992, and subsequently, confidence in the banking system remained shaky at best.

The remarkable thing about the case of the Bank Duta was the manner in which that institution was rescued. Since it was partly owned by a number of foundations set up over the years by President Suharto to raise funds for social and religious activities, the president himself organized the rescue operation. He requested a close business associate to provide fresh capital to inject into the bank in the shortest time possible. This received a favourable response, but within a few months it was reported that the associate was being granted a licence to build one of the largest of Indonesia's petrochemical complexes, Candra Asri. This complex enjoyed the privileges of foreign direct investment, and was subsequently given tariff protection.

The Bank Duta episode illustrates the direct involvement of, and intervention by, the president in business affairs, bypassing institutions and ignoring established rules and regulations. The few years up to 1990 had seen an increase in such behaviour, which continued to be unchecked. The larger and worrying picture suggested a gross lack of independent and effective institutions, including legal organizations. In fact, what was puzzling was that this lack of effective governance had not produced a situation where the country was seen to have priced itself out of international investments. Addressing this issue, MacIntyre and Ramli (1997) listed the many problems with the formal legal system as well as with systemic cronyism and corruption in the government administration. They also noted that the business community in Indonesia had largely abandoned the notion that the legal system was an effective vehicle for arbitrating commercial disputes. How was it then that the weak legal guarantees of property rights and widespread corruption did not discourage private foreign investors from entering the country?

MacIntyre and Ramli offered three explanations for such lack of discouragement (MacIntyre 1992; MacIntyre and Ramli 1997). First, high rates of return to investors would make them accept some increased costs associated with bribery, and some increased risk associated with uncertainty over formal property rights. Second, relating to the nature of governance, President Suharto's position in Indonesia's political architecture that concentrated and centralized power on the presidency was much like that of a unified monopolist. He was able to monitor and control circumstances so that the pricing of bribes by agencies did not drive down investments. Third – and this concerns the needed assurance that this strong leader would not reverse his decisions – MacIntyre and Ramli proposed that the government had effectively tied its own hands so as to make a credible commitment to the investment community. This was done through the open capital account, which created a powerful early warning of investor discontent and hence exercised strong discipline on government behaviour.

The current financial crisis shows that the disciplining mechanism should not be relied upon, since markets (and investors) can react so abruptly. That is particularly true of portfolio investment and short-term capital flows, rather than foreign direct investment. Indeed, recent developments suggest that it is ultimately the existence of good governance, including the development of solid legal institutions, which should be relied upon. Will the issue of good governance now become a priority in Indonesia's national agenda? Why in fact, and following the question of Goodpaster (1997), would a country such as Indonesia which had been able to achieve political stability and economic growth with little regard to the state of its laws and legal system, all of a sudden become convinced that the rule of law and regulated behaviour is necessary to ensure the sustainability of its development efforts?

It may not be difficult to find answers to these questions. One response is that successful development itself creates a more complex society that then requires a rule-based social ordering system to provide social stability, harmony, enhanced personal freedom, economic growth and even democratization (ibid.). MacIntyre and Ramli (MacIntyre 1992; MacIntyre and Ramli 1997) argue similarly that change is imperative because the political underpinnings of the present system would otherwise give way. It is true also that in an increasingly integrated global economy, Indonesia cannot allow itself to maintain a system in which transactions costs are excessive because of a lack of rule-based behaviour. This may not be self-evident yet to many Indonesians, but will be brought about sooner or later by the process of competitive liberalization in

East Asia. The latter process was as noted the driving force for Indonesia's third phase of deregulation from 1994.

THE THIRD PHASE

After the sweeping trade and financial deregulation from 1986 to 1988, Indonesia experienced 'reform fatigue'. During the early 1990s the average rate of nominal tariffs stayed at the same level, and no efforts were made to eliminate non-tariff barriers. Things began to change in 1994 following a poor non-oil export performance and a marked decline in approvals of foreign direct investment. It was felt that Indonesia was beginning to lose out to such nations as China, Vietnam and India in the competition for foreign direct investment. In addition, the country began to experience declining export competitiveness, which was another possible reason for the slowing of foreign investments.

A major change in investment regulation was instituted in June 1994, and again allowed for 100 per cent foreign ownership. This provision had originally been contained in the 1967 Foreign Investment Law, but had been amended in 1974 following the emergence of strong nationalist sentiments. In addition, nine sectors previously closed to foreign direct investment – including ports, power generation, shipping, air transport, railways and telecommunications – were opened up. Mass media were also originally included among these sectors, but later withdrawn.

Instead of an improvement, the 1990s saw a rapid deterioration in governance. As mentioned, the president granted help to the rescuer of Bank Duta, with the Candra Asri complex as a *quid pro quo*. Such awarding of protection was seen to violate the spirit of the ASEAN (Association of South East Asian Nations) Free Trade Area, on which Indonesia had recently embarked with other countries. The circumstances were made more awkward because the Candra Asri protection was announced only a few days after President Suharto had successfully engineered the Bogor Declaration of APEC (the Asia Pacific Economic Cooperation) to achieve free and open trade and investment in the region. This Declaration had been enthusiastically received by most governments concerned. The then Minister of Finance, Mr Mari'e Mohamad, who was also (as stipulated by law) the *ex officio* head of the Tariff Board (*Tim Tarif*), was removed from the latter position because he did not favour tariff protection to Candra Asri.

By the mid-1990s the technocrats were no longer so favourably placed in advising the president. Faced with the deterioration in governance, they pulled together their remaining strengths to make liberalization of the economy a regionally-binding commitment. They could not state this openly, but that was what they aimed for by supporting the idea of forming a Free Trade Area, which previously had not been promoted by Indonesia or even by the technocrats themselves. The technocrats had also been behind the efforts to bring about the Bogor Declaration, and further trade liberalization packages were introduced in May 1995 and June 1996. Yet, while on the whole significant progress was made in reducing tariffs, a few sectors such as steel, chemicals, automotive and agriculture remained highly protected for an extended period, and were exposed by the new deregulation packages of 1998. The dismantling of protection in these sectors had become politically very difficult, for the struggle to do so was no longer just a matter of competing concepts of development and industrialization between different government ministers, but also a fight to eliminate the rampant and entrenched cronyism.

The crisis that hit Indonesia in the second half of 1997 was initially seen by technocrats as another blessing in disguise, since it could provide a new opportunity to redress problems and continue the deregulation process that had actually come to a halt. The government began introducing fiscal and monetary measures to cope with the crisis quite early, and numerous large government and private infrastructure projects were cancelled for balance-of-payments reasons. Many of these projects involved businesses belonging to cronies of the president and even to his own children.

Despite the introduction of these measures, however, the currency remained unstable and continued to depreciate, in part due to the contagion effect, and this led the government to seek assistance from the International Monetary Fund (IMF). An agreement was reached in October 1997, involving an IMF-organized financial package of US\$ 43 billion in support of a reform programme to be undertaken by the government of Indonesia. The programme included a structural reform agenda that would end the monopolies. Yet the inclusion of this agenda carried a risk, because the entire programme could become entangled in complex and sensitive political problems.

CONCLUSION

It is interesting to speculate whether the crisis has provided a new stimulus for the further deregulation of the Indonesian economy. Should this be the case, Indonesia may enter a fourth phase of deregulation and liberalization under the tutelage of the International Monetary Fund, at least for the coming three years. The agreement with the IMF stipulates a continuation of deregulation measures, including the further removal of tariff and non-tariff barriers, opening up the wholesale, retail and banking sector to foreign direct investment, withdrawing all import and marketing monopolies (except for rice) over the next three years, and phasing out price controls and domestic monopolies, including cement and plywood. The process will now also focus on institutional development to promote greater transparency and competition, more institutional autonomy, and a stronger legal and regulatory environment.

It is ironic that an agreement with the IMF is needed for the Indonesian government to pledge autonomy for the central bank, Bank Indonesia, to formulate and implement monetary policy. However, the question remains: who will monitor this? Will it be necessary to rely on the IMF? The agreement with the IMF also suggests a number of laws that need to be improved, and others that should be introduced. Yet on paper there is no shortage of meaningful laws, including those that could help promote corporate governance. The Banking Law of 1992 could secure prudential supervision of banks, if it was enforced. The Corporate Law of 1995, which came into operation in 1996, clearly stipulates the new duties of directors, the rights of shareholders and disclosure requirements that match high international standards. The critical issue, however, is the enforcement of these provisions. The weak enforcement of the law has a lot to do with the patrimonial nature of the system of government and governance. In the end it is the Indonesians themselves who will have to work out a way of changing their system

NOTES

1. The Indonesian government over the period from President Suharto's effective assumption of power in October 1965, until his resignation in May 1998.
2. The Indonesian government over the period from the Declaration of Independence (from the Netherlands) in 1945 to the effective transfer of power from President Sukarno to President Suharto in October 1965.
3. This allusion parodies the famous term 'agricultural involution' coined by Geertz (1963). Geertz applied the term to the turning in on itself of an Indonesian agricultural system that (in the 1950s and early 1960s) could not cope with demographic and other pressures.
4. West Irian finally reverted to Indonesia in 1963, following American mediation and its transfer by the Dutch colonial power to United Nations administration the previous year. But this event had been preceded by a big military build-up and limited fighting between Indonesia and the Netherlands. *Konfrontasi* in 1963–5 refers to the tensions with Singapore and the newly-formed Malaysia, as well as with the perceived imperial sponsors of these countries (which included the United Kingdom and Australia).

9. The Institutions of Transition from Central Planning: The Case of Vietnam

Adam Fforde

In our new market economy, we are not worried ... (for) we will play by the same rules as everybody else, but in our own way (intervention by a Vietnamese participant at the Conference on Socio-Economic Strategy, Hanoi, 1990).

This chapter examines institutional aspects of the emergence of the Vietnamese market economy in the late 1980s. It argues that this emergence was the outcome of various processes,[1] accessible both through systemic and historical logics.[2] The systemic logic of Vietnam's transition adds to insights from the institutionalist framework. Its historical character points to various limitations in that approach.

The socioeconomic development of communist Vietnam since World War II is complicated and little understood, especially its political and popular aspects. This chapter draws upon a wider secondary literature to tell two basic stories: first, how and why Soviet-style agricultural producer cooperatives operated under north Vietnamese conditions; second, how and why Vietnam under communist rule possessed systematically adapted institutions which, under certain conditions, spontaneously shifted the system from central planning to something far more market-oriented. These two stories are interrelated, since Vietnam was and remains a largely rural country, and ways in which farming communities coped with collectivization had profound effects upon the operation of central planning at national level. For example, if farmers were powerful enough to threaten rice procurement, an acute systemic crisis would inevitably result. The 'micro' of the cooperativized villages contrasts with and supplements the 'macro' of the logic of systemic change.

Soviet 'state socialism' is now, for those who wish to study it in reality, primarily a historical phenomenon. Leaving aside Cuba and North Korea, all is in the past; this includes the great weight of academic literature devoted to central planning and collectivized agriculture, covering their complexities and their variations over time and in different places. Habits of thought live on, as do political and organizational structures, but economic structures do not. Human experience has tended to show that market-based economies are more efficient both in their static and dynamic aspects. Yet in not a few countries of the ex-Soviet Union, the costs of transition are high. Steep output drops have occurred and social welfare indicators have fallen dramatically. Whether these are the result, or the cause, of poor policies needs discussion. There is a gap between the promise and reality of market economies, which matches the fact that capitalist countries with similar per capita gross domestic product levels offer very different things to their citizens.

Like differences between countries in market economies, transitions to the market by different nations also vary significantly. Why this is so is a major issue, as witnessed by tensions in discussions around 'big bang' policies.[3] It is clear too that appeals to universal theories to explain such differences have limited applicability, for when societies are changing radically and rapidly many factors, including those of cultural, historical and social origin have importance. Human relations of reproduction, which are typically excluded from economic analyses but deeply nested in culture and history and profoundly significant to well-being (Robertson 1991), illustrate this. Thus Soviet socialism offered much (although delivering less) in the socialization 'beyond the family' of various functions, such as social welfare, job security, child care and care for the aged, leading to high female participation rates. People possessing such structures for generations found chaotic shifts to a market system placed great stress upon such human relations. What compensation did increases in real wages offer to an overburdened primary carer, when and if they occurred?

China and Vietnam both shifted their economies from central planning to market systems without the communist party losing power, and in both countries real incomes and welfare increased. The drops in income seen in Central Europe and the ex-Soviet Union did not happen. It is commonly argued that different economic starting conditions enabled Vietnam and China to avoid such costs (Sachs and Woo 1994), for when their rulers decided to shift to a market economy they had different 'stuff' to work with. It is claimed too that the parameters of their centrally-planned economies were favourable, with fewer state-owned enterprises and a rural population more sensitive to market opportunities. Such reasoning attributes to policy the main responsibility for change. Other strands in the literature maintain policy was neither so important nor the main source of change, and this is clear in the case of Vietnam. Thus when the market economy emerged (in Vietnam by 1989, when the final elements of central planning were abolished) 'the economy was already capable of a much more flexible response to market opportunities than the highly bureaucratized and centralized Soviet system' (van Arcadie 1993, p. 437).

The literature hovers around the basic issue of whether change is best viewed as endogenous, or policy-induced. Different authors come at this in different ways. Thus the above 'flexible response' covers notions of the microeconomic behaviour of the main economic agents, as well as ideas of macroeconomic structure and factor mobility. Where had such behaviour and such ideas – the outcomes of investments in institutional change – come from? Perhaps not from 'policy', but if not, from where? The answers tend to be that they emerge from some endogenous process or processes. Again, the literature about transition from socialism to capitalism often reflects ideas of the nature of nation-states, where communist regimes are assumed to exist in essential opposition to their populations.[4]

A corollary of this is that their rulers are assumed to have had such a high degree of relative autonomy from 'civil society' (see the discussion of Justin Lin's analysis below) that they can act in response to political logics for which the wider society is irrelevant. Such a non-democratic position explains (and justifies, if referring to some notion of a 'national interest' accessible to the leadership) central planning as much as any other elitist ideology. From an analytical rather than an ethical perspective, this elitist approach places too little emphasis on the power of non-elite groups in national politics. If collectivized farmers refuse to do what the party thinks they should do, and if this forces national policy changes, then farmers are exercising political power. They are not doing so through formal political channels – the mass organizations – for those are precisely designed to stop such things from happening. But power they still have.

Such non-elite influences can be seen in modern Vietnamese history, with ignorance of them permitting ignorance of endogenous change processes and encouraging misguided overestimation of the role of policy. This must be avoided if what happened and why are to be understood. The main question to be asked is how institutional change took place, and how the underlying processes were structured and organized. It is quite inadequate in this perspective to tell the story of change merely in terms of policy shifts.

HISTORICAL INTRODUCTION

The following chronology of events provides the basic historical logic of change. More background is given by Marr (1981), Woodside (1971, 1989), Beresford (1989) and de Vylder and Fforde (1996).

After the defeat of the French at Dien Bien Phu in 1954, Vietnamese communists took control of north Vietnam, ruling through the Democratic Republic of Vietnam. As Soviet bloc members, they sought to implement the neo-Stalinist development model (Fforde and Paine 1987), and following land reform in 1945–55, rural collectivization took place in 1959–60. Also, in the late 1950s 'socialist transformation' attacked the free market and private capital, and by the beginning of the 1960s the orthodox institutions of central planning were in place. The First Five-Year Plan (1961–5) saw a typical programme of forced industrialization fed by foreign aid, mainly capital goods. But what was actually happening in the north of Vietnam prior to national reunification in 1975 and the establishment in 1976 of a unified state, the Socialist Republic of Vietnam, incorporating both north and south sections of the country? The short answer is that it was something a long way from the Russian and Chinese textbooks.

Despite debate, the literature appears increasingly to argue that political compromise eased pressures upon the population and was reflected in institutional 'endogenization'. The economic manifestation of this was a structured coexistence: this entailed shortage phenomena familiar from other centrally-planned economies obtaining alongside pervasive market-type relations in an 'aggravated shortage'– the coexistence of adverse plan–market incentives with widespread market opportunities.[5] An important element was an equilibrium between plan and market that depended, amongst other things, upon the volume of resources controlled by the state. These included external assistance, which was large.[6]

The realities of the system in the north of Vietnam were applied in the south after 1976, but hopes for 'one country, two systems' were not realized. However, integration of the south with its different intellectual background and lifestyles, not to mention political loyalties and administrative systems, had profound effects. In the late 1970s military activities embracing Vietnam's occupation of Cambodia and China's punitive attack on Vietnam's northern provinces coincided with the loss of Chinese and Western aid. This changed important exogenous parameters of the system, and led initially to the endogenous institutional adaptation explored below. Yet policy changes from early 1981 introduced 'partial reforms' that marked a fundamental shift in the rules of the game, supporting dynamic transition processes under a formal 'transitional model'. Only at its 1986 Sixth Congress, however, did the communist party adopt *doi moi* (literal meaning: 'renovation') as a slogan, signalling the overt intention of moving to a market economy. The collapse of communist regimes in Eastern Europe in 1989, and the loss of Soviet aid in 1989–91, helped cause the eradication of what remained of central planning, and the twin-track price system vanished in 1989–90. From 1989 Vietnam possessed a market economy, but with weakly developed factor markets. This was to have a major impact upon growth in the early 1990s, which was nevertheless rapid and macroeconomically stable.

INSTITUTIONAL CHANGE

It thus appears that processes of institutional change in Vietnam have been determined by the interplay of various factors, which excepting the imported neo-Stalinist model were predominantly domestic in character. The important external 'shocks' of the late 1970s and late 1980s altered the domestic equilibrium, and initiated and then terminated the transition process whose end was marked by the final removal of twin-track pricing. Vietnam therefore offers fertile soil for those interested in how human societies change. This chapter examines institutional change in two settings – those of the pre-reform collectivized rural economy prior to initial partial decollectivization in 1981, and of the 'transitional model',[7] formalized by the partial reforms package of 1980–81. But first Justin Lin's tools and framework in relation to institutional change are considered.

A Critique of Lin

First, Lin's distinction in Chapter 2 of this volume between an 'institutional arrangement' and 'institutional structure' (p. 10) makes it possible to consider how particular arrangements may change whilst certain institutional elements in the structure are kept constant. It is necessary to ask: just what stays unchanged?[8] In analysing institutional change in collectivized agriculture, this can be seen in the notion that cooperatives existed within a wider and less altering social and economic institutional structure – a 'collectivity' defined in terms of all socioeconomic institutions of a given village or commune. In macro-level analysis it can be seen in the notion of 'aggravated shortage' where the key endogenous variable is the balance between plan and market. The market is viewed as embodying a package of institutional arrangements (for example, the emergence of commercial capital) within a more or less stable structure associated with the market economy.

Second, Lin places great stress on the notion of 'efficient' institutions, also introducing cognition, power and politics into the discussion where 'when government places a new constraint on the institutional choice set ... a less efficient arrangement may become dominant in the restricted set' (p. 14). But it is not clear to what the notion of 'efficiency' reduces in the final analysis. It is well known, for example, that capital cannot be measured easily, and there are innate and insoluble problems involved in interpersonal and intertemporal comparisons of welfare. Yet the general statement of efficiency made by Lin, and his portrayal of economic performance in a reasonably non-positivistic manner, are probably sufficient in underpinning his framework of institutional change.

Third, institutions matter for Lin since they lead to different economic performances, with the consequences of particular institutions depending in an endogenous manner not only on their own particular nature but on the functions of other arrangements in the overall institutional structure. Thus, institutional arrangements such as a neo-Stalinist cooperative or central-planning organization will depend for their resulting operations upon the structure within which they find themselves. Since neo-Stalinism was of its nature essentially foreign in all countries except the Soviet Union, this way of looking at things is useful for countries such as Vietnam and China.

Fourth, Lin sees the source of institutional change as being a search for efficiency, positing the idea of institutional 'disequilibrium' with profitable opportunities arising from four main sources including changes in the institutional choice set, technology, relative factor and product prices and other institutional arrangements. Such disequilibrium was clearly large in the context of neo-Stalinist Vietnam until the late 1980s. However, the circumstances were complex, where the institutional choice set was not absolutely given but contingent on such political aspects as material interests, forces linked to feelings of paralysis, the power and prestige of leaders, and cognitive processes. These latter processes involved not only the evolution of domestic ideas in the face of Vietnamese reality, but external factors such as the ebb and flow of ideological debate within the socialist world and interpretations within Vietnam of contemporary global events. It is difficult indeed to see how 'institutional disequilibrium' could be measured, although given the wide range of possible institutional changes that 'might' occur, their different impacts should clearly be gauged.

Fifth, on the gains from innovation, Lin assumes squarely and optimistically the national interest of society as a whole (p. 16), also arguing that whether a particular innovation takes place depends upon expected gains and costs to the innovators (p. 17). He states as well that although there is a potentially important role for the state in facilitating institutional change, this implies neither that the state will inevitably take the initiative nor that its policies are bound to succeed; although most states in less developed countries dominate civil society and have substantial autonomy in policy making, they will institute a new institution only when the benefits to them are higher than the costs. However, it is again hard to see how costs to the state of alternative outcomes can be measured, or how cognitive issues and their related political expression, which at least appear important in the Vietnamese case, can be integrated into this analysis.[9] Indeed, the nature of the state remains vague in Lin's discussion and it is not clear, for example, whether it is separate from the party or if state-owned enterprises are part of it.

The Collectivized Rural Economy

It is puzzling that source materials revealed a striking gap between reality and policy prescription in the collectivized economy of the late 1970s (Fforde 1989; Kerkvliet 1996). While this is surprising in the indigenous literature of a communist country which had just defeated the United States in war, 'systemic policy failure' now appears as a simple but powerful and enduring theme relevant in contemporary debates over land law and state-owned enterprise policy. One can posit the general phenomenon in communist Vietnam of a constitutional order within which, through a concept of process (*qua trinh*), widespread illegality or non-compliance is acceptable; this is subject to its forming a resource to be exploited as a basis for institutional change and also regime survival. Thus the institutional order could – and did – change radically.[10] The rules of the game governing Vietnamese cooperatives came to be quite different from those in Soviet textbooks.

The system of agricultural producer cooperatives adopted in the Democratic Republic of north Vietnam was basically Soviet (Fforde 1989). Land and labour were brought into the cooperative and were to come under cooperative management committees which would control processes of production and distribution: people worked in brigades and were paid in work-points. In this system transaction costs were high, for establishing the economic value of alternatives was heavily constrained by two sets of factors. One of these were the rigid requirements of a plan imposed from higher levels under the expectation that producers and consumers would follow it as a socialist duty while not exploring other opportunities. Another was the existence of grey, black and other markets, which were both frowned upon and weakly developed.[11]

The sources of the time reveal conflicts over control of production, distribution and access to production inputs of land, fertilizer and livestock, with farmers responding to collectivization by preventing policy implementation. The terms of trade facing cooperatives were such that the value of participating in the plan was very low compared with market opportunities, under circumstances of aggravated shortage. The fact that state prices in the 1970s were typically one tenth of those on the free market meant that rather extensive economic activities operating at high prices existed outside the plan. Hence although the '5% land' which farmers were allowed to use as they wished was set officially at 5 per cent of the cultivated area, its actual extent in any village reflected the equilibrium marking the balance between plan and market. It is clear that this influence was endogenous, not exogenous, and dependent on the free market–state price differential.

The cooperative form imposed under neo-Stalinist conditions possessed inherent institutional weakness. It was economically inefficient, incapable of realizing socially-valuable alternatives which were well recognized even if their exploitation was prohibitively expensive. It also had incentive structure difficulties, with familiar 'free-rider' problems where work-points were allocated without adequate labour supervision and the lazy were paid as much as the hard-working. These problems could be reduced by community commitment or charismatic local leadership, but such local initiatives were uncommon.

The imposition of the cooperative form could be seen as close to an institutional experiment. For collectivized farmers, the primary issue was not whether to join the cooperatives, since membership was quasi-compulsory (Anon 1992), but what to do when they had joined (Fforde 1987). The responses of these farmers opened the way for institutional change, but in a particular sense with nothing to do with 'policy'. A major issue was the unworkability of policy (Fforde 1986), with the official stance being one thing, but reality another, and in line with the saying that 'peasants do not understand the Party's line…'. The circumstances as they developed certainly demonstrated how the cooperative institutional form was influenced by surrounding institutional structure, in the manner suggested by Justin Lin's third point above.

The outcome of this difference between official policy and peasants' requirements drew upon historical elements deep within the political culture, as well as factors such as the prospects of further armed struggle to unify the country. The result was a 'political compromise' – under pressure, policy would change (Beresford and Fforde 1997). The Democratic Republic of North Vietnam could at one level be seen as a 'weak' state (a contentious thesis), where this was associated with the macroeconomic impact of an orthodox, neo-Stalinist, forced industrialization programme upon an area with a low economic surplus. Rapid industrialization and urbanization created demands for wage goods that the resource-starved and low-efficiency collectivized agriculture was not generating. Without recourse to force, this had to mean a rise in free-market prices and a fall in urban real incomes, but this begs the question of why the authorities did not follow the standard solution of sending in the armed forces to get rice from the villages at the point of a bayonet.

It had originally been hoped that land reform would create a loyal local political basis for the new regime, thereby preventing the rise of a rural middle class with interests hostile to the regime. However, this goal does not appear to have been achieved, because the communist leadership lacked firm political control of rural areas on the eve of collectivization. The strength of rural communities in resisting extractions of surplus imposed by higher levels had also not been anticipated. Unfortunately the antecedent circumstances are still unclear, and there is as yet no proper economic analysis of the first Five-Year Plan (1961–5).

The Development of Alternatives

In any case, as free-market prices rose in the early 1960s, farmers' wives and daughters who brought rice into Hanoi were not shot and a balance was struck. The existence of a high-price, outside economy had profound effects, generating substantial incomes. Transactions costs in the free market would also have been lower than in the pure neo-Stalinist system, with it being easier and less risky to carry out private deals, often from within state-owned enterprises or cooperatives themselves. Thus Lin's fourth point of institutional disequilibrium, which in this instance flowed largely from relative factor and product prices, did result in some institutional change which nonetheless took many years more to become formalized.

However, despite opposition to the official line from important figures with impeccable reputations, the stance remained that neo-Stalinist institutions were correct. The tension created by systematic unworkability was 'written in stone', but was nonetheless creative, with the reigning institutional disequilibrium entailing a possibility for change, if factors holding it in place were to alter. Given the attractive material incentives pertaining to alternatives, violations to the official line tended to produce higher output, and therefore could attract support from pragmatic leaders. Policy was profoundly conservative until 1979–81, seeking to push back local adaptations and fly in the face of material incentives that were shifting economic power away from the cooperative leadership down to brigades and farming families. Cooperatives that did not take advantage of alternatives often benefited from favourable resource allocations as 'models'. Following Lin's fifth point, the state did not, despite the benefits of fence-breaking to individuals, consider it was advantageous to facilitate institutional change.

Yet at the end of the 1970s as the economic crisis associated with the Cambodian and Chinese conflicts and loss of Chinese and Western aid ran its course, the macro environment shifted the balance of incentives further against the cooperatives. Also, the political options and conceptions of policy-makers were changing, with the former being perhaps better researched than the latter. Cuts in resource flows through official channels combined with floods in the south, procurement difficulties (where troops were again not sent in) and a minor regular development-strategy reassessment by the Party to create conditions in which spontaneous de-collectivization gathered strength.

Out of this came, in an example of basing proposals for reform on illegal reality, Order CT-100 of the Party Secretariat of January 1981[12] announcing a shift to household contracting 'to save the cooperatives'. Contracting had already been done, it was said, in Hai Phong. Brigade structures were no longer seen as essential to socialist construction, and with other changes the balance moved decisively to a new approach. However, the work-point system remained, as did many local cadre jobs, but the changes were sufficient to generate significant gains in outputs of staples in 1980–82 (Fforde 1989, Chapter 12).

Order CT-100 exemplifies well the way in which Vietnamese policy-makers generated institutional change within the constitutional order. It recognized the facts of life of policy unworkability, aggravated shortage and inherent institutional weaknesses of the cooperative form within the particular macroeconomic environment. It also identified more economically-efficient incentives 'beyond the margin', including a property-rights structure embodying farmers' own-account activities to replace collective production and procurement. It provided fertile ground for institutional innovation 'over the fence', to be exploited in policy debates. Relating to Lin's fifth and second points, the regime now saw gains from institutional change and relaxed its restrictive practices to permit more efficient organization.

The 'Transitional Model' 1979–89[13]

In moving to a market economy, Vietnam resembled China in defining a set of transitional institutions in law. These institutions emerged as pure central planning was abandoned, and were in part a means to effect that abandonment. They were marked by official documents defining the emerging forms as 'household contracts' and the 'three-plan system'. As suggested, the institutions existed in practice before being expressed in policy documents, with reform 'coming from below' but being mediated by intellectual and political activity. Cognitive issues were involved, for order existed both in terms of 'the textbooks' and 'reality'.[14] Such *post-hoc* policy documentation seems lacking in countries which changed their constitutional before their institutional order.

Why were transitional institutions with endogenous processes increasing the scope of the market at the expense of the plan accepted? The basic answer is that increasing orientation towards the market contributed to better economic performance along lines argued by modern institutional economics. It was also true that political forces of increasing power pushed for further expansion of markets, and that 'fence-breaking'[15] activities proved extremely difficult for conservatives to prevent. Once the gap between reality and policy existed and had been admitted, there was a fertile source of institutional innovations for policy-makers to research and then introduce into formal policy if political circumstances were appropriate; this in turn allowed another round of changes to begin.

In January 1981, there was a package of partial reforms, including both CT-100 and a fundamental decree in state-owned enterprise reform, 25-CP (Beresford and Fforde 1997). This package was of central importance, introducing a dynamic element into the system by permitting state enterprises to engage in free market transactions for inputs and outputs. In 1989 25-CP's three-plan arrangement combining plan and market was abandoned, effectively relinquishing central planning and introducing a market economy. In combination, these two decrees gave the state enterprises and farming households greater freedoms.[16] A further important factor was steps from around 1981 to reduce the extent of consumer goods rationing, which also helped reduce distributional tension and improve economy. The state enterprises' enhanced freedoms permitted them to accumulate capital under their own direct control, which was a prerequisite for the development of stable markets.[17] Since such capital was by its nature part of the market and not the plan, its growth implied a shift to a market economy.

The period of the transitional model is complicated, and one has to factor in such issues as the ebb and flow of collectivization drives in the Mekong area of south Vietnam, the similar advances and reversals in the decentralization of foreign trade, and the effects of the Soviet aid programme.[18] Ideologically, the period divides into two stages: a 'hard' reform socialism up to around 1985, and a 'soft' reform socialism subsequently (de Vylder and Fforde 1996, Chapter 4). What is striking, though, is how the 'rules of the game' were set from the outset through the introductions of CT-100 and 25-CP. These defended the core institutions of the state through tactical concessions that permitted a lessening in transaction costs by permitting a significant expansion of 'unplanned' activities.

If the emergence of rural reforms drew upon years of policy unworkability and macroeconomic shocks, then much the same thing explains state industrial reform. As early as 1964, during debates that 'wrote the neo-Stalinist model in stone', various state-owned enterprises were 'running to the market'. The real difference between aggravated shortage and the transitional model concretized by CT-100 and 25-CP is that the shortage was essentially static, once the basic political compromise had been reached. The transitional model, on the other hand, was dynamic, leading in time to the demise of traditional socialism.[19]

The transitional model permitted rapid institutional change, but was dysfunctional in the sense that under it resources were consistently sucked from the planned to the unplanned sectors. It was highly functional in that it preserved the regime and offered avenues for personal enrichment to many close to it. As it had in the development of alternatives to rural collectivization before 1979–80, the economy became more efficient. This time, however, the change was driven by politics and capital accumulation rather than by adaptation to Stalin's development model. It seemed to work in the end, however.[20] An intriguing economic question here is why under conditions of aggravated shortage, with market prices that reflect the extant state of the economy and its complicated plan–market balance, the overall dynamic of the economy should move prices closer to those that will clear markets when the plan eventually vanishes? One answer is the existence of 'undistorted' price signals produced by the widespread use of gold and dollars.[21]

The issue of the 'end-game' implied in the transitional model is also of interest from a political economy perspective, especially bearing in mind problems that have faced many countries of the ex-Soviet Union. Here it is helpful to refer to the work of de Vylder and Fforde (ibid., Chapter 1), who make a distinction between 'plan' and 'market' distortions. The former refer to the distance the resource allocation pattern must move for the economy to have generalized commodity exchange which replaces central planning, while the latter alludes to the extent of distortions in the final market economy outcome. These two authors feel the 'transitional model' reduced 'plan' distortions so that, in 1989, administrative resource allocation could be abandoned rather easily. Again, prices by that time were near market-clearing levels, so required resource reallocation was not very great and real consumption rose.

CONCLUSION

Let us take a step backwards. The partial reforms of 1981 (of which CT-100 and 25-CP were the most important) helped change the rules of the game. These changes were not 'policy-driven' in strict terms, but the outcome of spontaneous institutional change; thus 'fence-breaking' was recognized, intellectually ordered and brought into formal policy. They also prevented the collapse of the system, and were preceded by a period where adaptation of pure neo-Stalinist forms had become accepted and normal, if not exactly concordant with leaders' wishes. The 1981 measures marked, but did not of themselves create, an institutional order that was dynamic but did not seem to change the constitutional order. They comprised in effect a 'transitional model'.

One reason for the successes —and limitations — of the transition was that it occurred within a framework that had two aspects:

1. A formal model that could be discussed and objectified, and which gave enhanced but still constrained freedoms to economic agents – this allowed economic performance to be improved, at root by reducing transaction costs and encouraging capital accumulation.
2. A more 'cultural' approach to institutional development that tacitly if not overtly accepted change as a process, with policy having to follow willy-nilly rather than leading reality.

'Legalization' gave justification both to fence-breakers and to intellectuals, who grasped their activities and expressed them in policy-relevant terms.

The processes of institutional change in Vietnam tend to confirm basic insights from the approach of Justin Lin and others contributing to this volume. They likewise support the view that the great increase in accumulation marked by rapid growth in gross domestic product in the early 1990s should be seen in the context of the way in which the market economy emerged. Respecting the politics involved in processes of institutional change, economic analysis shows how differing incentive and economic structures influence the outcome. It appears likely that 'orthodox' Western political science is to blame for the excessive 'policy' focus found in much of the transition literature; the latter ignores political processes and, so, to an important extent, is blind to associated political compromises between people and government. This analysis of the Vietnamese experiences can help in perceiving that error.

NOTES

1. The initial 'revisionist' position maintaining that socialist Vietnam was a far more adaptable and adapting society than Western researchers had realized is found in Fforde (1982). Despite the weakness of the sources upon which this position was based, its relative proximity to north Vietnamese critiques of the Democratic Republic of Vietnam model, albeit largely implicit, tended to confirm a reality that later research has shown to be largely correct. For this I owe much to those Vietnamese who managed to maintain their wits despite enormous ideological pressures, and to farmers and others who simply did things despite Party dogma, giving the critics a base for their thinking.
2. Systemic logic involves addressing the efficiency and viability of social and economic systems, while historical logic entails a chronological scrutiny of how systems either change or reproduce themselves.
3. Early debates about policies that should be adopted by countries moving from central planning to market economies typically polarized around the values of rapid and complete 'big bang' abandonment of central planning, or a step-by-step approach that saw partial reforms adopted'. For a clear presentation, see Naughton (1995), p. 13 *et seq.*
4. For a review of the literature see de Vylder and Fforde (1996), pp. 246–53. For an analysis in terms of opposition or 'resistance', see Fforde (1989), Thayer (1992) and Marr (1994).
5. See Kornai (1980) for the classic analysis of systemic shortage in traditional centrally-planned economies, and Fforde and Paine (1987) for a discussion of 'aggravated shortage'. The latter is a situation where endemic micro-shortage phenomena common in centrally-planned economies, and analysed in Kornai's classic, coexist with relatively widespread market-oriented activities that are analytically important. Kornai explicitly excludes such behaviour from his theoretical framework, thus ruling out the possibility of spontaneous, endogenous – and therefore policy-independent – transition to a market economy. It is worth pointing out that aggregate econometric analysis of East European centrally-planned economies has tended to conclude there was little evidence for aggregate chronic shortage (Portes et al. 1983), although Kornai has argued against this that his concept of shortage is essentially microeconomic and not aggregate. The notion of 'aggravated shortage' is close to that of the 'institutional disequilibrium' which Lin posits in Chapter 2.
6. Such an endogenously-determined equilibrium between plan and market can be explicitly modelled, and has been by Fforde (1984). The main free resource – that which can be allocated in response to local incentives and thus acts as a main determinant of the plan–market equilibrium – is labour effort. The model remains to be tested empirically.
7. No suggestion is made here that this 'model' was in any sense a conscious one: it is a notion that comes from the reflections of the outsider or scholar, not the policy-maker.
8. This approach is reminiscent of the application of late Wittgensteinian notions of human behaviour as being rule-governed, with game metaphors often used. Winch (1963) uses these ideas in the context of social science theory and practice. The metaphor of games is a nice one.
9. Cognition is interpreted here as a combination of awareness and understanding, which comes from the Vietnamese sense that these features are important and vary, and cannot be expected to do otherwise. 'The horse must not only know that it is thirsty, but that the trough contains water it can drink', i.e. cadres must not only want the dollars but also see they will stay in power. 'Cognitive issues' refer to the sense that understanding is not fixed, but limited and changing, with people learning, so that what they do alters.
10. The conventional distinction is made here between institutional and constitutional order, as being between 'changing the rules' and 'changing the rules about changing rules' (e.g. Ostrom et al. 1988. p. 120).

11. Thus the costs of policing and enforcing 'outside' deals were high. In compensation, personal links were valuable, leading to the emergence of networks to which newcomers could gain access.
12. CT-100 permitted cooperatives to shift the production and organization base from collective brigades to the family. This was done by dividing work into various tasks, some of which would be performed collectively, but most not. Households were allocated land to farm, and contracted with the cooperative to pay for collective inputs, with any excess after taxes and other 'duty-sales' to the state freely saleable on the market. Payments to the cooperative were still based upon work-points, however, and the value of these tended to rise subsequently, reducing farmer incentives and slowing rural incomes growth in the mid-1980s.
13. This section draws heavily upon de Vylder and Fforde (1996).
14. Beresford and Fforde (1997) suggest that these policy changes were inexplicable without consideration of the accompanying political process. In that process, material interests interacted with feelings of paralysis, the power and prestige of leaders, and cognitive processes. The interactions did not always work in the same direction, being marked by compromises which meant the early reforms were necessarily partial in nature.
15. I first found this phrase in an early and interesting article by Dam van Nhue and Le Si Thiep (1981). It refers graphically to a penetration of the boundary between plan and market.
16. Private non-agricultural producers were not formally accepted until 1987–8.
17. Any notion of constrained maximization requires that the unit's choice be backed up by an effective command over resources. In a simple Marshallian cross model both consumers and producers must be capable of allocating resources to alternatives. For producers, this means capital, and the ability to use it. Thus for state-owned enterprises a shift to commodity production in this sense has profound implications for both what they control and how they control it. If the nature of the dominant transaction changes, so must that of the production and consumption units.
18. By around 1985–6 this was running at around $10 per capita.
19. It seems to me through informal discussion that the precise circumstances through which the categories of 'output contracting' and the 'three-plan system' arose were similar in many ways.
20. It goes almost without saying that Vietnamese experience confronts exponents of the need for 'big bangs' with severe problems in sustaining their position, both over the political economy of change and their assumptions of micro-behaviour and evolution of real incomes in economies emerging from central planning. These exponents expected micro-behaviour to resemble that in heavily distorted market economies, with rather rapid supply responses attributed to prior investment of resources in a wide range of market-supporting institutions like sales and accounting sections within enterprises. But lags in many parts of the economy were in fact longer, for resources were required to establish effective and normally operating markets. The resources needed were relatively large, meaning important societal decisions had to be made about where they were to come from, and the effects on incentives of their diversion from consumption.
21. Widespread use of gold and dollars helped link Vietnam's domestic price system to world markets, guiding spontaneous resource reallocation towards patterns that were not only closer to domestic market-clearing distributions but also those consistent with Vietnam's position in the globalizing economy.

10. Executive–Legislative Relations in the Philippines: Continuity and Change

Emmanuel S. de Dios

It has often been casually observed that the processes inherent in a formal democratic system such as that in the Philippines may have a counter-developmental impact. During a famous visit to the Philippines in 1995, senior minister Lee Kuan Yew advised Filipinos to practise 'less democracy and more discipline'. In particular, the system of checks and balances that prevails between Congress and the president – and increasingly also the judiciary – is thought to lead to either policy gridlock or inconsistency and accordingly to produce inferior economic outcomes. At least until the Asian economic crisis in 1997, this wisdom appeared vindicated by the Philippines' mediocre economic performance compared to its neighbours.

Yet Philippine economic growth since 1987 has by most accounts been moderate and acceptable, although not as vigorous as that of adjacent countries. Economic reforms have been implemented with a quality of public decision-making that may be judged fairly responsive to changing global conditions. Moreover, in the recent economic crisis the Philippine economy proved more resilient and less vulnerable than those of its neighbours. These developments would seem, *ex post,* to transcend any simple dichotomy between democracy and authoritarianism.

This chapter argues that evaluations of governance institutions should proceed beyond merely analysing the relative strengths of democratic versus authoritarian structures in the abstract. They should in addition inquire into changes in civil society that affect the interests represented and the influence of these on the balance of power in public decision-making. The fruitfulness of this line of analysis is illustrated using the Philippines as an example.

THE PHILIPPINE POLITICAL SYSTEM

After gaining independence in 1946, the Philippines set up a republican system under a constitution drafted in 1935. In a pattern closely resembling that in the

United States, three separate but equal branches of government – the presidency, Congress, and the judiciary – exercised power under an arrangement of checks and balances. Congress comprised a House of Representatives, whose members were elected through local votes, and a smaller Senate whose members were elected nationally. The president and vice-president were elected by direct vote in national polls. Members of the judiciary were appointed by the executive, but held office indefinitely, while lower court judges were supervised by the Supreme Court. As in the United States, elections were contested mainly between two parties favoured by electoral rules, which were the Nacionalista and Liberals.

This system existed from the Philippines' independence in 1946 until martial law was declared in 1972 by President Ferdinand Marcos (1964–86), who originally assumed office under the previous electoral system. Notwithstanding the existence of a unicameral parliament since 1981, the entire 1972–86 period may for practical purposes be regarded as a dictatorship built on Marcos's control and use of the military. Probably the best evidence of this was the continued use of presidential decrees as means of legislation. This was despite the formal existence of a parliament which ultimately functioned as a rubber-stamp body, dominated as it was by the Marcosian party, the New Society Movement.

After the 1986 popular revolution overthrowing the Marcos regime, however, the previous three-branch system of checks and balances was re-established according to a constitution promulgated under the new president, Mrs Corazon Aquino (1986–92).[1] The 1987 Constitution, which is described by Nolledo (1997), introduced significant changes, notably one involving the term limits of officials. In particular, the terms of the president and vice-president were lengthened from four to six years, but the option for re-election was closed. This was regarded as a means of precluding a return to dictatorships like that of Marcos.

The restoration of formal democratic institutions under Aquino has been widely regarded, especially from a left perspective, as a simple continuation of the style and substance of pre-authoritarian politics and society (see, for example, Wurfel 1988). In particular, the end of the Marcos regime and the advent of constitutionalism was viewed as restoring the influence of the old economic elite or 'oligarchy' which the dictatorship had initially sought to supplant by its own coterie of cronies.

FACTIONAL POLITICS AND RENT-SEEKING

Ample consensus exists that pre-dictatorship politics and society facilitated patronage politics and extraction of rents by competing factions of a fractious elite. This pre-martial law era has been extensively analysed from the aspect of its political system, the character of the state and the economic interests of the elite. The central theme of what may be regarded as the dominant reading of

Philippine political economy is the likelihood of the state being 'captured' by vested interests, which were traditionally those of local elites with wealth based on agrarian concerns.[2] This theme continues an earlier tradition in Philippine political literature that has come to be known as the 'factional model' of Philippine politics (Lande 1965). The economic elite is seen as divided into various factions and alliances, cutting across class lines and based on the political and economic power of local elites originating in agrarian land ownership and personalistic patron–client relations. Such local interests and influences are then successively consolidated upwards and ultimately expressed in national political factions. Elections are perceived as periodic contests among factions for gaining access to state resources.

Notwithstanding his observation of politics being dominated by the elite, Lande's assessment of the prospects for the Philippine system were sanguine. In emphasizing the vertical rather than class basis of patron–client relations, he argued that this could lead in principle to enfranchisement, albeit imperfect, of the masses. In contrast to this, however, the influential radical tradition in Philippine political writing proceeded from a Marxian view which saw the state as reflecting the dominant interests in society, and as an 'executive committee' of ruling classes which monopolized politics. The natural implication of this was that the anti-developmental character of governance could not be changed without radical alteration of the social structure itself. Radical writing has accordingly tended to emphasize needs to reframe the social structure, beginning with wealth and income redistribution.

Without denying requirements for social restructuring, however, more recent work has focused on the possibility and desirability of an 'autonomous' or 'strong' state. The central problem is regarded as the state's susceptibility to manipulation by particularistic social interests, especially factions of the elite seeking opportunities to accumulate wealth through access to the official machinery. The development of a Weberian autonomous bureaucratic state, in contrast to the current 'patrimonial' one based on personal authority (Hutchcroft 1998), is seen as the main institutional solution.

The economic repercussions of an elite-dominated state founded on access to corruption rents, such as that described above, conform readily with some results in the literature. Models of competitive rent-seeking (Krueger 1984; Findlay and Wellisz 1982) fit certain aspects of the struggle for spoils among factions of the elite. Such models suggest this struggle for state rents causes a dissipation of resources otherwise available for investment. This is thought likely to be especially pronounced in a regime of economic controls, like that in the Philippines during the period of import substitution. It can be argued, moreover, that the system of political contests embodied in elections which are venues for rewarding political entrepreneurship draw undue resources and talents away from more productive activities.

Similar conclusions are suggested by the literature on corruption and bribery.[3] In a well-known article, Shleifer and Vishny (1993) argue that the likely level of corruption increases when power is diffuse compared with when it is centralized. Where agencies provide complementary services – such as when their concurrence is required to secure a licence or a franchise – their attempt to maximize revenues independently results in higher bribes and lower levels of service than if bribery were centralized. The reason is that independent monopolists fail to take account of what their counterparts do.

As Bardhan (1997) points out, moreover, the situation is worsened by 'free entry', when other agents are not prevented from setting up additional regulations beyond those originally anticipated. Thus when an investor has paid off certain key people, others suddenly emerge who also need to be rewarded. In the Philippines, congressional investigations or legal suits are typical means for other institutions to involve themselves in executive decisions, leaving room for additional bribes. The total bribes to be paid cannot be easily foreseen, leading to fundamental investment uncertainty. Ultimately, higher political bribes per unit discourage investment, providing another channel for institutions to affect economic growth. It is insufficiently noted that such potential economic losses are distinct from those occasioned by rent-seeking itself, although they may occur concurrently with it.

In the growth industry that sought to explain the economic success of authoritarian states in enabling the Asian miracle, the advantages of democratic regimes were typically neglected. To be sure, many analyses were made before the Asian economic crisis, when it was thought necessary to explain the connection between authoritarianism and superior economic growth. Moreover, in what came to be known as the 'corruption puzzle' (World Bank 1997), it was thought deserving of explanation that economies where corrupt authoritarian regimes existed (for example, Indonesia, or China) still managed to post large gains in economic growth. As suggested, the answer appeared to lie first in the narrower scope for competitive rent-seeking under authoritarian regimes, and second in the predictability and centralization of such corruption where it was present.

These analytical models accordingly seemed to denote that highly centralized authoritarian regimes may deliver greater efficiency than democratic regimes. The prediction arising from this is that the Philippine transition from dictatorship to democracy was bound to raise levels of bribery and rent-seeking, and by extension to affect static allocation and economic growth. Indeed, Shleifer and Vishny (1993) explicitly concluded that corruption – and implicitly the costs associated with it – may increase with the return of liberal democratic institutions.

BEYOND THE 'DEMOCRACY–AUTHORITARIANISM' DICHOTOMY

The dichotomy between democracy and authoritarianism found in the literature has failed to distinguish sufficiently between formal political institutions and the social structure underlying them. To explain the present Philippine political economy adequately, one must distinguish between alterations in the form of the *political system* and more fundamental *societal changes* which influence the system's content. Hence, while it is certainly true that the post-Marcos regime restored formal democratic institutions, it would be a mistake to conclude that the economic consequences and prospects of post-martial law democracy would simply be the same as those under the system introduced by the 1935 Constitution. The Philippine system does not fit in static categories, since it is caught up in a process of evolution where the main factors have been institutional learning from experience under the Marcos regime and a changing underlying social reality or 'civil society' in the sense used by Hegel as well as Marx ([1843] 1975).[4]

The principal relationship to analyse between the legislative and executive branches in the Philippines is that between the fragmented goals and activities of traditional elites represented in the legislature, especially the House of Representatives, and the more global viewpoint embodied in the executive and the bureaucracy. Doronila (1992) refers to these respectively as the 'localist' and 'centralist' tendencies. It is not denied that rents can be and are generated on both sides, and could even represent the major incentive for political activity. Indeed, as Persson et al. (1997) point out, politics inevitably generates rents owing to the incomplete contracts and informational asymmetry that exist between representatives and the represented.

But while rents doubtless represent just as powerful a motive for the presidency as for the legislature, it is posited that the former is inherently more conscious of *whole-system* imperatives as well as global opportunities for securing such returns. Hence, the executive would control rents from large infrastructure projects, privatization of national assets and so on, but, at the same time, it would be more keenly aware of overall requirements for internal and external balance, including the need for revenue collection, rational allocations of spending, and for addressing the consequences of large fiscal and external deficits and pressures from multilateral agencies. System requirements accordingly place greater constraints on the executive than on the legislature. In contrast, local politicians with their interest in local rents seek to maximize the proportion of local relative to national projects as well as to tilt the bias of national projects in favour of their localities. Not all this is cynical, for local lobbying does, after all, help correct some of the bias in the distribution of public goods. In a sense, therefore, whole-system imperatives were only just fulfilled to facilitate the achievement of the localist objectives of the traditional elite.

The elite factionalism and rent-seeking, regarded as outstanding features of Philippine politics, refer primarily to the dominant localist influence embodied by Congress, as well as the subordination of the executive's functions to these influences. The next three sections describe how this relation has changed in the periods before, during and after the dictatorship.

CHANGES IN EXECUTIVE–LEGISLATIVE RELATIONS

With the United States system as benchmark, and notwithstanding obvious similarities, the Philippine executive has always been historically powerful. This was no accident but rather a consequence of design, and clearly featured relations in the pre-dictatorship period now under consideration. The executive branch descended historically from the office of the colonial governor-general, the direct representative of an occupying power (Wurfel 1988). Relative to this authority, the role of the Commonwealth legislatures – the Philippine Assembly and subsequently the bicameral Congress – through which the local elite was gradually allowed to participate in politics, should be seen as qualified concessions to what was essentially executive domination. The presence of a foreign occupying power set obvious limits on the rent-seeking and rent-generating activities of the traditional elite, simply because the latter were not entirely in control of the state.

From this viewpoint, formal independence after 1946 resulted in a relative weakening of the executive, which now came from the same constituency as the legislature. Analytically, therefore, the entire system would have been less constrained in generating larger rents in the manner that Shleifer and Vishny (1993) have described. This constitutes a simple explanation for the traditionally observed rise in corruption coinciding with the end of World War II.[5]

The domination of the post-independence process by rent-seeking activities of localist elites was bound to lead to unsustainable macroeconomic and development trajectories, however. In particular, it was conducive to the prolonged pursuit of a protectionist policy for both agriculture and industry, and a macroeconomic bias for deficit-spending. Both are associated with enlargement of the government's capacity to dispense privileges and allocate resources discriminatorily, leading to the existence of disposable rents. The aggregate effect of the domination, however, was to undermine the basis for long-term growth, a fact evident in successive balance-of-payments crises which began in 1949 and were repeated in 1957, 1969, 1980–83 and 1990.

The exact relationship between legislature and executive in the pre-dictatorship period is ambiguous. To be sure, the executive was politically dominant in setting the legislative agenda and controlling resource allocation. But, as Wurfel (1988, p. 85) notes, 'presidential domination of the legislative process would never again be as complete as it was under Quezon' (Manuel Quezon, 1935–44), suggesting a reduction of domination relative to the Commonwealth period.[6] The Philippine Congress, before the beginning of authoritarian rule in 1972, was considered 'one of the most influential legislatures in the Third World' (Wurfel 1988, p. 81). Its power derived primarily from the ability of its members to strike political bargains with the president, in whose re-election their support at local level was indispensable. The Senate, on the other hand, was elected nationally, and consisted of potential presidential rivals or valued national political allies.

An implicit task of the executive in this scheme was to secure the larger viability of the system with respect to internal and external challenges, such as ensuring the observance of constraints imposed by external and internal balance and managing social protest. This amounted to limiting negative externalities arising from the rent-seeking of elite factions. In this sense, the executive, for all its power, merely played a facilitating role, supporting the activities of a traditional elite.

Dictatorship and Overweening Executive Power

The Marcos dictatorship, beginning in 1972, represented a fundamental break in pattern. In political terms, the dictatorship's principal legacy was reasserting the powers of the executive, both in form and in practice. The executive's dominance over the legislature is seen most vividly in the disbandment of Congress between 1972 and 1981, during which Marcos ruled by decree alone. Indeed, the president's decree-making powers were retained through the entire period, notwithstanding the creation of a rubber-stamp parliament in 1981.

This shift in political institutions matches a corresponding one in civil society. It is worth recalling that Marcos justified his 'revolution from the centre', using a rhetoric that hit out against the 'oligarchy' comprising the traditional landed elite, including such families as the Lopezes (McCoy 1994). In significant ways, the situation reversed that existing prior to the dictatorship, in which the role of the traditional, locally-based agrarian elite was more open and direct, with representatives of the aristocracy taking a prominent role. The powers of this elite were weakened relative to those of Marcos himself and his selected 'crony capitalists', many of whom did not originate from that stratum. In the pre-martial law period the local elites, typified by the powerful sugar interests, exercised a dominant influence over the executive. Consistent with obvious oligarchic dominance at the time, the circumstances approximated that frank 'identity' between political and civil society observed by the early Marx in the case of the feudal 'Estates-General' and before the triumph of capitalism.[7]

Civil-society Changes since 1987

The restoration of democratic institutions since 1987 has been generally regarded as a simple return to institutions existing before the dictatorship. The picture is not as unambiguous as it first seems, however. Both formal changes in governance institutions and deeper shifts in civil society have acted to dilute the influence of traditional localist elites relative to that prevalent during the 1935 regime.

Significant economic and demographic changes have occurred, and have tended to undermine patron–client relations that earlier formed the foundation of traditional politics. The appearance of new sources of wealth outside traditional agriculture (the classic locus of the patron–client relationship) created opportunities for new, more heterogeneous forces to gain access to the political process. These forces included members of the professions, such as lawyers, former military personnel and people from the media. The effect of globalization, both as a preferred policy direction and ineluctable trend, also cannot be denied, since the stronger links of localities to larger markets changed the valuation of assets and the nature of wealth-accumulating activities.

Urbanization and agrarian reform – notwithstanding the fitful and uneven implementation of the latter – have also contributed greatly to the shift in civil society. Between 1970 and 1990, the proportion of population living in urban areas increased from 32 per cent to 49 per cent. Moreover, while industrial employment has still not become predominant, significant economic differentiation has occurred with services (including wholesale and retail trade, real estate, finance, government and other community services) now accounting for the bulk of both domestic output and employment, while agriculture has declined drastically in significance from 29 to 21 per cent of gross domestic product over the two decades (National Statistical Coordination Board 1973–98; and National Statistics Office 1971–91).[8]

In addition, the middle class has grown in size, especially as a result of incomes from overseas employment. Even more important, the spread of a free mass media and mass education has given middle-class values an influence disproportionate to that stratum's small numbers and actual economic power.[9] All these trends have made it more costly and difficult but admittedly not impossible to build political bases on the type of particularist patronage that traditional politicians long cultivated.

Finally, it is important to note that the imposition of dictatorship itself spawned a high degree of mass resistance and organization, both armed and unarmed, that permeated all social strata. This culminated in the 1986 uprising, with the confrontation between people and troops in the main Manila thoroughfare, Epifanio de los Santos Avenue or 'EDSA'. This is a legacy that has been preserved, if recast. A crucial post-Marcos element not present in the

1935 system is the great number of cause-oriented groups and non-government organizations; these act both as development cooperators and the core of extra-parliamentary opposition. Normally heterogeneous and diffuse, this 'people's power' element is nonetheless occasionally capable of being mobilized to respond to critical debates on national issues. Notable examples of this included the huge controversies over the proposal in 1997 to amend the 1987 Constitution and extend term limits for elected officials, and over the decision in 1998 to bury Marcos in the Philippines.

FORMAL INSTITUTIONAL CHANGES

It becomes possible in the social context just described to look beyond the purely legal and subjective in assessing the significance of institutional changes in the political system since 1987. A primary concern of the 1987 Constitution was certainly to weaken presidential power and discretion, so as to prevent the re-emergence of one-person rule. This was done through such new provisions as the prohibition on presidential re-election, additional safeguards against declaring martial law and the power of judicial review in matters involving the broadly interpretable 'grave abuse of authority'. On the other hand, many traditional prerogatives of the presidency were retained or even expanded, such as discretion over budgetary disbursements, disposal over large lump-sum funds, authority to draw up implementing rules and regulations for legislation and the 'line-item' veto further discussed below.

Even measures meant to weaken executive power at times have had the ironic effect of *strengthening* it. Thus the prohibition on the president's re-election (Art. VII, Sect. 4 of the 1987 Constitution), together with additional safeguards against the declaration of martial law, were meant to preclude attempts at term extension. It is to be recalled, however, that an important source of Congress's influence *vis-à-vis* the president was the need for local support for re-election, and reducing the presidency to a single term actually undercut congressional bargaining power. Moreover, with the president's six-year term spanning the shorter three-year terms of representatives and senators, it was the members of Congress seeking re-election that tended to become beholden to the executive for favours and endorsement. In this respect, the direct election of the president – already provided for in the 1935 Constitution – assumed an added significance. The chief executive now derived his mandate not from parliament but from the electorate at large,[10] with the only provision for recall being a difficult impeachment process.

A visible expression of the shift that has occurred is the change from the traditional two-party to a multi-party system. The 1987 Constitution (Art. IX (c), Sect. 6) provides for 'a free and open party system', which was subsequently implemented through relaxing the requirements for accrediting new parties and granting them representation in the relevant electoral bodies. The 1935 electoral rules, by contrast, were biased in favour of the two major political parties. Notwithstanding obvious deviations from developed-country benchmarks,[11] the previous two-party system represented a predictable process of turnover for elite factions, with factions in the opposition party having an even chance of gaining power in the next elections.[12] While the phenomenon of 'turncoatism' in favour of the party in power existed even then,[13] a minimal level of allegiance to the two major parties remained, with one always maintaining the role of a significant opposition and being driven by the prospect of contesting the next elections.[14] This state of affairs resulted in a degree of independence of Congress from the executive.

The current multiplicity of political parties tends, however, to dilute the potency of the legislature as an independent body. The present large number of parties raises the transactions costs of forming stable coalitions, and provides an opportunity for the executive to exert external influence through the selective distribution of political largesse, thereby tilting the process of coalition formation in its favour. The regimes of all three post-dictatorship presidents have notably been accompanied by great instability of party formations after the elections, wholesale turncoatism and the formation of broad coalitions to support the incumbent executive. This is especially true for the lower house, where local political interests dominate.[15] Significantly, therefore, practices commenced under the dictatorship have continued.

The effects of both societal and formal political changes have begun to have palpable influences in elections as well. Elections under the 1987 Constitution have witnessed many 'new' faces and groups not previously connected with politics running for electoral office. An early study of the results of 1987 and 1988 elections by Gutierrez et al. (1992) concluded pessimistically that little had changed, and that clan-based traditional politics continued its sway. This conclusion was based on the large number of representatives of established political clans that ultimately won the elections. However, a significant result from the same study but not emphasized was the fact that 21 to 56 per cent of the total vote in all regions had gone to newcomers, although this was often not sufficient for such persons to win.[16]

Nor has this phenomenon been confined to local levels. The past two presidential elections saw candidates not closely associated with localist politics posting strong showings against administration-backed candidates. Fidel Ramos (1992–8) won narrowly in 1992 over Miriam Santiago, a former professor, judge and bureaucrat. Joseph Estrada won in 1998 over the administration-backed Jose de Venecia, the epitome of traditional politics and candidate of choice for a large number of traditional political clans. Most of these events are fairly recent and merit closer analysis. They are nonetheless consistent with the hypothesis of a turning point in Philippine politics.

The foregoing discussions suggest that both societal and formal political changes have laid the ground for a weakening of the legislature and the particularist politics it represents, relative to the central function of the presidency. The next section examines an important means by which the influence of the presidency is exercised.

PORK-BARREL POLITICS AND PARTICULARISM[17]

The true relationship between the presidency and Congress is nowhere better reflected than in the budget process. The 1987 Constitution provides that, in the third week of July each year, the president should present the proposed budget incorporating the government's priorities and a list of 'urgent bills'. Both houses of Congress then deliberate on and finally approve the budget. Following the principle of checks and balances, moreover, the president may veto the budget although this veto may in turn be overturned by a two-thirds' majority of Congress.

Press coverage and investigative analyses (Coronel 1998) have focused public attention on the distortive effects of congressional power and the huge potential these create for corruption. The implied assessment is that the scope for congressional intervention is excessive. The most prominent negative example in recent times has been the issue of the 'pork barrel', and this is now explored.

Philippine practice is novel in giving individual members of Congress unusual leeway in identifying projects to be implemented through both the so-called Countrywide Development Fund and system of Congressional Initiative Allocations (commonly termed 'congressional insertions'). The Countrywide Fund was set up in the budget of 1994 to formalize a previous system allowing members of the legislatures and the vice-president to identify favoured projects up to certain ceilings: these are 12 million pesos ($ 284 000) per representative, 18 million pesos ($ 427 000) per senator, and 20 million pesos ($ 474 000) for the vice-president. In what is essentially a lump-sum appropriation, the nature and location of projects for which these amounts are used are unspecified and left to be decided by each legislator, thus effectively short-circuiting normal selection and evaluation.

A recent study of the Countrywide Fund concludes that the bulk of allocated amounts were devoted to local projects, with a bias towards infrastructure and equipment purchases. Social development projects, by contrast, were given low priority. Public opposition to the Fund system, however, revolves around the opportunities for graft it is thought to afford. The wide discretion given to legislators in specifying projects to be financed from 'their' Fund means requirements may be tailor-made to favour chosen contractors, making it much easier to obtain kick-backs. The capital bias in the choice of Countrywide Fund projects is consistent with the conjecture that they afford ample opportunities for graft.[18]

Compared with the Countrywide Fund, the Congressional Initiative Allocations or congressional insertions are more involved, affect a greater portion of the budget and have a less uniform distribution among members of Congress. These insertions essentially involve augmenting the president's budget to support new initiatives or projects selected by individual congressmen. That this can happen might seem strange in the light of a constitutional provision that Congress 'may not increase the appropriations recommended by the president for the operation of the Government as specified in the budget (Art. VI, Sect. 25(1)). Curiously without challenge from the executive, however, Congress has chosen to interpret this provision as a stricture merely on increasing the *total* amount of the budget, and not as prohibiting reallocations across individual appropriations. Congress therefore feels that as long as it can reduce appropriations for some items, it is justified in increasing those for others, or in introducing completely new items not included in the president's budget.

The key item for reduction and an indispensable part of the farce played by Congress over many years has been the ritual slashing of debt-service appropriations, in the guise of 'progressive' opposition to an onerous debt burden.[19] Operating under the transparent fiction that amounts struck off have been 'saved', Congress then feels free to reprogramme them for more favoured purposes or introduce new items. Some appropriations may accordingly be cut drastically during congressional deliberations, with the proceeds reallocated to items which implementing agencies themselves have not requested (Gutierrez 1998). Agencies such as education and public works that benefit from such insertions become beholden to certain legislators for augmenting their funds, and the lump sums involved are tagged as being 'owned' by or allocated to certain legislators.

As an illustration, in 1997 the president submitted a budget totalling some 441 billion pesos ($ 15.8 billion at the concurrent exchange rate), but Congress then struck off 16 billion pesos ($ 573 million) from the debt-service appropriations, and used this amount to expand existing appropriations or to insert new ones. Since the president was constrained to restore the full amount of debt appropriations in any event, the total approved budget became 457 billion pesos ($16.4 billion), which was 3.6 per cent larger than the total originally submitted.

Some important differences may be highlighted between the Countrywide Development Fund and congressional insertions. First, the Fund allocations are uniform across members of Congress, while the insertions are unevenly distributed. Thus a press exposé in 1996 revealed that the larger part of the insertions fell to members of the House Committee on Appropriations, and that these cut across party lines (ibid., p. 71). Twelve members of the House

Committee on Appropriations were responsible for some 5.7 billion pesos' ($ 204 million) worth of insertions in the budget, or some 6 per cent of capital outlays for that year. Information regarding funds available for insertions is a source of patronage within Congress itself.

Second, the Fund and insertions differ in their overall impact on the budget and the macroeconomy. In principle, the availability of predetermined amounts from the Fund leaves the bulk of the president's budget unchanged. Indeed, according to a earlier personal interview with B. Diokno who is now the government Budget Secretary, the rationale for systematizing the Countrywide Fund under the Aquino regime was to minimize the distortion of the president's budget. By contrast, congressional insertion amounts are less transparent and more distortive, being able to reorder priorities drastically through the manipulation that takes place. In this sense, insertions enhance the legislature's prerogatives more than the Fund.

Third, insertions represent a larger bias for fiscal expansion. As already described, the practice of slashing debt service to maintain a total budget constraint and reallocating 'saved' amounts is illusory, since the president must either ultimately restore the debt service allocation or choose to exercise a veto. This leads to a total appropriation that is larger by the original cut in the debt service. The expansionary bias of insertions is also easily seen when the magnitudes of the two are compared: the fixed-amount Countrywide Fund accounted for no more than 0.5 per cent of the approved 1997 budget, while the insertions took up 3.5 per cent.

A key element of both the Countrywide Fund and Congressional Initiative Allocations is the discretion by individual legislators over selection of projects (and often contractors as well). This allows legislators to satisfy their local constituents' need for visible contributions, as well as providing them with obvious vehicles for patronage, if not graft. In a larger framework, therefore, the Fund and insertions are clear examples of mechanisms to implement the politics of particularism.

Executive Leverage

It would be a mistake to conclude as others have done, however, that the practice of pork-barrel politics is sufficient to prove excessive legislative prerogatives relative to the executive branch. That assessment is only possible if several key aspects of current practice are ignored.

Pork-barrel politics implicates the executive branch either through design, acquiescence or active collusion. The Countrywide Fund arose as a mechanism designed by the executive branch to limit congressional interference with executive priorities. With the congressional insertions it is clear that passive acceptance or collusion is needed between officials of the executing agency and the legislator. Indeed, the agency could be ordered by the administration to refuse to host pork-barrel projects.

In the extreme, the Philippine presidency, unlike its United States counterpart, has the right to a 'line-item', which carries 'the power to veto any particular item or items in an appropriation, revenue, or tariff bill, but the veto shall not affect the item or item to which he does not object.'(Art. VI, Sect. 27(1)). Legal commentators including Nolledo (1997) point out that the present constitution – like Marcos's 1973 Constitution but unlike that of 1935 – removes Congress's power to override the president's *partial veto* although there is a procedure for overriding the veto of a particular bill. Beyond a line-item veto, the president may also veto the entire appropriations Act. The consequences of doing so would not be as catastrophic as it might be in some countries, since the constitution provides that in such a case the previous year's budget is automatically enacted. Game theory suggests that this safeguard against severe dislocation serves to make the veto threat even more credible.

The president's office also disposes of large discretionary funds, which congressmen derisively call the president's 'pork barrel'. These include the calamity fund, contingency fund, social fund, intelligence fund and other lump-sum appropriations.[20] The president is also allowed to augment appropriations in some items from savings in others.[21] In other instances, one-off special lump-sum appropriations may also be requested from Congress. The effect of all these provisions is to allow the executive substantial leeway in undoing the effects of congressional intervention in budget priorities by restoring appropriations cut by Congress.

Probably the most important of the president's prerogatives relating to the budget, however, is the power to disburse funds. The president may impose special provisions in disbursement of funds. This prerogative includes, among others, a requirement to maintain budgetary reserves, which is typically applied to agencies across the board, but, following high-level clearance, may then be relaxed on a case-by-case basis allowing much discretion. This expedient of controlling financial releases was especially utilized when the country needed to conform with International Monetary Fund conditionality. In particular, cash disbursement control by the Department of Budget and Management also applies to legislators' pork-barrel funds, enhancing the executive's powers over them.

Owing to such discretion, budgets actually disbursed or implemented differ significantly from 'obligated' budgets, which are official budgets passed by Congress and signed by the president. Thus in 1987–8 about 20 per cent of obligated appropriations were *not* disbursed, while the gaps in 1990–91 and 1994 were 16 per cent and 13 per cent respectively. It is notable that these gaps only became pronounced *after* the Marcos period, when explicit executive influence over the legislature was no longer possible.

In short, tighter administrative control over departments, the line-item veto and the power to withhold funds are among various presidential expedients that partially or fully offset legislative prerogatives. Hence while Congress may increase total appropriations and change the priorities proposed by the executive, this power may be largely diluted, if desired. Ample recourse is available to the executive to offset if not terminate the practice of pork-barrel politics.[22]

The arguments and evidence therefore suggest that pork-barrel politics serves the purposes of the executive and is tolerated, if not actively encouraged, for this reason. Far from representing excess legislative prerogatives, the pork barrel signifies congressional weakness and a susceptibility to manipulation by the executive. The consequent regime of overbudgeting-cum-rationing permits the executive to exercise selectivity in the release of funds, thus reasserting the importance of presidential patronage to individual members of Congress. By the same token, of course, it opens the door more widely to possible abuses of power by the executive. An assessment of the extent of current corruption in the Philippines would be anecdotal at best, and is beyond the scope of this paper. It would be a testable proposition of the present hypothesis, nonetheless, that the shift of power in favour of the executive means opportunities for graft also become biased in its favour.

There is no denying, however, that the expedient of presidential patronage can and has occasionally served a development role. Especially during the Ramos administration, congressional votes on crucial national issues were often mobilized by the executive through implicit appeals to forthcoming pork-barrel releases. In the typical pattern, the House Speaker, also the leader of the amorphous pro-administration coalition, presides at a closed-door meeting to discuss a vote in frank conjunction with forthcoming political largesse. Prominent examples of successful executive persuasion through this means include the passage of a controversial law expanding the commodity coverage of the value-added tax and of a law deregulating the oil industry.

Ironically, therefore, the mechanism for patronage could be reoriented to push difficult reforms over particularist objections, and at times even mass protests. From a larger view, the emergent relationship between Congress and the executive (of which pork-barrel politics is symptomatic) has allowed the political system to devise a means of cobbling together a consensus unthinkable in the pre-martial law period.

CONCLUSION

A basic hypothesis advanced here is that the Philippine political system is undergoing change, initial appearances notwithstanding. Over a long, tortuous period, the system has swung from legislative licence, to unabashed authoritarianism, to the present regime of executive first-mover advantages. These changes could not have occurred without more profound shifts in the economy and civil society, which have modified the earlier patron–client base of traditional politics. Particularist rent-seeking and the motives of economic rewards from political office have not ceased, but executive dominance of the patronage game limits negative externalities from such trends, and provides a serviceable if crude mechanism to elicit strategic and informed decision-making. This development in governance must be considered part of the explanation for the acceptable economic performance of the Philippines since the dictatorship period, and for its economic resilience even during the Asian economic crisis.

The changes have been a mixed blessing, however. The strong presidency reduces the importance of Congress, allowing the latter to abdicate responsibility for a large part of decision-making. What looms in fact is a trivialization of the legislature. With congressional voting records being unimportant for re-election,[23] the incentive is all the greater for Congress to concentrate on activities leading to local public goods provision, rent-seeking or both, with the national agenda initiated entirely by the executive. The extent of Congress's abdication of its functions is seen in the ill-considered, contradictory or vague character of a number of recent laws. Repair of this critical defect is, however, waved off to the executive which it is assumed will always 'fix' the situation through the specific 'implementing rules and regulations'.

The obvious danger under these circumstances lies in the possibility of executive manipulation of Congress, where this was illustrated in the acrimonious debate in late 1997 over attempts to change the constitution. At that time, circles close to President Ramos initiated moves to circumvent the constitutional limit on the president's term by calling for a charter amendment. Congressional cooperation was crucial in that enterprise, with Congress needing to form itself into a constituent assembly and propose amendments. Congress's preferences on this matter were only whetted by the prospect that its members too could extend their terms beyond constitutional limits.

There was no reason in the background described why such confluent interests could fail to assert themselves, and only a massive show of force from 'people's power' and media criticism exposed the plan and made it so politically untenable that it had to be abandoned.[24] These and other episodes indirectly show the critical significance of other civil-society institutions, such as the press and non-government organizations, the church, the courts and even outlawed rebel groups, in helping to check abuses by authority.

It thus appears that, while a purely abstract description of current trends would suggest the start of a return to the authoritarianism of the dictatorship period, this is prevented from happening by the very development and influence of civil society itself. This aspect relates to the distinction made earlier in this chapter between the formal political structure and the more fundamental factor of the society underlying it. Aside from the economic–demographic changes already described, the state violence and absolutism under the Marcos regime elicited a powerful reaction from societal forces which sought legitimate outlets but, finding none, expressed themselves in extra-parliamentary and at times extra-legal forms. Once unleashed, however, these forces are difficult to reverse.[25]

The politically vocal and active churches, the mushrooming of non-government and peoples' organizations and the rise of independent mass media now constitute an amorphous extra-parliamentary force that continues to exist notwithstanding the disappearance of the original catalyst of the dictatorship. This force stands distinct from and alongside the restored political institutions of formal democracy. The current system having a different starting point is thus not simply fated to repeat the path of pre-Marcosian democracy in degenerating into dictatorship.

The political and social system of the Philippines, in short, has evolved to a situation in which formal institutions are dominated by the presidency, but where a check is provided – albeit only imperfectly and occasionally – by the threat of civil protest and public exposure. Yet it remains to be seen whether this new force will be absorbed into the formal political system, gradually dissipated or maintained.

NOTES

1. From February 1986 until elections were held under the new constitution for legislative and local government positions in May 1987, Mrs Aquino ruled using *de facto* authority under a revolutionary government.
2. This is not to preclude changes in the economic nature of these elite interests. Hence, writers such as Rivera (1995) document the shift of wealth from landowning classes towards import substitution, which in turn created a powerful lobby for protectionism.
3. Bardhan (1997) provides a recent survey.
4. For Hegel and Marx, civil society was the sphere of economic life in general. In particular, it was the sphere of conflict where the individual's relations with others were governed by selfish needs and individual interests (*bellum omnium contra omnes*). In contrast, political life in the state evoked unity and common interest. Marx made it clear in Hegel's *Philosophy of Right* that it was bourgeois society in general he was referring to. But the loose sense in which 'civil society' is used nowadays in the Philippines seems to identify it only with the non-government sector.
5. It is also true that received wisdom has attributed the worsening corruption problem to cultural causes, i.e. the decline in moral values during the war due to the permissibility of cheating and deceiving a government run by an enemy.
6. The Commonwealth was a period of wide-ranging self-rule under the American occupation, which was meant to prepare the country for full independence. It lasted from 1935 until the Japanese invasion in 1942. Full independence was gained in 1946.
7. 'The spirit of the Middle Ages may be summed up in this way: the classes of civil society were identical with the Estates in the political sense, because civil society was political society...' (Marx [1843] 1975, p. 137)
8. The rapid expansion of the services sector relative to industry has raised questions by some economists regarding the quality and sustainability of growth.
9. The recent electoral successes of media and show business personalities with little or no previous connection to politics or politicians from traditional political backgrounds is a significant indication of this shift.

10. Individual votes matter directly in the Philippine system, as distinguished from the United States electoral college, where the winner takes all at each state level.
11. For example, political 'turncoatism' to join the party in power was common even then.
12. As an indication of this, no president before Marcos had ever been re-elected under the 1935 Constitution.
13. The 1987 Constitution removed a prohibition on turncoatism that was originally part of the changes contemplated in the 1973 Constitution.
14. An economic analysis of the dynamics between the party in power and that in opposition is beyond the scope of this paper. Suffice it to say, however, that future electoral prospects confer some benefits on a party in opposition, justifying its refusal to participate in the short-term division of spoils available from collaborating with the party in power.
15. These were the Laban ng Demokratikong Pilipino, the Lakas–NUCD and, most recently, the Laban ng Masang Pilipino under the Aquino, Ramos and Estrada presidencies.
16. Unfortunately, the study failed to inquire why the total vote share was not translated into electoral victory. The large number of non-traditional candidates is one possible reason for this.
17. 'Pork barrel' is a Philippine and North American colloquial term, defined in Webster's dictionary as 'government appropriations for political patronage'. 'Particularism' is another word in Philippine–North American usage, connoting 'the policy of allowing each member or state in a federation to govern independently without regard to the interests of the whole'.
18. The last budget secretary under President Ramos, Salvador Enriquez, is quoted as estimating that as much as 40 per cent of the Countrywide Development Fund goes to graft.
19. This operation may also be done subtly by changing the underlying exchange rate or tax revenue assumptions in the financial programming exercise.
20. In 1994, for example, the Office of the President alone disposed of over 1.3 per cent of total appropriations.
21. Art. VI, Sect. 25(5). The same paragraph also allows the House Speaker, Senate President, and Chief Justice to use savings according to their discretion, but given the much larger amounts appropriated for the president's office, it is clear whose prerogatives are most enhanced.
22. Indeed, imbued with confidence in its own power, the newly-elected Estrada administration is pushing for abolition of the existing form of the pork-barrel system.
23. This is because the agenda of the Congress is largely determined by the president for each session, being removed from the immediate needs of local constituents except for minor bills of local application. The pork barrel, on the other hand, delivers more tangible or visible benefits which local constituents have come to expect.
24. The same threat of massive demonstrations forestalled a controversial decision to have Marcos interred in a heroes' cemetery.
25. As an illustration of this same principle, the military politicized under Marcos also became an 'overdeveloped' force, whose refusal to return to the barracks posed a continual threat to the Aquino government, culminating in attempted *coups d'état* in 1987 and 1989.

11. Global Economic Institutions from the Southeast Asian Perspective

David Vines

At the beginning of 1997, a paper on 'global economic institutions' as seen from the Southeast Asian perspective would have begun by discussing the East Asian miracle. It would have argued that this miracle was achieved with little explicit help from global economic institutions.

First, the growth of the East Asian region was based fundamentally on industrialization for the *world* market. Because of their global orientation, East Asian economies understood that their growth was fundamentally dependent on the strength and continuity of an open global trading system. However, there was a shared concern about the slow progress of multilateral trade negotiations in the Uruguay Round of the General Agreement on Tariffs and Trade (GATT), which was later to become the World Trade Organization (WTO). This led to a turning away from a focus on global trade liberalization and the establishment, through 'open regionalism', of a *regional* institution for trade liberalization.

Second, it was argued that East Asian growth was underpinned by stable macroeconomic policies – high savings rates to make way for high levels of investment and fixed exchange rates as a nominal anchor to keep price inflation low. These policies were conducted nationally, without great reliance on the International Monetary Fund (IMF, in this chapter hereafter referred to as 'the Fund'), other than through an annual consultation process.

Third, it was increasingly argued that high-growth, 'middle income' developing countries no longer need or want the World Bank (hereafter referred to as 'the Bank'), because they disliked the conditions attached to its loans and because they have little difficulty in borrowing from other sources.

How things have changed! The Asian crisis of 1997 has led to the largest rescue operation in the history of the International Monetary Fund. This prompted a sustained questioning of the role of that institution and of the World Bank, and of relations between them. It has also had significant implications for the durability of the regional process of open regionalism and for the relations between that process and the global trade regime administered by the WTO.

This chapter has been written in the light of the changes of 1997–8. It lays out the traditional conception of the roles of the Fund, the Bank and the WTO, and asks how the recent crises have changed our views of what these institutions should do.

THE INTERNATIONAL MONETARY FUND AND THE ASIAN FINANCIAL CRISIS

The Fund began as a multilateral institution which administered the global international monetary system. It presided over a specified system of rules about fixed exchange rates, explicitly constraining the macroeconomic policies of member governments.

The Fund now has a very different role. It still operates limited surveillance over global macroeconomic conditions, primarily through its *World Economic Outlook*, but its operations are essentially confined to providing macroeconomic assistance for developing countries with underdeveloped policy-making capability. First, it offers detailed advice on macroeconomic policy. Second, it provides lending to countries with adjustment difficulties, subject to conditionality. Third, in the 1980s and 1990s it has been drawn into tne management of debt crises.[1]

The Fund's Traditional Role: Research Analysis and Policy Advice

Although there has been much questioning of the Fund's analysis of the Asian crisis, there remains no question that the Fund is the world's premier institution for research about and analysis of macroeconomic policy, and for the provision of advice on macroeconomic adjustment policies (Fischer 1995). In its consultations, the Fund brings to bear macroeconomic analysis and forecasting to determine the adequacy of national macroeconomic policies, traditionally concentrating on the core macroeconomic areas of fiscal and monetary policy.

There are three reasons why an institution such as the Fund is important for this process. First, there are very significant economies of scale and scope in the provision of such analysis. This analysis is also an international public good (because the theory of macroeconomic policy is partly comparative). Second, many national governments of poorer countries cannot afford or cannot get access to the necessary resources themselves. Thus the advice becomes a form of 'technical assistance'. Third, Fund advice, to be useful, must frankly stress both weaknesses and required remedies, and Fund assistance consists in working with a country to help it solve its problems, including the building of policy credibility. This involves not merely one-off advice, but continuing policy assistance. It is this twin feature – the need for frank diagnosis by the Fund followed by continuing work together to solve the problems identified – which makes the advice and assistance relationship between the Fund and its client countries a peculiar one.

In good times, research and analysis, plus recommendations on policy, will be all that a client country needs from the Fund. When this works well, current problems are clearly identified and a commitment is established by the client government to solve them, with assistance from the Fund.

Second Traditional Role: Adjustment Lending

In bad times, when a country gets into macroeconomic adjustment difficulties, the relationship with the Fund goes beyond that of analysis, advice and assistance. Instead there may be recourse to a Fund adjustment package with associated conditionality requirements. In these circumstances, Fund staff can then effectively – subject to negotiation – dictate the policies appropriate for the borrowing country to follow. Again it has to be asked: what is it that the Fund contributes as an institution in such adjustment-difficulty circumstances?

The classic case of macroeconomic imbalance is caused either by excess demand which has been reflected in inflated goods and asset prices and in a deficit on the current account of the balance of payments, or by reduced export demand. What is needed in either of these cases is a mixture of a reduction in national spending (by a combination of fiscal and monetary contraction) and a currency depreciation to get the country's international competitiveness back into line. The actual mix of policies needed depends on whether the sources of the imbalance were primarily internal or primarily external. A country's government may not have the capacity, either technically or politically, to deal with the problem, and may not take this necessary corrective action until too late, when that country is already faced with financial pressures.

The Thai crisis of 1997 was one among the Asian crises in which elements of this 'classic' pattern were strongly present (Chote 1998). There had been a long period of very large current account deficits which became more serious in 1996 in the face of a downturn in export revenues. At the same time, although price inflation was under control, buoyant demand over a number of years had led to rising wage costs in the export sector. The Thai authorities were reluctant to abandon their pegged exchange rate, even though the need for this became increasingly obvious in 1996, and they were urged to do so by the Fund. Once they had done so, with the onset of the crisis in the middle of 1997, there was great uncertainty about the ability of the authorities to take the necessary corrective action. They were, in fact, reluctant either to tighten fiscally by a sufficient amount, to suspend bankrupt finance companies, or to pursue consistently a sufficiently tight interest-rate policy. All of these actions were needed to ensure that the devaluation was effective and did not merely lead to inflation.

In such circumstances, a 'liquidity support' is needed, with an explicit conditionality attached: that money will not be forthcoming unless the country agrees to the Fund's diagnosis and prescribed solution. Such conditionality – besides tying a wavering government to the Fund's advice – provides a 'commitment' device which the borrower government can offer to private markets in its search for additional funds. Without such a device, the country is unable to give firm and credible commitments to its creditors that loans will in fact be used for adjustment. The outcome of relying on private creditors at a time of adjustment difficulty, even if adjustment efforts are under way, may be no loan at all.

The ability to combine policy advice and financial assistance, with conditionality attached, is something which private financial markets cannot match. The Fund's ability to impose conditionality arises fundamentally from its legitimacy as a multilateral Bretton Woods Institution.[1] There have been few attempts to apply such conditionality by private financial markets and no known example of private markets doing this effectively. In one example, in 1976 the Peruvian government allowed a consortium of United States banks to impose conditions on it, and to monitor their implementation, in return for a $240 million loan. The conditions were not met, the stabilization was a failure and the Fund was called in the following year (Rodrik 1995).

The Asian Crises: Financial Vulnerability, Financial Crises and 'Orderly Workouts'[2]

The Asian crises have stretched the Fund's role well beyond the two functions just described, with implications not yet fully apparent.

Apart from the crisis in Thailand, the Asian crises have not been primarily caused by macroeconomic imbalances, although almost all countries in the region suffered from the export downturn in 1996. The crises were instead caused by financial vulnerability, and, unlike the Latin American crises of the early 1980s and the Mexican crisis of late 1994, were attributed to an overhang not of public but of private debt. Borrowing was in foreign currency and short term, as companies sought to escape high domestic interest rates by borrowing in dollars at lower rates; these companies chose to believe implicit guarantees that the fixed exchange rates of currencies in the region would not be altered, and that revenue growth would continue so that the rolling over of loans would not be problematic. Thus firms had high debt-to-equity ratios, with the debt being in foreign currencies and liquid.

When weaknesses became apparent, creditors became unwilling to roll over loans and attempted to move out of the national currencies into dollars, ahead of other creditors. In Korea, Indonesia and Malaysia this happened for two reasons. First, to some degree there were the same kinds of weaknesses that had afflicted Thailand. Second, contagion set in: a belief that if currency collapse could happen in Thailand it could also happen elsewhere. As the crises developed and currencies plummeted, the value in domestic currency of outstanding obligations rose beyond what companies could afford to pay, making creditors all the more unwilling to roll loans over. Countries suffered from what were effectively national 'bank-runs'.

The Fund has responded to these crises with packages containing its two traditional components: macroeconomic tightening and financial assistance. However, this has led the IMF into two deep problems.

First, the Fund's traditional remedies — tight monetary and fiscal policies — have not appeared directly to address the panic problems, since these have not been essentially problems of excess domestic spending. Indeed, it has been argued that Fund remedies may make the problems worse (Stiglitz 1998). Tight monetary policies will reduce, not improve, the creditworthiness of indebted firms, and fiscal contraction, by exacerbating the downturn in the face of panic, causes revenues to fall. The Fund has replied that halting and reversing currency collapse is a precondition of crisis resolution, and that traditional polices are essential for that purpose because there is no effective alternative (see the discussion in Chote 1998). Many have nevertheless argued that the fiscal tightening required in the packages was excessive: and that the fiscal tightening in the packages was overtly contractionary.

Second, it appears that the Fund's financial assistance effectively enables international bank lenders to escape without bearing an appropriate proportion of the losses which the crises cause. In the Mexico crisis of 1995, that country received a \$17.8 billion standby programme,[3] in combination with \$20 billion from the United States Stabilization Fund and \$10 billion from the Group of Ten nations lending money to the Fund. This funding enabled Mexico's debts to be rolled over in full, and the loans are in the process of being paid in full. Similarly, in 1997 and 1998 Korea received a rescue package — again of unprecedented size — of over \$50 billion; this came partly from the Fund and the Bank, and partly direct from the United States and from other Group of Ten countries). This did enable bank debts to be rolled over: it looks likely that, *ex post*, debts will be serviced and the injection repaid.

The problem is that there is no orderly workout procedure available which would ensure that losses are borne by those that made the mistakes. In the Latin American debt crisis of the early 1980s, rescheduling and partial default led to a problem which took ten years to solve — Latin America's 'lost decade'. The crisis greatly added to poverty and there were ten years of low investment. Resolution took so long both because of free-rider problems — each lender seeking to profit from concessions made by competitors — and because creditors held out for injection of funding from the governments of advanced countries.

Similarly in the case of Indonesia in 1997 and 1998, it appears likely that repayment in full will not be possible. Even putting aside the severe political difficulties apparent at the time of writing, it will be in principle a more difficult task to organize an orderly workout of Indonesian debt than to overcome the difficulties posed by the Latin American debt crisis of the early 1980s. Although all Indonesian debtors are hit by the same macroeconomic crisis — a collapsed currency and depressed domestic demand — the positions of individual borrowers are all different. Thus, as well as the free-riding problem already mentioned, lenders are reluctant to initiate rescheduling because of fears that offering concessions to one debtor will encourage others to demand similar treatment.

There are very significant obstacles, including serious legal ones, to organizing the necessary workout process. There is no clear agreement that the Fund is the right institution to oversee it, since it would be required both to oversee the workout procedure and to advise and assist the indebted country. Nevertheless, some orderly workout seems essential in order that a failure to repay in full does not lead to an extended period of debt deadlock, both in Indonesia, and in future similar circumstances elsewhere. If such a workout process is not established, significant moral hazard remains in the international system — lenders, still expecting to be bailed out, will persist in not taking sufficient care in lending.

Challenges for the Fund

The Asian crises have presented the Fund with perhaps the greatest challenges in its history. First, if countries are to move away from pegged to floating exchange rate systems, they will need advice in the redesign of macroeconomic policy frameworks that this implies. Second, there are challenges of crisis management: how to devise macroeconomic adjustment packages in response to debt crises which are not excessively contractionary, and how to include within crisis rescue operations the procedures for debt workouts which can make lenders better aware of the problems. Third, the crises have made the strengthening of financial systems a matter of urgency: if borrowing had been in securities, and hedged against currency risk, or if exchange rate systems had been floating in such a way as to make apparent the risk attached to foreign borrowing, then these crises would not have happened or would have been much less severe. Finally, surveillance of financial systems must, as a matter of urgency, be added alongside more conventional macroeconomic concerns in the research, analysis and advice role of the Fund.

THE WORLD BANK AND DEVELOPMENT POLICIES

The Bank began as an institution for funnelling capital to the global periphery in the face of liquidity-constrained capital markets. With the integration of global capital markets in the past thirty years, this initial conception of the Bank now makes much less sense. The Bank owes its strength and distinctiveness to combining a number of activities in one institution. The core International Bank for Reconstruction and Development (IBRD) bundles the functions of (a) lending, (b) development research and (c) development assistance — all glued together by the Bank's ability to exercise conditionality. The International Development Association (IDA) function delivers a similar bundle, except that the lending is 'concessional' and is effectively aid (Gilbert et al. 1997).

The Bank's First Traditional Role: Research, Analysis and Policy Advice

The Bank is the premier global institution for research and analysis on development economics and on the *microeconomics* of development. In this it complements the Fund's advice on macroeconomics.[4] Gavin and Rodrik (1995, p. 7) argue that it is difficult to overemphasize the part played by the Bank 'as a conveyor belt of ideas about development policy to the borrowing countries ...Thanks to its far-flung lending operations, the Bank is the single most important source of ideas and advice to developing country policy-makers'.

As has already been argued in relation to the Fund, such provision of advice to individual governments is an appropriate role for a worldwide international institution because of economies of scale and scope in the provision of such analysis. The reasons why such provision needs to be sustained, and why private markets will not provide the required types of analysis in each individual country, have already been discussed in the section above on the Fund.

There are several major issues on which the Bank's work and advice have traditionally been important. The most well known is infrastructure provision: the design, organization and implementation of large-scale projects in, for example, transport, power and irrigation. The second issue is trade liberalization. Nogués (1998) documents the transformation of the Bank's intellectual thinking in the early 1980s towards open, liberal trade policies, concluding that the Bank made a fundamental contribution to understanding in developing countries of the importance of this area. The third important issues is the mobilization of savings, including the design of taxation and advice on pension schemes. The fourth issue concerns privatization and regulation, where many developing countries have inefficient state sectors subject to extreme political interference but lack the necessary entrepreneurial capacity for running those activities to be taken over by the private sector. It may be that well-designed foreign investment schemes are essential. Also, although experience with privatization in OECD countries has shown that the regulatory environment is crucial in order that post-privatized corporations pursue socially-desirable objectives, the capacity in Third World countries for firm and credible regulation is extremely limited. A final issue is that there are other more general aspects of infrastructure which fall under the title of 'institution-building'. 'To a greater or lesser extent, a market-based economy requires law and order, a legal system which allows aggrieved parties to seek redress, security from extortion and from preferential treatment, and standard reporting and accounting conventions' (Gilbert 1996, p. 6). The work of the Bank in assisting with the establishment of these institutions can be crucial.

Second Core Role: Lending, Subject to Conditionality

It might have been thought, and was argued before the Asian crisis, that, as emerging economies in the Asia–Pacific region engaged with financial market liberalization, there was no longer a need for Bank lending. The argument for actual Bank lending is similar to that made for Fund lending in the previous section.

The importance of Bank lending derives from two things. First, the Bank has the ability to monitor loans and projects and so to ensure that contractual lending terms are met. Second, because of its large research staff and its institutional knowledge about development-improving strategies, it is able to devise conditions on loans and to impose these. In the absence of these conditions, the overall return to the project may not be such as to make it worth undertaking. In particular, in the absence of Bank surveillance, loans may be used in ways which have an anti-development bias, or rent-seeking may suck away the returns. The effect of policy conditionality is thus to raise expected investment returns (both social and private) and so to make possible lending which would not have occurred with purely private-sector financing. The ability to impose conditionality is therefore central to the Bank's effectiveness. This ability — again, like that of the Fund — arises fundamentally from its legitimacy as a multilateral Bretton Woods Institution.

In sum, the distinctiveness and strength of the Bank derives from its combination of lending, development research and development assistance functions. By lending for approved development projects on which it can impose conditionality, it can help governments to benefit from its development experience. That experience ensures a higher success rate on loans than might otherwise be attained. This success pays for the research which underpins the assistance.

Implications of the Asian Crisis

In March 1997, just before the Asian crisis, the president of the World Bank, James Wolfensohn, conducted a review of the Bank's activities which was presented to the Executive Board under the banner of a new 'Strategic Compact'. This review focused on the fact that, at a time when private capital flows to developing countries were booming, the IBRD was only lending at 55 per cent of its capacity. The response embodied in the Strategic Compact to these issues was, first, that the Bank needed to update its product range, and, second, that it needed to reorganize, with a greater presence on the ground and a replacement of existing staff by new recruits having better financial skills and more development experience.

It could be argued that this represented part of a required strategy. It asked the right questions: what products should the Bank be selling to which clients, and at what prices? Full answers, however, required the Bank to keep in mind its core roles. The Asian crisis has necessitated a redefinition of these.

The crisis has shown that financial vulnerability can put in jeopardy the fruits of years of rapid economic growth: countries which open their international capital markets as they industrialize must strengthen their financial institutions. The previous discussion identified advice, assistance and lending associated with such institution-building as lying at the core of the Bank's mandate. Since many of the financial weaknesses have been associated with corrupt crony capitalism, the required reforms will be difficult, and Bank conditionality will have a key part to play.

The crisis has also exposed the need in the countries involved for social 'safety nets' — in particular, forms of unemployment insurance, pension provision, and medical insurance — that can best protect workers from hardship at times of downturn. There is a fund of international expertise in these matters. There is an important role for the Bank in promoting this and in seeing that best-practice ideas are implemented.

If these two issues give the Bank a strengthened new mandate, they will also create challenges. Giving advice on social safety nets takes the Bank further along a spectrum from the provision of technical expertise towards what are intrinsically issues of national politics. If the Bank is to become deeply involved in financial reform, this presents a difficulty for its division of labour with the Fund. The Fund is responsible for macroeconomic, and the Bank for microeconomic, development issues, but these demarcations are essentially blurred when dealing with the banking and financial sectors.

One other way of attempting to define the division of labour is to suggest that the Fund deals with short-run crisis resolution and the Bank with longer-term structural reform, but these tasks are interrelated. For example, in dealing with the Indonesian crisis the Fund was forced to take rapid action which resulted in the closure of 16 banks, but it was not possible to say whether those banks which remained open were subject to closure in the longer-term reform process — and the result was widespread panic. There are suggestions that, because of the importance of sound financial systems to effective macroeconomic policy, all the financial-sector expertise of the Fund and the Bank should be concentrated in the Fund. This is unlikely, but much closer cooperation between the two institutions will be essential.

THE WORLD TRADE ORGANIZATION, TRADE LIBERALIZATION AND OPEN REGIONALISM

The central activity of the WTO is trade liberalization. Unlike the Fund, whose primary output is advice, adjustment assistance and crisis management for individual countries (through advice and loans), or the Bank, whose primary output is development assistance for individual countries (again through advice and loans), the primary activity of the WTO is rule-writing and enforcement of liberalized global trade. Again, unlike the Fund and the Bank, whose effectiveness ultimately stems from a combination of an internal knowledge base and an ability to exert conditionality on individual countries, the effectiveness of the WTO rests upon something quite different: it combines a global forum in which rules can be brokered with a disputes-settlement process in which they can be enforced.

Trade Liberalization and the Challenge of Reciprocity

Neoclassical trade theory argues that free trade is first-best for individual nations considered separately, and so unilateral trade liberalization is desirable for individual countries. Much of the worldwide drive to liberalization in the past ten years has indeed been genuinely unilateral. If this were all that there was to liberalization, however, there would be no collective action problem for an international organization to solve.

The collective action problem which the WTO addresses arises from the need for reciprocity in trade liberalization: the fact that there are kinds of trade liberalization which individual states will not pursue unilaterally (Arndt 1994; Johnson 1976; Bhagwati and Irwin 1987). For such liberalization to occur, it is necessary for states to make 'exchange concessions': state A desiring liberalization of a particular kind from state B must make an offer of liberalization itself, where this is something which it would not do otherwise. When there is a need for reciprocity, trade negotiations take on the nature of a prisoners' dilemma, in which only cooperative solutions can yield liberalization outcomes.

There are a number of circumstances in which this can be so. First, if a country has market power, either because the country is large or because traded products are imperfect substitutes, then, when trade liberalization leads to a shift in demand towards imports, this raises their price.[5] In this case, the unilateral 'optimal tariff' is not zero. Second, 'strategic protectionism' can arise as a result of imperfect competition. If there are large economies of scale, or where there are large gains from research and development and from learning economies, prices will in general be above marginal costs; where there are entry barriers because products are imperfect substitutes, or because of network externalities or threat of predatory pricing, prices can also be above average costs. In this case there are rents which a nation as a whole can earn from protection. The third, and most difficult, circumstance arises when trade policies are subject to rent-seeking: when products are intensive in the use of factors of production whose political support is important for election, protection can be a device for increasing perceived governmental welfare, even if it does not raise national welfare. All of these cases are different in detail, but they share the common feature that governments may be unwilling to abandon protection, without reciprocal concessions from trading partners.

Difficulties in the WTO Process

The structure of the WTO is a strange one and there are significant weaknesses in the WTO liberalization process. The General Agreement on Tariffs and Trade was simply a contract signed by governments which became 'contracting parties' to it: the GATT was clearly understood to be an organization in which the secretariat intrinsically had no power. Only contracting parties could initiate new moves towards liberalization and the implementation of existing ones could only be through a dispute-settlement panel (Sampson 1996; Jackson 1997; Quraishi 1996). The WTO is now gradually evolving away from this original GATT model. In particular, the dispute-settlement process has been strengthened in an important way by the removal of veto by the offending party on the establishment of a panel and on the adoption of a panel's report. Nevertheless, this evolution is in its early stages; the WTO remains, like the GATT before it, a very peculiar organization, essentially a structure of committees in which liberalization is negotiated.

Because of the way in which the WTO works, all progress must be made through negotiations between the contracting parties. In the late 1980s, countries in the Asia–Pacific region came to believe that these negotiations, although vitally important, did not fully serve their interest in reciprocal liberalization. Such negotiations are extraordinarily laborious (the Uruguay Round of GATT negotiations took ten years) during which participants are tempted to hold back on liberalization which they might otherwise have undertaken, using this as 'coin' in negotiations. Although in the Uruguay Round there was significant input from developing countries, particularly from the 'Cairns group' of primary commodity exporters, the negotiations were finally concluded as a result of a bilateral deal between the United States and Europe, an endgame in which participants from other parts of the world were excluded.

Open Regionalism as an Alternative Form of Liberalization Strategy?

In the late 1980s and early 1990s, trade policy in the East Asian region found its own way of responding to the challenges of reciprocity in trade liberalization.

This was through 'open regionalism', which involves a country dismantling trade barriers against *all* imports, on a most favoured nation (MFN) basis. This entails removing barriers on imports from trade partners, both outside and inside the region. Such a process has been promoted by the Asia–Pacific Economic Cooperation (APEC) 'club', whose membership is very broad.[6] The regionalism of the club contrasts sharply with the approach taken in most regional cooperation initiatives, including the European Union and North American Free Trade Agreement, which are trade blocs involving preferential discriminatory arrangements.

Members of the Asia–Pacific club have known that, as they open their own markets, they are benefiting from reciprocity, as markets are being simultaneously opened in partner countries. However, the reciprocity is 'diffuse': countries can act in their own way in their own time, without reference to external formal treaties. The club participants have also avoided trade diversion since, after liberalization, the region continues to trade both with the rest of the world and within the region on a level playing field. Regional integration of this kind, without external barriers, can likewise enable a process of successful regional integration with neighbouring countries. Before the recent crisis, the open structure of the APEC club was helping a cumulative process of industrial relocation through foreign investment to take place throughout Asia.

Open regionalism has a further advantage: it avoids putting the kind of pressure on the WTO system which is caused by preferential blocs. Article 24 of the WTO Charter allows the creation of preferential blocs only if they are all-or-nothing affairs. Participants in preferential blocs must completely liberalize, across 'substantially all trade', according to an agreed timetable, and they must do this by negotiating a formal trading bloc for which they obtain explicit sanction from the WTO.[7] Since agreement on this in the diverse Asia–Pacific region would certainly be impossible, the most likely outcome would be a 'dirty bloc', in which there was backsliding into partial preferential liberalization, and picking and choosing the sectors to liberalize, at different times, by different players, in bilateral deals. Such behaviour would fundamentally compromise the region's respect for WTO principles, something which participants have so far been determined to uphold.

Over the past ten years the kind of positive environment created by open regionalism has produced a degree of liberalization which has surprised almost all observers and even many participants. The ultimate aim of this process under the APEC club was declared at the Bogor summit in November 1994: free trade by 2010 amongst developed countries in the region and by 2020 for developing countries.

What has been constructed is a form of regional trade integration which avoids trade diversion, is in unproblematic conformity with WTO principles, is consistent with freedom of individual action, promotes unhindered integration of the region with its periphery, and is actively pushing towards further progress at the WTO. This is a significant achievement.

Open Regionalism, WTO Negotiations, and the 'Free-rider Problem'

Even before the crisis, a problem was emerging in the relation between the open regionalism of the APEC club and the WTO. This is because of what has become known as the 'free-rider' problem. Countries in a region which are liberalizing their domestic markets and concentrating on exporting create opportunities for foreign firms at home which home firms are not at the same time getting outside the liberalizing region. The perception of this problem in the United States has been at the centre of its discussions of trade policy and drives American demands for reciprocity in trade policy liberalization. Concretely, it has produced fear in the United States that truly open regionalism in the Asia–Pacific would offer Europe access to a liberalizing East Asian market without any corresponding opening of markets being offered by Europe.

As a result of this concern, influential commentators have suggested that the Asia–Pacific club might collectively reserve the right *not* to press on towards full free trade, unless the rest of the world joined it in a new WTO round of trade negotiations and thus in a move to global free trade. Bergsten has suggested that the Asia–Pacific club would make clear that, in the final stage of the trade liberalization process, it would retain external tariffs and move to a discriminatory free-trade area rather than most-favoured-nation free trade. The prospect that external tariffs would not be removed until the rest of the world joined with the Asia–Pacific countries, Bergsten argues, would create a powerful incentive for outsiders to ally with them in liberalizing trade.

This proposal, however, has struck at the very heart of the APEC agenda. It threatens the distinctive and successful way in which APEC has been operating, with its absence of trade diversion, its unproblematic conformity with WTO principles, its consistency with complete freedom of individual nations and its promotion of unhindered integration with the periphery.

Since the United States' fears about Europe seem to be at the core of this problem, it appears that the European Union can make moves which would have really significant implications here (Drysdale and Vines 1998). The European proposal for a 'transatlantic marketplace', put forward by Leon Brittan, the then European Commissioner responsible for international trade, might provide a starting point for such negotiations. The proposal calls for the removal of tariffs on trade in industrial goods on a most-favoured-nation basis in Europe and the United States by 2010; the reduction of technical barriers to trade; and the creation of a North Atlantic free trade area in services, which — at least in principle — others would be free to join.

The proposal would in effect take on the challenge of the Asia–Pacific club's open regionalism and apply it across the Atlantic and hence almost globally. It would involve a deliberate move towards the kind of regional liberalization which the club has been promoting. The explicitly stated aim is that Europe and the United States would take tariffs to zero, providing that a critical mass of other trading partners joined in. Although the document is not specific, it is clear that it has the Asia–Pacific club in mind. Such an offer by Europe could be crucial in allaying continuing United States' fears regarding European protectionism and could create the positive environment which would break down political resistance to trade liberalization in America. It is cleverly designed to reassure the United States polity that continual working by the Asia–Pacific club towards its agenda of free trade by 2010 will not be accompanied by 'free-riding' in a Europe reluctant to liberalize.

It may be that some such global move is necessary to resolve the regional tensions within the open regionalism process, and that the successful continuation of the latter, which was begun to circumvent difficulties in the WTO, will itself come to depend on that WTO process.

Finally, the Asian financial crisis also represents a significant challenge to the Asia–Pacific club's open regionalism. Protectionism is a common response for economies in times of crisis. So far this has not been the response in Korea, Thailand or the Philippines, while in Indonesia, at the time of writing, the outlook remains highly uncertain. It is nevertheless optimistic to expect further rapid progress with liberalization through open regionalism at the present time of crisis. There is resistance to liberalization under such circumstances, since resources freed from import-competing sectors can be less rapidly re-absorbed elsewhere. And the reciprocity benefits obtainable from other economies also in crisis will be that much smaller.

Keeping the open regionalism process of trade liberalization on track in the Asia–Pacific region may thus require external assistance. A further push towards global liberalization at present, orchestrated by Europe and the United States through the negotiations discussed above, could make a significant contribution. This constitutes a second reason why the open regionalism may well have become dependent on the success of the global WTO process.

AGENDA ISSUES IN THE LIGHT OF THE ASIAN CRISIS

The Asian crisis has reminded us that global economic institutions have a vitally important part to play, even though one might have believed, up to 1997, that countries of the Asia–Pacific region — including Southeast Asia — had outgrown the need for strong international institutions. First and fundamentally, the role of the Fund has become crucial, and both its policy advice and its function as crisis manager have come under close scrutiny. Second, the World Bank has been propelled to the fore as provider of advice and assistance on financial-sector reform, and on social safety nets. Third, the crisis has meant that the open regionalism process of regional trade liberalization may well have become dependent on stimulus from elsewhere in the global trading system, and this might be a push to transatlantic liberalization. The passage of one year has changed our views on global economic institutions very considerably.

NOTES

1. The World Bank and the International Monetary Fund were established at a conference on the postwar international monetary system held at Bretton Woods, New Hampshire in 1944, after much planning between the United States and the United Kingdom over the previous three years. They are entirely separate from the United Nations system. It was envisaged that there would be a World Trade Organization alongside these two bodies, but this was not ratified by the United States Congress and so the General Agreement on Tariffs and Trade became the only international trade institution until 1994 when the World Trade Organization was established.
2. This section builds on the discussion in Portes and Vines (1997).
3. This programme amounted to what was then an unprecedented 688 per cent of Mexico's quote in the Fund.
4. It is worth noting in this context that in 1994 the Bank had a research budget of $25 million, compared with the United States National Science Foundation budget for economic research of $17 million.
5. Put another way, to pay for the extra imports associated with trade liberalization, exports must be increased; if the nation is of non-negligible size in export markets then the extra export volumes will require lower prices.
6. Members include not only the Association of South East Asian Nations (ASEAN) six comprising Brunei, Indonesia, Malaysia, the Philippines, Singapore and Thailand, but also Japan and Korea, China, Hong Kong, Taiwan, Australia, New Zealand, Canada, the United States, Mexico and Chile.
7. The reasons for this are entirely understandable. Formal constraints on bilateral liberalization are essential if the most-favoured-nation principle which underpins the WTO rules for a liberal world trading system is to be protected. The particular set of rules embodied in Article 24 states that non-MFN liberalization is allowed if – and only if – it seeks to create a fully integrated market such as exists within a single country.

PART IV

Conclusions

12. Conclusions

Colin Barlow

The studies of institutions in this book raise critical issues regarding their role in economic change, also throwing light on the processes of institutional inducement and adaptation. This last chapter addresses the role and functioning of institutions in relation to events treated in individual chapters, doing this largely in reference to ideas set out by Justin Lin. It finally summarizes some indications about institutions arising from the discussions, looking as well at directions of institutional development now appearing desirable in Southeast Asia.

ISSUES AND PROCESSES

Justin Lin, in reviewing the theory of institutional change in Chapter 2, treats many issues pertaining to later presentations in the book. He highlights as a start the existence of institutions side by side with markets, performing the major roles of coordinating production and allocating resources (p. 8). Such coexistence is illustrated by many examples in the book, and on the institutional side extends from the Javanese rice-harvesting systems to the arrangements of Thai bureaucracy treated by Krongkaew and functions of the Philippine legislature scrutinized by de Dios. Lin's delineation of the 'security function' of institutions flowing from bounded rationalities and personal uncertainties of individuals (p. 9) is probably reflected in all institutions described, but does not emerge explicitly in the cases analysed. Yet his exposition of the parallel 'economy function' secured through collective action is depicted by all institutions treated, ranging from the small Indonesian tree-producing nurseries described by Barlow to the big business pressure groups reviewed by Krongkaew. Other aspects of the economy function are identified by Mackie quoting Leff (1976, 1978), who emphasizes the critical part of the economic group in integrating imperfect markets and dealing with problems of risk and uncertainty.

Lin's depiction of the problems of free-riding and moral hazard springing from lack of conjunction between individual and group rationality in collective action (p. 10) are widely portrayed, highlighting the significance of designing institutions that cope with the likely opportunism of agents operating within them. It does in fact seem inevitable that most institutions will be featured by incomplete contracts and informational asymmetries, leaving scope for rent-seeking by actors concerned. Thus Soesastro and Manning deal respectively with violations of the Indonesian financial market and industrial labour-control arrangements aimed at securing a more progressive economy. Fforde cites the prevalence of free-riding within the neo-Stalinist Vietnamese cooperatives, where lack of supervision meant too many work-points were allocated to lazy individuals. De Dios provides examples of 'pork-barrel politics' entailing the securing of patronage appropriations in Philippine legislative activities, while Vines indicates difficulties when trade policy formulation is subject to rent-seeking because the products at issue are associated with actors whose political support is required by those doing the formulation. All such problems arose because the pertinent institutional arrangements were public goods, and hence available to those who did not bear or only partly bore the costs of introduction and maintenance.

There is likewise plentiful evidence that, where appropriate institutional frameworks are not formed, politically powerful groups will organize themselves effectively to pursue their own narrow interests. Krongkaew describes, for example, how Thai auto makers and dealers employed their oligarchic power in arrangements to discourage imports of competing models by preventing the latter from being serviced. The editor noted during a recent study of potentials for private investment in eastern Indonesia that substantial initiatives by local entrepreneurs were frequently 'stopped' by dominant business interests in Java, using mechanisms restricting credit access and making official key permissions impossible to get. De Dios reports how the Philippine state was 'captured' (pp. 133–4) during the pre-dictatorship period by local agrarian elites, which extracted substantial rents for their own purposes. It is further manifest that the tortuous nature of most institutional evolution gives rein to actors who devise means of deriving benefits during the very process of adjustment, while simultaneously derailing progress towards improvement.

Although Lin notes that managerial discretionary behaviour in modern corporations is greatly mitigated by competitive product markets, managerial labour markets, stock markets, constitutions and property rights systems (p. 12), there is doubt whether markets and systems as they now exist effectively constrain such behaviour in Southeast Asia. Hence Soesastro in addressing the widespread institutional meltdown in the last few years of the Indonesian New Order also observes that 'there is no shortage of meaningful laws, including those that could help promote corporate governance' and help control discretionary behaviour (p. 116). Doing these things adequately is a complicated matter, entailing as a key component the elimination of such elements as patrimony, which itself requires the institution of other effective governance systems. The actions of the new Indonesian government towards this end have been heavily constrained by political elements, and have yet to prove effective.

It is nonetheless significant that free riding and various corrupt processes stimulate both public and private efforts at containment, including the emergence of control mechanisms. Thus the new 1998 government in Indonesia tried to impose more discipline on the banking system and introduce more flexibility into labour markets, while popular disillusion with the unfair distribution of work benefits in Vietnam was a key element in the subsequent upsurge of fence-breaking. Attempts were made to limit pork-barrel items in the Philippines through the quantity and administrative controls embodied in the Countrywide Development Fund and Congressional Initiative Allocations. The government of Anand Panyarachun that came to power in Thailand in 1991 moved immediately to reverse the corrupt practices associated with auto industry interests, although these provisions were unfortunately short-lived.

Another significant aspect of containment is the growth cited by de Dios in the Philippines of countervailing civil society institutions, including politically-vocal churches, independent mass media and community organizations. Often the latter have political as well as ethical and development goals, as illustrated by the two examples of the Indonesian Nahdatul Ulama, an Islamic group with some 25 million members (Fealy and Barton 1991), and the non-government Philippine Rural Reconstruction Movement with large development projects and important political connections (Clarke 1995). These two bodies were quasi-political forces in their own right in the late 1990s, seemingly poised to become more influential. Indeed, even the anti-Japanese riots occurring within the centralized and patriarchal Indonesian system of 1974 represented a wave of public opinion forcing the official adoption of more restrictive investment policies. While civil institutions and popular expressions often do not act directly to control particular practices, they are frequently instrumental in the setting up of bodies that will.

Lin's distinction between specific 'institutional arrangements' and the 'institutional structure' embodying a totality of arrangements (p. 12) is significant, being illustrated by most cases in the book. Fforde accordingly portrays the existence in Vietnam of Soviet-style producer cooperatives within a 'wider and less altering ... institutional structure' (p. 122) entailing all socioeconomic institutions of a given commune. Certainly, it seems that the element of institutional structure entailing family units and social relations may not have changed much, and greater recognition of this structure when cooperatives converted to the new arrangement based on household contracting may have explained the subsequent economic success. Again, de Dios distinguishes between 'formal political institutions' and the social structure underlying them, arguing the need to recognize that the restoration of formal democratic institutions following the Marcos dictatorship should be viewed against a background where fundamental and much more widespread structural alterations had occurred from the pre-dictatorship position (p. 139). It is crucial to appreciate the wider structural position if useful assessments of the role of particular arrangements are to be made.

Lin also points out that the nature and function of any new proposed arrangement must be carefully assessed in relation to the wider structure (p. 13), one critical instance of this being the introduction of an institution successful elsewhere but not necessarily suiting the broader economic and other circumstances. This is exemplified by Krongkaew's description of the insertion into Thai governance of a British-style legislature, which although working excellently in the United Kingdom has proved less effective in Thailand owing largely to the dominant bureaucracy. Another aspect of this same issue is that local institutions with international implications need to be properly linked to the global structure. Fitzgerald (1998) has accordingly proposed improvements to the institutional arrangements and links of international financial markets, suggesting a central bank, collective prudential regulation of intermediaries, and a sound and transparent legal system as 'missing institutions' that should now be set up.

Another aspect of association with the structure connects again with the question of providing for incentive-compatible collective action through matching institutional design to the cultural and other traditional characteristics of surrounding society. Thus, the patrimonialism featuring in all Southeast Asian societies demands recognition in design, with appropriate measures being taken to counter the negative effects of certain elements including cronyism and undue respect for particular actors who may be high in the patrimonial hierarchy. On the other hand, institutional design can benefit from using societal characteristics to its advantage, as where the marked inclinations of Indonesian and Malay peoples to work together in *kelompok* or small cooperatives can be harnessed through incorporating this advantageous economic feature.

Disequilibrium

Lin's sources of disequilibrium-inducing institutional change entail factors that act to raise profits, lower transaction costs and enhance efficiency. They comprise alterations in (a) the institutional choice set; (b) technology; (c) long-run relative factor and product prices and (d) other institutional arrangements (pp. 13–16). The sources are illustrated by many cases in the book, as where desirable adjustments to the International Monetary Fund indicated by Vines have been caused primarily by steep rises in the price of capital and the need for debt workouts under (c) and alterations in the world financial system under (d). Again, changes in Javanese rice-harvesting reward systems outlined by Manning were chiefly attributed to yield increases promoted by green revolution technology under (b) and a weakening of patron–client and other social ties under (d).

It is also evident, however, and portrays the characteristically wide array of causes for change, that all the four sources of disequilibrium normally affect what takes place. Regarding the example of the Fund, increases in knowledge of market participants about how to manipulate financial systems under (a) and changes in technology allowing markets to work faster under (b) had roles additional to those of main factors. Concerning harvesting-reward systems, increases in knowledge of overall economic and social circumstances under (a), and expected difficulties and costs of handling increasingly militant labour forces under (b), played further parts.

Lin likewise intimates that institutional change takes time and resources, additionally confronting social constraints against violating rules and being subject to differing perceptions from persons involved (p. 16). All these features are well portrayed by the switch from cooperatives to household contracts in Vietnam, with struggles between party officials and 'fence-breaking' actors at field level through the 1970s being succeeded by a decade-long transition to a stage of final dominance by contracts in the 1990s. The diverging views of actors caused political struggles, but eventually policies were formulated entailing ways of partitioning gains from the change, with the balance of advantage shifting decisively from officialdom to household members. It should be mentioned too that, despite the relatively constant nature of the rural segment of the wider Vietnamese institutional structure, the switch to household contracts was accompanied by major modifications in other segments of that structure. There was accordingly a move from the Stalinist centrally-planned nature of the structure in the early 1970s to a form of market economy in the 1990s, creating an atmosphere which further promoted the household emphasis.

Lin furthermore proposes following North (1990) that institutional change takes place in an historically-determined political and social structure which causes it to exhibit path-dependence. This is instanced by the Philippine legislative development addressed by de Dios, where both Congress and the presidency evolved in ways visibly depending on what went before. As one example, the elite factionalism and rent-seeking often seen as characterizing Philippine politics have persisted and influenced ongoing events. De Dios nevertheless stresses that these features have also been slowly overtaken by the growth of a multi-party system, the emergence of other institutions in civil society and the strengthening of the presidency; these indeed are another side of the coin, and path-dependence is rarely dominant in any situation.

Lin's externality problems, which mean that private institutional innovators do not reap full profits from their efforts because others imitate and reduce their costs of organization (p. 17), rarely appear significant in the contexts of this book. Undoubtedly innovators of the private tree production and marketing arrangements described by Barlow were subsequently copied, but such action was limited by difficulties in acquiring knowledge about operating relatively sophisticated ventures in places with poor communications and information. Similar circumstances, and a consequent lack of constraint on private institutional enterprise, appear true of many underdeveloped regions although they would certainly not obtain in a modern developing sector.

Political constraints and influences on institutional change are amply depicted in the book. Thus, respecting the development of automobile industries, Tham and Mahani underline the constraint imposed by official government policies supporting the need for a national car and prepared to provide subsidies for this, while Krongkaew points to the powerful business lobby backing and generally getting high protection. Again, the key role in national institutional change of the relevant power equation emerges vividly in several scrutinies. During the period addressed, this equation entailed a combination of government and business interests in Malaysia; a vying of government technocrats with a coalition of government political figures and business against the background of military influence in Indonesia; contention between the army, bureaucrats and business in Thailand; a clash of party officials with grass-roots agriculturists in Vietnam; and a struggle of Congress members with the presidency in the Philippines. These power equations, which were variously and sometimes highly influenced by national leaders, essentially determined policies for change in what were often political struggles only partly conditioned by economic judgements.

Lin's recognition of the critical role of 'political entrepreneurs' in innovating institutions and overcoming problems of change (p. 17) is depicted by several cases, including Mackie's exploration of entrepreneurship by overseas Chinese and others. Mackie also reviews the work of several authors on this issue, analysing the institutional connections of Chinese entrepreneurs and stressing the supports provided by small family firms and speech-group networks, as well as cultural connections. He likewise perceives how entrepreneurship has emerged under many circumstances, given the crucial existence of profitable opportunities. He further makes the important observation that entrepreneurial dynamism inheres in the structures of large-scale, impersonal corporate enterprises regardless of the chief executive, with entrepreneurs arising inside corporate, government and other big institutions once the framework is there. The latter is indeed exemplified by such entrepreneurial technocrats as Dr Snoh Unakul of the Thai National Economic and Social Development Board (Krongkaew, p. 93), and Dr Ali Wardhana the Indonesian economist helping to plan and implement official economic policies (Soesastro, p. 111).

An interesting issue associated with disequilibrium is the relative role of endogenous and exogenous factors in institutional change, where Lin notes that 'a number of economists have attempted to extend the neoclassical framework to endogenize the choice of institutions' (p. 8). While such extension is desirable and realistic, it is true as well that most institutional change embodies manifold economic, social and political connections. Particular changes in arrangements may rarely be ascribed to solely endogenous or exogenous causes. Some factors may be clearly endogenous, as exhibited by Tham and Mahani's assignment of low labour costs as a factor encouraging the first stage of electronics industry development in Malaysia. But an unambiguously exogenous factor is what de Dios terms the 'ineluctable trend' of globalization (p. 139) as localities become ever more strongly linked to world markets; this indeed applied to Malaysian electronics, with fluctuations in international demand being most significant for that industry. Because many factors including lagged effects are usually involved, Field (1981) has cautioned against ascribing institutional changes solely to endogenous and largely economic influences, arguing that all main causes should be considered. Barlow explores this matter in some detail in his chapter.

The Government Role

Lin sees the state as having a 'potential role as an intervenor in institutional change', because the latter is a public good and free-rider and externality problems are intrinsic to the innovation process (p. 18). The state as 'the most important institutional arrangement in society' which tends to dominate events in less-developed countries can itself be viewed as a major actor in institutional formation and change. Certainly the state is pre-eminent in Southeast Asia, with this going well beyond Weber's original concept of its function and being well reflected in the book. Lin's concept of the state in a 'multiple-level, principal–agent framework' provides useful insights, and probably matches closest to President Suharto's early Indonesian command economy described by Soesastro. The competing forces in the Philippines are seemingly furthest from this concept. Clearly the actions of government in each national case revolve to a fair extent around the relevant political power equations, albeit often modified by further outside elements in what are usually dynamic situations.

Such dynamism was exhibited as the Indonesian command economy was later overtaken by more independent influences on government of technocratic, business and other groups, including especially the armed forces, all of which have continued to vie with one another in the post-Suharto period. The successive and often military-imposed governments in Thailand also contained the partly autonomous element of a strong bureaucracy, while the power of business rose and that of the military declined during the period covered by Krongkaew. The initial control of the Vietnamese socialist regime by conservative groups in Hanoi and elsewhere came to be more strongly opposed by grass-roots movements favouring an altered ordering of affairs at the rural level, while the original dominance in the Philippines of conservative agrarian interests was progressively cut away as power within the framework tended to be broadened.

Each competing group in these power equations embraced a particular viewpoint, which at one level can be regarded in the vein of an ideology. Hence bureaucracies generally wished to protect the interests of the state and work for general welfare, while business interests looked to maximizing profits through appropriate measures including eliminating bureaucratic restrictions. Certain actors within groups followed rather more specific components of ideology, as portrayed by the desire of some leading persons in both Malaysia and Indonesia to establish heavy industries including cars and steel. The civil organizations cited above also demonstrated specific ideological thrusts, which with Nahdatul Ulama was a moderate brand of Islam and with the Philippine Rural Reconstruction Movement, a populist belief in empowering people towards change which bettered their economic and social circumstances.

Plainly, the institutional arrangements seen as desirable by each competing group will differ, while actual arrangements emerging from connected political processes will vary in 'appropriateness' for securing economic and social progress. It is indeed true that appropriateness is itself hard to define, since even excluding the divergent attitudes of local political groups it will be viewed disparately by outside analysts. The contributors to this book tend to have contrasting interpretations, despite the fact that fundamentally all follow a neoclassical economic interpretation looking to a measure of profit or net economic return. It should also be observed that the kind of ideology just treated differs from the variety noted by Lin (p. 19), who sees it as a tool of a ruler to encourage commitment by bureaucrats and others to their office; this latter variety is common, however, being exemplified through the use mentioned by Manning of five *pancasila* principles in 'guiding Indonesia's path of development' (p. 43).

It is pertinent in examining the role of the state in institutional change to scrutinize the institutional arrangements of governance and position of the bureaucracy in their historical perspectives, where doing this further exemplifies partial path-dependence. Thus, the relatively strong position of the administrative arm in Thailand during the period examined seems attributable to its long history of relatively autonomous existence and its firm place in the social hierarchy. This contrasts with the Indonesian situation where, although a governing apparatus was well established in the colonial period, it was by the late 1960s 'no longer functioning owing to ideological and political conflicts during the Old Order' (Soesastro, p.106). Although the bureaucratic structure was rehabilitated and included a strong core of technocrats, it remained firmly under central power and was consequently susceptible to pressures from cronyism and other influences acting through that nexus. The earlier destruction of Indonesian governance also meant that ongoing business and armed forces' influences on government tended to be exercised informally and in hidden ways; this compared with Thai circumstances where although things were certainly not straightforward pressures were more formally channelled. The latter is illustrated through the activities of the Joint Public–Private Sector Consultative Committee of government and business interests described by Krongkaew.

Philippine arrangements were again very distinct, with the long history of elected parliaments and American colonial influence leading to an essentially weak bureaucracy much subject to the politicians in power. Similar circumstances springing from the British colonial heritage characterized the Malaysian bureaucracy, which has not been dealt with in this book; there the dominance of the political arm was especially marked by the weight of four straight decades in power of essentially the same coalition dominated by the United Malay National Organization. Finally in Vietnam, with its autocratic regime dominating the bureaucratic apparatus, there nonetheless seems to have been a strong strain of pragmatism amongst the dominant Party leaders, meaning that fence-breaking pressures were ultimately able to move the administration in radically changed directions. Such background aspects are highly pertinent to the working out of national power equations and the policy-making finally emerging.

Lin's question of 'whether the state has the incentive and ability to design and set up suitable institutional arrangements when these cannot be provided by the induced innovation process' (p. 18) is addressed in discussing several government-associated developments. Thus Barlow indicates complementary roles for public and private sector initiatives in the crucial sphere of introducing new technologies to the incomplete rural markets of Sumatra. The critical contribution of public institutions was to provide centres of new-technology diffusion under conditions where inferior knowledge and high uncertainty meant perceived private benefit–cost ratios were much lower than those evident to actors at the state level. Barlow (1997a) in studying rubber production across a range of poorer countries has also observed the clear economic advantages of state-promoted research and extension in enabling small farmers to reach higher technological planes. The establishment by Malaysian authorities of training and technological support for developing rubber-manufactured products was another instance of effective public-goods supply, stimulating the vigorous growth of small local companies unlikely otherwise to emerge so vigorously and to contribute to the international status of that industry.

Thai official assistance for health, education and other social development was clearly a 'proper role of the state', albeit one given minimum priority by business interests involved in the Joint Committee cited above (Krongkaew, p. 94). The Philippine presidency's motivation and ability to address 'whole-system imperatives' in economic policy (de Dios, pp. 136–7) portrayed another effective official and public-goods role not attractive to other parties, including members both of the legislative branch and business organizations. The International Monetary Fund's ability to combine policy advice and financial assistance with conditionality was a further public-goods example cited by Vines; here conditionality raised expected social and private investment returns, thus enabling lending which would not have occurred with purely private-sector financing. This ability of the Fund sprang from its legitimacy as an official global financial institution and was 'something which private financial markets cannot match' (p.153), with the latter being instanced when a consortium of United States banks attempted unsuccessfully to impose conditions on the Peruvian government in return for a loan.

Lin's discussion of sources of 'policy failures' – mainly regarded as a failure to introduce institutional reforms that result in sustained economic growth (p. 19) – is amply illustrated by the text. Here the undue influence of certain actors in relevant power equations and inappropriate organizational arrangements both frequently appear as basic causes. Krongkaew describes undue business influence within the institutional arrangements for formulating Thai automobile policy, leading to the uneconomic protection of vehicle-parts making and car fabrication; this policy of distributing undue returns to manufacturers was only reversed in the early 1990s, when the balance of power and means of policy arrangement changed briefly in the technocrats' favour. Again, Soesastro covering the Indonesian institutional meltdown depicts policy problems in regulating financial markets. These sprang from the predominance of business interests in policy-making mechanisms, but were again countered to an extent by comparable rectification attempts on the part of technocrats.

Vines diagnoses the institutional problems of the International Monetary Fund, criticizing one organizational feature – that of a lack of orderly workout procedures including measures constraining international lenders to bear a portion of losses caused by the regional financial crisis. Fforde discusses the inappropriate nature of earlier Vietnamese central planning imposed by the party apparatus, entailing serious economic policy failures which condemned the agricultural sector to years of poor performance. Tham and Mahani appraise Malaysian government initiatives to sponsor cluster development, entailing vertically integrated networks of firms supported by appropriate infrastructures and institutions; they indicate that despite the success of rubber technology promotion by the state, other initiatives failed to adjust adequately to emerging economic and technological conditions.

Lin's denoted causes of policy failures, including the desire of 'the ruler' to maintain power, the machinations of bureaucrats, the actions of powerful groups and inadequate social science knowledge (p. 20), all have a bearing on these institutional deficiencies. Thus, the centrally-oriented policies of the Vietnamese regime were connected with maintenance of the Party's control, while the business interests in Thailand and Indonesia were examples of powerful groups. The failure of centrally-planned policies in Vietnam were a reflection of poor social knowledge on the part of the ideologically-motivated persons who formulated them.

Although a key issue arising from policy failures is that of how the state can improve its public goods institutional role, this tricky question is perhaps unsurprisingly not fully answered by either Lin, other contributors or further scholars addressing it in the wider literature. Krongkaew implicitly suggests that giving greater weight to bureaucratic interests would produce better policies, while Soesastro quoting Goodpaster argues for a 'rule-based ordering system'. Fforde denotes that fence-breaking by local interests was a desirable answer to rectifying manifestly unsuitable policies.[1] De Dios in discussing the growing influence of civil society institutions on Philippine government policies, intimates that this is likely to lead to better policies.

The arguments of Fforde and de Dios broadly suggest more democratic participation in policy-making, which seems a good direction to this editor although it runs counter to the notion of Campos and Root (1996) quoted by Soesastro (p. 108) that 'insulating' economic policy-making is important to its success. Channelling such participation effectively is hard, however, as exemplified by Thai and Philippine governance arrangements. While both arrangements seemingly provide for a wide engagement of parties, their actual working leaves much to be desired. It is also crucial that policies once formulated are effectively implemented, and this requires an administrative apparatus that responds efficiently to policy demands. Lin's comment that institutional reform must commonly proceed as 'trial and error', with great dependence on luck and political ingenuity (p. 21), is certainly germane to the present evolution of policy and other governance institutions.

Lin's component of political ingenuity is crucial, having to emanate from entrepreneurs who devise suitable ways of designing organizations to achieve relevant goals while avoiding externality and free-rider problems and recognizing pertinent cultural and social contexts. However, more is needed than his second component of luck to influence institutional change in participative directions, since this entails the establishment of representative institutions and forums in which views can be considered prior to formulating policies. Administrative mechanisms that enable such policies to be implemented successfully have likewise to be built, and this is no mean task. Although many Southeast Asian governance mechanisms appear to be moving in ways that could ultimately produce such development, the difficulties of evolution remain very evident.

SYNOPSIS

Several critical indications arise from these scrutinies of institutions and economic change in diverse Southeast Asian contexts. One is confirmation of the central role of institutions, with their associated ability both to facilitate and to obstruct economic and social alterations. Manifestly, assessments of societal improvement must take relevant institutions into account, examining ways in which they need to alter to enable it to occur productively.

Beyond this it is evident that institutional adjustments usually spring from a wide complex of endogenous and exogenous factors, and that particular institutional arrangements should always be considered in relation to the economic, social and political attributes of their wider surrounding structures. It is clear too that adjustments are characteristically slow, being featured by substantial trial and error and conditioned by previous circumstances in a form of path-dependence. This said, it may be seen that most institutions tend to be in states of dynamic change, continuously albeit gradually altering in response to disequilibriating pressures.

It is further evident that institutions are most susceptible to free-riding, moral hazard and other collective-action problems, with these highlighting the importance of entrepreneurs who can negotiate and fashion incentive-compatible institutional designs that help minimize such problems and assist the achievement of primary goals. It is patent as well that institutional change and the operation of institutional arrangements have a regular political element, with conflicting groups of actors possessing different ideological positions and with their activities in defence of these becoming institutionalized through the relevant power equations. It is likewise apparent that where serious collective-action problems occur, this commonly gives rise to efforts at containment, resulting in new evolutions in the dispositions of power.

Government emerges as a most important institution, having a potentially key role as an intervenor in institutional change as a public good. Part of this role is in directly supplying infrastructures and services, and part in creating a regulatory and facilitating environment where various groups can contribute fruitfully to economic progress. Often, however, this role does not seem to have been fulfilled successfully, with difficulties being attributed both to the nature of the relevant power equation and to poor institutional design with concomitant free-rider and other problems. It seems that more participative government is desirable from the viewpoint of getting better policies, but this is hard to achieve.

Numerous other private organizations ranging from community groups to big business enterprises are also significant in providing institutional bases for productive economic and social change. The cultural attributes of society including the widespread tradition of patrimony and other customarily recognized behaviour patterns are likewise institutional aspects that heavily influence societal organization and need careful recognition in fashioning effective new institutional designs.

Future Directions

The disastrous effects on Southeast Asian economies of the recent financial crisis have emphasized the grave inadequacies of many regional institutions, stressing the need for change to secure economic and social recovery and renewed advance. The drastic lowering of living standards following the crisis[2] has provided major new stimuli to institutional improvement, including fresh political pressures likely to force the pace of such reform.

The present book does not attempt to specify detailed directions for institutional change in Southeast Asia, apart from adjustments proposed for given situations by individual contributors. The main goal of the book as stated in the Introduction is to use the case studies in successive chapters to examine how institutions have performed in given areas of economic and social development, matching these performances against the theoretical framework provided by Lin and noting certain other elements of institutional contribution and adjustment. The case studies also denote the responses of institutions to disequilibria, illustrating in addition problems of collective action and how designs to achieve this might be improved. The cases further permit the role of government in several Southeast Asian countries to be scutinized, looking at this mainly in terms of the performances of particular official institutions of economic and social change.

It seems nonetheless useful, on the basis of discussions, to briefly indicate spheres where improved Southeast Asian institutions concerned with economic change may be seen as required. These spheres are judged to be the working of government institutions, the arrangement of financial markets and the organization of rural and regional development. Although improvements seen as desirable in these spheres are now only framed generally, it should be noted that tasks of institutional betterment are always complex, with arrangements having to be fashioned carefully to the differing circumstances in each country and being subject to continuous political manipulation.

Respecting government, it seems important, as indicated, for it to become more participatory, with consequent modifications to the structure of relevant power equations and particularly to ways in which policies are formulated. Government has a clear public-goods function in providing macroeconomic and sectoral policies and associated administration, all of which can be bettered through strengthening the role of relevant institutions. It also needs to improve its other public-goods institutions, including not only those furnishing infrastructures and social services but also those regulating financial markets and promoting targeted rural development.

Concerning financial markets, there are strong needs especially apparent since the financial crisis to enhance the effectiveness of official institutions controlling domestic capital flows and permissions for investment projects, with additional persuasive arguments for more transparency in operation. It is necessary too to strengthen the regulation of financial flows on international markets, improving the global superstructure of institutions so as to lessen the huge surges of short-term foreign investment capital. This may well entail setting up regional institutions which assist in countering political influence from an axis between the International Monetary Fund and the Washington administration.

Finally, regarding rural and regional development, with its incomplete information, capital and other markets, there are convincing arguments for more government intervention to promote appropriate economic activities which are often extremely underdeveloped or non-existent. These activities could include the supply of technology-generation institutions as well as of extension organizations providing information and limited credit in targeted development areas. Here the active participation of other community institutions and small private enterprises is also important in its own right as well as for government to encourage.

Little has been said in these closing comments about the private sector, although it is highly evident that the business and other institutions which motivate it, and the entrepreneurs who help direct its economic development, are very basic elements in economic advance, without which the activities of government would generally amount to very little. Most contributors to this book have a major interest in government or government-related institutions, which is a characteristic helping to explain the preoccupation with these aspects.

Lin has indicated that 'theory of institutions and institutional change is one of the least developed spheres of modern economics' (p. 21). It is hoped that the association between institutions and economic change in this book, and the attempts in this chapter to relate different empirical experiences to the framework of theory, will help to usefully extend the understanding of how institutions operate in real life.

NOTES

1. Although Fforde implies that fence-breaking, entailing the unsanctioned introduction of innovative social practices which are subsequently legalized, is peculiarly Vietnamese, it actually takes place in most societies. The recent recognition in Indonesia of a key role for burgeoning trade unions is another example of this, as is the onset of official support for the cluster approach in Malaysian manufacturing following the 1987 industrial policy change. Tension between existing officially-promoted systems and new privately-arising institutional innovations is indeed a key feature of institutional disequilibrium, reflecting Lin's first source of a change in the institutional choice set. It is probably more noticeable in socialist societies, where breaking the official line has historically appeared as a sacrilegious act meriting severe sanctions.
2. Thus the World Bank (1998) has estimated gross domestic product drops in 1997–8 of: -15 per cent for Indonesia; -5.5 per cent for Malaysia; -8.0 per cent for Thailand; and -1.0 per cent for the Philippines. These compare with rapid advances averaging over 7.0 per cent per year over the previous decade for the first three countries, and have extremely serious implications for employment levels.

References

Aitken, H.G.J. (1963), 'The future of entrepreneurial research', *Explorations in Entrepreneurial History*, 2nd series, **1** (10), pp. 3–9.

Alchian, Armen A. (1950), 'Uncertainty, evolution and economic theory', *Journal of Political Economy*, **58** (June), pp. 211–22.

Alchian, Armen A. (1995), 'Some economics of property rights', in S. Medema (ed.), *The Legacy of Ronald Coase in Economic Analysis*, Vol. II, *Intellectual Legacies in Modern Economics Series*, Aldershot: Edward Elgar (previously published 1965), pp. 193–206.

Alchian, Armen A. and Harold Demsetz (1972), 'Production, information costs, and economic organization', *American Economic Review*, **62** (December), pp. 777–95.

Alexander, Jennifer and Paul Alexander (1982), 'Shared poverty as ideology: agrarian relationships in rural Java', *Man* (New Series) **17**, pp. 597–619.

Allen, G.C. and Audrey Donnithorne (1957), *Western Enterprise in Indonesia and Malaya*, London: Macmillan.

Anderson, Terry L. and P.J. Hill (1975), 'The evolution of property rights: a study of the American West', *Journal of Law and Economics*, **18** (April), pp. 163–79.

Anek Laothamathas (1992), *Business Associations and the New Political Economy of Thailand: From Bureaucratic Polity to Liberal Corporatism*, Singapore: Institute of Southeast Asian Studies.

Anon (1992), 'General report on the Party's position, 1945–1980' (in Vietnamese), mimeo dated 16 November, Hanoi.

Aoki, T. (1992), 'Japanese FDI and the forming of networks in the Asia–Pacific Region: experience in Malaysia and its implications', in S. Tokunaga (ed.), *Japan's Foreign Investment and Asian Economic Interdependence*, Tokyo: University of Tokyo Press (Chapter 3).

Arndt, H. (1994), 'The political economy of reciprocity', *Banca Nazionale Quarterly Review* (September), pp. 259–69.

Arrow, Kenneth J. (1974), *The Limits of Organization*, New York: W.W. Norton.

Ayal, E. (1969), 'Value systems and economic development in Japan and Thailand', in Robert Tilman (ed.), *Man, State and Society in Southeast Asia*, New York: Praeger, pp. 535–49.

Ayres, Clarence (1944), *The Theory of Economic Progress: A Study of the Fundamentals of Economic Development and Cultural Change*, Chapel Hill: University of North Carolina Press.

Bardhan, Pranab (1984), *Land, Labor and Rural Poverty: Essays in Development Economics*, New Delhi: Oxford University Press.

Bardhan, Pranab (1989), *The Economic Theory of Agrarian Institutions*, Oxford: Clarendon.

Bardhan, Pranab (1997) 'Corruption and development', *Journal of Economic Literature* **35** (3) (September), pp. 1320–46.

Barlow, C. (1986), *Oil Palm as a Smallholder Crop,* Occasional Paper No. 21, Bandar Baru Bangi: The Palm Oil Research Institute of Malaysia and Ministry of Primary Industries.

Barlow, C. (1997a), 'Growth, structural change and plantation tree crops: the case of rubber', *World Development,* **25** (10), pp. 1589–107.

Barlow, C. (1997b), 'The market for new tree crop technology: a Sumatran case', *Journal of Agricultural Economics,* **48** (2), pp. 193–210.

Barlow, C. and T. Tomich (1991), 'Indonesian agricultural development: the awkward case of smalholder tree crops', *Bulletin of Indonesian Economic Studies,* **27** (3), pp. 29–53.

Barzel, Yoram (1982), 'Measurement costs and the organization of markets', *Journal of Political Economy,* **69** (3), pp. 213–25.

Basu, Kaushik, Eric Jones and Ekkehart Schlicht (1987), 'The growth and decay of custom: the role of the new institutional economics in economic history', *Explorations in Economic History,* **24** (1), pp. 1–21.

Battacharya, Amar and Mari Pangestu (1996), 'Indonesia: development transformation and the role of public policy', in Danny M. Leipziger (ed.), *Lessons from East Asia*, Ann Arbor: The University of Michigan Press.

Bauer, P.T. (1984), *Reality and Rhetoric*, Cambridge, MA: Harvard University Press.

Becker, Gary S. (1976), *The Economic Approach to Human Behavior*, Chicago: University of Chicago Press.

Beresford, Melanie (1989), *National Unification in Vietnam*, London: Macmillan.

Beresford, Melanie and Adam Fforde (1997), 'A methodology for analysing the process of economic reform in Vietnam: the case of domestic trade', *Journal of Communist Studies and Transition Politics,* **13** (4), pp. 99–128.

Bhagwati, J. and D. Irwin (1987), 'The return of the reciprocitarians: US trade policy today', *The World Economy* (June), pp.109–30.

Binswanger, Hans P. (1978), *The Economics of Tractors in South Asia*, New York: Agricultural Development Council; and Hyderabad: International Crops Research Institute for Semi-Arid Tropics.

Binswanger, Hans P. and Mark R. Rosenzweig (1981), *Contractual Arrangements, Employment and Wages in Rural Labor Markets: A Critical Review*, New York: Agricultural Development Council and ICRISAT.

Binswanger, Hans P. and Mark R. Rosenzweig (1986), 'Behavioral and material determinants of production relations in agriculture', *Journal of Development Studies*, **22** (April), pp. 504–39.

Binswanger, Hans P. and Vernon Ruttan (1978), *Induced Innovation: Technology, Institutions, and Development*, Baltimore: Johns Hopkins University Press.

Boeke, J.H. (1930), 'Dualistic economics', reprinted in W.F. Wertheim (1966) (ed.), *Indonesian Economics. The Concept of Dualism in Theory and Policy*, The Hague: W. van Hoeve, pp. 165–92.

Booth, Anne and Peter McCawley (1971), 'The Indonesian economy since the mid-Sixties', in Anne Booth and Peter McCawley (eds), *The Indonesian Economy During the Suharto Era*, Kuala Lumpur: Oxford University Press, pp. 1–22.

Booth, Anne and R.M. Sundrum (1985), *Labour Absorption in Agriculture: Theoretical Analysis and Empirical Investigations*, Oxford: Oxford University Press.

Boserup, E. (1965), *The Conditions of Agricultural Growth*, Chicago: George Allen and Unwin.

Bowie, A. (1991), *Crossing the Industrial Divide: State, Society, and the Politics of Economic Transformation in Malaysia*, New York: Columbia University Press.

Boyko, M.A. Schleifer and R.W. Vishny (1966), 'A theory of privatisation', *Economic Journal*, 106 (435), pp.–69–81.

Breman, Jan (1992), 'Kerja dan kehidupan buruh tani di pesisir Jawa" ('Work and livelihood of farm workers in coastal Java'), *Prisma* **21** (3), pp. 3–34.

Brewster, John M. (1950), 'The machine process in agriculture and industry', *Journal of Farm Economics*, **32** (February), pp. 69–81.

Campos, Jose Edgardo and L. Hilton Root (1996), *The Key to the Asian Miracle*, Washington, DC: The Brookings Institution.

Carroll, J.J. (1966), *The Philippine Manufacturing Entrepreneur*, Ithaca: Cornell University Press.

Chandler, A.D. (1962), *Strategy and Structure. Chapters in the History of the Industrial Enterprise,* Cambridge, MA: MIT Press.

Chandler, A.D. (1990), *Scale and Scope. The Dynamics of Industrial Capitalism,* Cambridge, MA: The Belknap Press.

Cheung, Steven N.S. (1974), 'A theory of price control', *Journal of Law and Economics*, **17** (1), pp. 53–71.

Chote, R. (1998), 'Financial crises: lessons from Asia', in *Financial Crises and Asia, CEPR Conference Report No. 6,* London: Centre for Economic Policy Research.

Christensen, Scott R., David Dollar, Ammar Siamwalla and Pakorn Vichyanond (1992), 'Institutional and political bases of growth-inducing policies in Thailand', paper prepared for the World Bank project on the Role of Government and East Asian Success, October.

Clarke, G. (1995), 'Participation and protest: non-governmental organisations and Philippine politics', unpublished PhD dissertation, Department of Political Studies, School of African and Oriental Studies, University of London.

Collier, William (1981), 'Agricultural evolution in Java', in Gary E. Hansen (ed.), *Agricultural and Rural Development in Indonesia*, Boulder, CO: Westview Press.

Commons, John (1934), *Institutional Economics: Its Place in Political Economy*, New York: Macmillan.

Coronel, S. (ed.) (1998), *Pork and Other Perks: Corruption and Governance in the Philippines*, Quezon City: Philippine Center for Investigative Journalism.

Crouch, Harold (1978), *The Army and Politics in Indonesia*, Ithaca: Cornell University Press.

Dam van Nhue and Le Si Thiep (1981), 'Integration of the workers' interests in local industry' (in Vietnamese), *Nghien cuu kinh te* (Economic Research), **5.**

Davis, Lance and Douglass C. North (1970), 'Institutional change and American economic growth: a first step toward a theory of institutional innovation', *Journal of Economic History*, **30** (1), pp. 131–49.

Day, Richard H. (1967), 'The economics of technological change and the demise of the sharecropper', *American Economic Review*, **57** (June), pp. 427–49.

de Dios, E. and H. Esfahani (1997), 'Political centralization, turnover and investment in the Philippines', unpublished manuscript.

Demsetz, Harold (1967), 'Towards a theory of property rights', *American Economic Review*, **57** (May), pp. 347–59.

de Vylder, Stefan and Adam J. Fforde (1996), *From Plan to Market: The Economic Transition in Vietnam, 1979–89*, Boulder, CO: Westview.

Devarajan, Shantavanan, Hafez Ghanem and Karen Thierfelder (1997), 'Economic reform and labour unions: a general equilibrium analysis applied to Bangladesh and Indonesia', *World Bank Economic Review*, **11** (1), pp. 145–70.

Direktorat Jenderal Perkebunan (1992), *Outline of the Crop Scheme Operations, 1992/93* (in Indonesian), Jakarta.

Doronila, A. (1992), *The State, Economic Transformation, and Political Change in the Philippines, 1946–1972*, Singapore: Oxford University Press.

Dorward, A., J. Kydd and C. Poulton (eds) (1998), *Smallholder Cash Crop Production under Market Liberalisation. A New Institutional Economics Perspective*, CAB International: Wallingford.

Drysdale, P. and David Vines (1998), *Europe, East Asia and APEC: A Shared Global Agenda?*, Cambridge: Cambridge University Press.

Fama, Eugene (1980), 'Agency problems and the theory of the firm', *Journal of Political Economy*, **88** (2), pp. 288–307.

Fealy, G. and G. Barton (eds) (1991), *Nahdatul Ulama, Traditional Islam and Modernity in Indonesia,* Clayton: Monash Asia Institute.

Feeny, David (1982), *The Political Economy of Productivity: Thai Agricultural Development, 1880–1975,* Vancouver: University of British Columbia Press.

Fforde, Adam J. (1982), 'Problems of agricultural development in North Vietnam', PhD dissertation, Faculty of Politics and Economics, University of Cambridge.

Fforde, Adam J. (1984), 'Macro-economic adjustment and structural change in a low-income Socialist developing country – an analytical model', Discussion Paper 163, Dept. of Economics, London: Birkbeck College.

Fforde, Adam J. (1986), 'The unimplementability of policy and the notion of law in Vietnamese Communist thought', *Southeast Asian Journal of Social Science,* 1, pp. 60–70.

Fforde, Adam J. (1987), 'Socio-economic differentiation in a mature collectivised agriculture – North Vietnamese agricultural producer cooperatives in the mid 1970s', *Sociologica Ruralis,* 127 (2/3, October), pp. 197–215.

Fforde, Adam J. (1989), *The Agrarian Question in North Vietnam 1974–79: A Study of Cooperator Resistance to State Policy,* New York: M.E. Sharpe.

Fforde, Adam J. and S.H. Paine (1987), *The Limits of National Liberation – Problems of Economic Management in the Democratic Republic of Vietnam, with a Statistical Appendix,* London: Croom-Helm.

Field, Alexander James (1981), 'The problem with neoclassical institutional economics: a critique with special reference to the North/Thomas Model of pre-1500 Europe', *Explorations in Economic History,* 18 (2), pp. 174–98.

Fields, Gary (1992), 'Labor institutions and economic development: a conceptual framework with reference to Asia', paper presented at the *International Workshop on Labour Institutions and Economic Development in Asia,* Bali, 4–6 February.

Fields, Gary and Henry Wan, Jr (1989), 'Wage setting institutions and economic growth', *World Development,* 17 (9), pp. 1471–83.

Findlay, Ronald (1990), 'The new political economy: its explanatory power for LDCs', *Economics and Politics,* 2 (2), pp. 191–221.

Findlay, R. and S. Wellisz (1982), 'Endogenous tariffs, the political economy of trade restrictions, and welfare', in J. Bhagwati (ed.), *Import Competition and Response,* Chicago: National Bureau of Economic Research.

Fischer, S. (1995), 'The World Bank and the IMF at fifty', in H. Gensberg (ed.), *The International Monetary System,* Heidelberg: Springer Verlag.

Fitzgerald, V. (1998), 'Global capital market volatility and the developing countries: lessons from the East Asian crisis', paper presented to the East Asian Crisis Conference at the Institute of Development Studies, Sussex University, July.

Fong, C. O., K.C. Lim and Z.A. Mahani (1985), 'Malaysia Industrial Master

Plan Study. Electronics sector. Draft final report', Kuala Lumpur.

Frohlich, Norman and Joe A. Oppenheimer (1974), 'The carrot and the stick: optimal program mixes for entrepreneurial political leaders', *Public Choice*, **19** (Fall), pp. 43–61.

Gavin, M. and D. Rodrik (1995), 'The World Bank in historical perspective', *American Economic Review*, **85** (2), pp. 329–34.

Geertz, C. (1956), 'Religious belief and economic behaviour in a Javanese town', *Economic Development and Cultural Change*, **4** (1), pp. 34–58.

Geertz, C. (1963), *Agricultural Involution; The Process of Ecological Change in Indonesia*, Berkeley: University of California Press.

Gilbert, C. (1996), 'The World Bank at Fifty', *Newsletter of the ESRC Global Economic Institutions Research Programme,* Issue No. 3, London: Centre for Economic Policy Research, July.

Gilbert, C., R. Hopkins, A. Powell and A. Roy (1997), 'The World Bank: Its functions and its future' (revision of a discussion paper of the ESRC Global Economic Institutions Research Programme, CEPR, London: 1996), mimeo.

Goodpaster, Gary (1997), 'Rule of law, economic development, and Indonesia', paper presented at a Conference, *Sustaining Economic Growth in Indonesia: A Framework for the Twenty-First Century*, organized by USAID, ACAES and LPEM–UI, Jakarta, 17–18 December.

Goodwin, R.E. and Brennan, G. (1991), 'Institutional design: an introduction', paper presented at the *Seminar Series on The Role of Institutions in Economic Development*, Canberra: Research School of Social Sciences, Australian National University, September.

Gouyon, A. (1991), 'Farming and social change in South Sumatra: an historical perspective', paper presented at the *Seminar Series on The Economics of Trade and Development*, Canberra: Department of Economics, Research School of Pacific and Asian Studies, Australian National University, August.

Gutierrez, E. (1998), 'The public purse', in S. Coronel (ed.), *Pork and Other Perks: Corruption and Governance in the Philippines*, Quezon City: Philippine Center for Investigative Journalism, pp. 56–79.

Gutierrez, E., I. Torrente and N. Narca (1992), *All in the Family: A Study of Elites and Power Relations in the Philippines,* Quezon City: Institute for Popular Democracy.

Hadiz, P. (1997), *Workers and the State in New Order Indonesia*, London: Routledge.

Harriss, John, Janet Hunter and Colin M. Lewis (eds) (1995), *The New Institutional Economics and Third World Development*, London and New York: Routledge.

Hart, Gillian (1986), *Power, Labor and Livelihood: Processes of Change in Rural Java*, Berkeley: University of California Press.

Hart, Gillian, Andrew Turton and Benjamin White (1989), *Agrarian*

Transformations: Local Processes and the State in Southeast Asia, Berkeley: University of California Press.

Hawkins, E.D. (1963), 'Labour in transition', in R. McVey (ed.), *Indonesia*, New Haven: Human Relations Area Files Press, pp. 248–71.

Hayami, Y. and M. Kikuchi (1982), *Asian Village at the Crossroads: An Economic Approach to Institutional Change*, Tokyo: University of Tokyo Press.

Hayami, Yujiro and Vernon W. Ruttan (1971), *Agricultural Development: An International Perspective*, Baltimore: Johns Hopkins University Press.

Hewison, Kevin (1989), *Bankers and Bureaucrats: Capital and the Role of the State in Thailand*, Monograph Series 34 (Yale University Southeast Asia Studies), New Haven: Yale Center for International and Area Studies.

Higgins, Benjamin (1989), *The Road Less Travelled*, Canberra: ANU, National Centre for Development Studies.

Hill, H. (1996), *The Indonesian Economy Since 1966: Southeast Asia's Emerging Giant*, Cambridge: Cambridge University Press.

Hugo, Graeme (1978), *Population Mobility in Java*, Yogyakarta: Gadjah University Press.

Hugo, Graeme, Terry Hull, Valerie Hull and Gavin Jones (1987), *The Demographic Dimension of Indonesian Development*, Singapore: Oxford University Press.

Husken, Frans (1979), 'Landlords, sharecroppers and agricultural labourers: changing labour relations in rural Java', *Journal of Contemporary Asia*, **9** (2), pp. 140–51.

Hutchcroft, P. (1998), *Booty Capitalism: The Politics of the Banking System in the Philippines*, Ithaca: Cornell University Press.

Indonesian Documentation and Information Centre (1981–87/88), *Indonesian Workers and Their Right to Organise* (main report in May 1981, and annual updates with the same title up to 1986 and for 1987–88), Leiden.

Jackson, J. (1997), 'Designing and implementing effective dispute settlement', in A. Krueger, *The WTO as an International Organisation*, Chicago: University of Chicago Press.

Jesudason, J.V. (1990), *Ethnicity and the Economy*, Singapore: Oxford University Press.

Johnson, H.G. (1976), 'Trade negotiations and the new international monetary system', in *Commercial Policy Issues*, No. 1, Graduate Institute of International Studies, Geneva and Trade Policy Research Centre, London. Leiden: W.W. Sijthoff.

Kerkvliet, Benedict (1996), 'Village–state relations in Vietnam: the effect of everyday politics on decollectivization', *The Journal of Asian Studies*, **54** (2), pp. 396–418.

Kilby, P. (1971), 'Hunting the Heffalump', in P. Kilby (ed.), *Entrepreneurship*

188   *References*

8References

188   *References*

188 *References*

and Economic Development, New York: The Free Press, pp. 1–42.
Kornai, Janos (1980), *The Economics of Shortage*, Amsterdam: North-Holland.
Krueger, A. (1984), 'The political economy of the rent-seeking society', *American Economic Review*, **64** (3), pp. 291–303.
Krueger, A. (ed.) (1997), *The WTO as an International Organisation*, Chicago: University of Chicago Press.
Krugman, P. (1993), 'Regionalism versus multilateralism: analytical notes', in J. de Melo and S. Panagariya (eds), *New Dimensions in Regional Integration*, London: CEPR.
Lande, C. (1965), *Leaders, Factions, and Parties: The Structure of Philippine Politics*, New Haven: Yale University Southeast Asian Program.
Leff, Nathaniel H. (1976), 'Capital markets in the developing countries: the Group Principle', in Ronald I. McKinnon (ed.), *Money and Finance in Economic Growth and Development*, New York: M. Decker, pp. 97–122.
Leff, Nathaniel H. (1978), 'Industrial organization and entrepreneurship in the developing countries: the economic groups', *Economic Development and Cultural Change*, **26** (94), pp. 661–75.
Leff, Nathaniel H. (1979), 'Entrepreneurship and economic development: the problem revisited', *Journal of Economic Literature*, **8**, pp. 46–64.
Leibenstein, H. (1968), 'Entrepreneurship and development', *American Economic Review*, **58**, pp. 72–83.
Lewis, Arthur (1954), 'Economic development with unlimited supplies of labour', *Manchester School of Economic and Social Studies*, **22**, pp. 139–91.
Lim, S.C. (1989), 'Technology and research facilities for the rubber-based industry', paper presented at the Federation of Malaysian Manufacturers' Seminar on *Investment and Business Opportunities in Rubber-based and Wood-based Industries in Malaysia*, Kuala Lumpur.
Limlingan, Victor S. (1986), *The Overseas Chinese in ASEAN: Business Practices and Management Strategies*, Manila: Vita Development Corporation.
Lin, J.Y. (1989), 'An economic theory of institutional change: induced and improved change', *Cato Journal*, **9** (1) pp. 1–33.
Luce, R. Duncan and Howard Raiffa (1957), *Games and Decisions: Introduction and Critical Survey*, New York: John Wiley.
MacIntyre, Andrew J. (1992), 'Politics and the reorientation of economic policy in Indonesia', in Andrew J. MacIntyre and Kanizhka Jayasuriya (eds), *The Dynamics of Economic Policy Reform in South-east Asia and the South-west Pacific*, Singapore: Oxford University Press.
MacIntyre, Andrew J. and Rizal Ramli (1997), 'Investment, property rights, and corruption in Indonesia', paper presented at the World Bank/Foundation for Advanced Studies on International Development Workshop on

Governance and Private Investment in East Asia, Hakone, 24–26 August.

Mackie, Jamie (1992), 'Overseas Chinese entrepreneurship', *Asia-Pacific Economic Literature*, **6** (1), pp. 41–64.

Mackie, Jamie (1998), 'Business success among Overseas Chinese: the roles of culture, values and social structures', in Robert W. Hefner (ed.), *Market Cultures. Society and Morality in the New Asian Capitalisms*, Boulder, CO: Westview Press, pp. 129–46.

Mahani, Z.A. (1996), 'The Malaysian experience in the automotive industry: some lessons and future directions', paper presented at the Seminar on *The Asian Age of Automotive Industry*, Jakarta.

Malaysia (1996a), *Seventh Malaysia Plan: 1996–2000*, Kuala Lumpur: National Printing Press.

Malaysia (1996b), *The Second Industrial Master Plan: 1996–2005*, Kuala Lumpur: Ministry of International Trade and Industries.

Malaysian Institute of Economic Research and DRI/McGraw-Hill (1995), *Malaysia's Quest for Competitive Advantage, Inception Report: Post-IMP Project*, Vol. II, Kuala Lumpur.

Manning, Chris (1979), 'Wage differentials and labour market segmentation in Indonesian manufacturing', PhD dissertation, Australian National University, Canberra.

Manning, Chris (1988), *The Green Revolution, Employment, and Economic Change in Rural Java: A Reassessment of Trends under the New Order*, Institute of Southeast Asian Studies, Occasional Paper No. 84, Singapore: ISEAS.

Manning, Chris (1998), *Indonesian Labour in Transition: An East Asian Success Story?*, Cambridge: Cambridge University Press.

Marr, David (1981), *Vietnamese Tradition on Trial 1920–1945*, Berkeley: University of California Press.

Marr, David (1994), 'The Viet Nam Communist Party and civil society', paper presented at the Vietnam Update Conference, November (mimeo).

Marx, K. (1843 [reprinted 1975]), 'Critique of Hegel's philosophy of the state', in *Early Writings*, The Pelican Marx Library, Harmondsworth: Penguin Books.

Marx, K.H. (1858 [English translation, 1972]), *Foundations of a Critique of Political Economy*, London: Lawrence and Wishart.

Marx, Karl and Frederick Engels (1818–83 [reprinted 1968]), *Selected Works*, New York: International Publishers.

Matthews, R.C. (1986), 'The economics of institutions and sources of growth', *Economic Journal*, **96** (384), pp. 903–18.

Mazumdar, Dipak (1989), *Microeconomic Issues of Labor Markets in Developing Countries: Analysis and Policy Implications*, EDI Seminar Paper No. 40, Washington, DC: World Bank.

McCloskey, Donald N. (1975), 'The economics of enclosure: a market analysis', in William N. Parker and Eric L. Jones (eds), *European Peasants and Their Markets*, Princeton, N.J.: Princeton University Press, pp. 25–38.

McCoy, Alfred (ed.) (1994), *An Anarchy of Families: State and Family in the Philippines*, Quezon City: Ateneo de Manila University Press.

Medhi Krongkaew, Pranee Tinakorn, and Suphat Suphachalasai (1992), 'Rural poverty in Thailand: policy issues and responses', *Asian Development Review*, **10** (1), pp. 199–25.

Metzner, J.K. (1982), *Agricultural and Population Pressure in Sikka Isle of Flores. A Contribution to the Study of Stability of Agricultural Systems in the Wet and Dry Tropics*, Monograph No. 28, Canberra: Development Studies Centre, Australian National University.

Miller, G. (1997), 'The impact of economics on contemporary political science', *Journal of Economic Literature*, **35** (3) (September), pp. 1173–1204.

Miller, M. and Lei Zhang (1996), 'A bankruptcy procedure for sovereign states' (mimeo), Warwick University.

Morris-Suzuki, T. (1992), 'Japanese technology and the new international division of knowledge in Asia', in S. Tokunaga (ed.), *Japan's Foreign Investment and Asian Economic Interdependence*, Tokyo: University of Tokyo Press (Chapter 5).

Muller, Dennis C. (1983), *The Political Economy of Growth*, New Haven: Yale University Press.

Murtopo, Ali (1975), *Labourers and Farmers* (in Indonesian), Jakarta: Center for Strategic and International Studies.

Myers, Ramon (1989), 'Confucianism and economic development: mainland China, Hong Kong and Taiwan', Taipei: Chung-hua Institution for Economic Research, *Conference Series*, **13**, pp. 281–302.

Nabli, Mustapha K. and Jeffrey B. Nugent (eds) (1989), *The New Institutional Economics and Development. Theory and Applications to Tunisia*, Amsterdam: New Holland.

Nancy, C., A. Gouyon and Maman Superman (1990), 'The smallholders' demand for planting material and the response from private nurseries', paper presented at the Lokakarya Nasional Pembibitan Karet, Pusat Penelitian Perkebunan, Sungei Putih.

Narayanan, S. and Y.W. Lai (1996), 'Towards a more matured technological base: R&D in Malaysian electronics', paper presented at the Federation of ASEAN Economic Association (FAEA) Conference, Bangkok, Thailand.

National Statistical Coordination Board, Republic of the Philippines (1973–98), *Philippine Statistical Yearbook* (various issues), Manila.

National Statistics Office, Republic of the Philippines (1971–91), Integrated Censuses of the Population, 1970, 1980 and 1990, Manila.

Naughton, Barry (1995), *Growing out of the Plan – Chinese Economic Reform*

1978–1993, Cambridge: Cambridge University Press.

Nelson, Richard R. and Sidney G. Winter (1982), *An Evolutionary Theory of Economic Change*, Cambridge, MA: Belknap Press of Harvard University Press.

Nogués (1998), 'Comment on paper by David Vines', in A. Krueger (ed.), *The WTO as an International Organisation,* Chicago: University of Chicago Press.

Nolledo, J. (1997) *The New Constitution of the Philippines Annotated*, rev. edn, Mandaluyong: National Bookstore.

North, Douglass C. (1981), *Structure and Change in Economic History*, New York: Norton.

North, Douglass (1990), *Institutions, Institutional Change and Economic Performance*, Cambridge: Cambridge University Press.

North, Douglass C. and Robert Paul Thomas (1970), 'An economic theory of the growth of the Western world', *The Economic History Review,* 2nd series, **23**, pp. 1–17.

North, Douglass C. and Robert Paul Thomas (1973), *The Rise of the Western World: A New Economic History*, Cambridge: Cambridge University Press.

Nozick, Robert (1974), *Anarchy, State, and Utopia*, New York: Basic Books.

Olson, Mancur, Jr (1965), *The Logic of Collective Action: Public Goods and the Theory of Groups*, Cambridge: Harvard University Press.

Olson, Mancur, Jr (1982), *The Rise and Decline of Nations: Economic Growth, Stagflation and Social Rigidities*, New Haven: Yale University Press.

Omohondro, John T. (1981), *Chinese Merchant Families in Iloilo: Commerce and Kin in a Central Philippine City*, Athens, Ohio: Ohio University Press.

Ong, E.L. (1996), 'Contributions of the Rubber Research Institute of Malaysia to the Malaysian Rubber Industry', in *Industry and Export Directory*, Kuala Lumpur: Malaysian Rubber Products Manufacturers Association.

Ostrom, V., D. Feeny and H. Pick (1988), *Rethinking Institutional Analysis and Development*, San Francisco, CA: ICS Press.

Paauw, Douglas S. (1963), 'From colonial to guided economy', in Ruth McVey (ed.), *Indonesia*, New Haven: HRAF Press, pp. 165–257.

Persson, T., G. Roland and G. Tabellini (1997), 'Separation of powers and political accountability', Working Paper.

Petcharee Thanamai (1985), 'Patterns of industrial policy-making in Thailand: Japanese multinationals and domestic actors in the automobile and electrical appliances industries', PhD dissertation, University of Wisconsin, Madison.

Pincus, Jonathan (1996), *Class, Power and Agrarian Change: Land and Labour in Rural West Java*, London: Macmillan Press.

Polanyi, Karl (1944), *The Great Transformation: The Political and Economic Origins of Our Time*, New York: Rinehart.

Pollak, R.A. (1985), 'A transaction cost approach to families and households',

Journal of Economic Literature, **23** (2), pp. 581–608.

Porter, M. (1990), *The Competitive Advantage of Nations*, New York: The Free Press.

Portes, Richard, Richard Quandt, David Winter and Stephen Yeo (1983), 'Macroeconomic planning and disequilibrium: estimates for Poland, 1955–1980' (mimeo 07/83), University of London.

Portes, R. and D. Vines (1997), *Coping with International Capital Flows*, London: Commonwealth Secretariat.

Posner, Richard A. (1980), 'A theory of primitive society, with special reference to law', *Journal of Law and Economics*, **23** (April), pp. 1–53.

Prayong Nettayarak (1992), 'The future of the Thai sugarcane and sugar industry' (in Thai), paper presented at the 1992 Annual Year-End Conference of the Thailand Development Research Institute, Chon Buri, December.

Quraishi, A. (1996), *The World Trade Organisation*, Manchester: Manchester University Press.

Ramsay, Ansil (1987), 'The political economy of sugar in Thailand', *Pacific Affairs*, pp. 248–70.

Rangsun Thanapornpan (1989), *The Process of Economic Policy Determination in Thailand: Analysis of Political Economic History, 1932–1987* (in Thai), Bangkok: The Social Sciences Association.

Rasiah, R. (1995), *Foreign Capital and Industrialisation in Malaysia*, London: St Martin's Press.

Rasiah, R. (1997a), 'Ethnic politics and economic development in Malaysia', in R. Robison, G. Rodan and K. Hewison (eds), *Political Economy of Southeast Asia*, Sydney: Oxford University Press (Chapter 5).

Rasiah, R. (1997b), 'Malaysia's National Innovation System', in K.S Jomo and G. Felker (eds), *Technology Issues in Malaysia*, London: Routledge.

Riggs, Fred W. (1966), *Thailand: The Modernization of a Bureaucratic Polity*, Honolulu: East-West Center Press.

Rivera, T. (1995), *Landlords and Capitalists*, Quezon City: University of the Philippines Press.

Robertson, Alexander F. (1991), *Beyond the Family: The Social Organization of Human Reproduction*, Cambridge: Polity Press.

Robertson, P.L. and R.N. Langlois (1992), 'Innovation, networks and vertical integration', paper presented at the Conference of Industry Economists, Canberra: Australian National University.

Robison, Richard (1986), *Indonesia: The Rise of Capital*, Sydney: Allen and Unwin.

Rodgers, Gerry (1975), 'Nutritionally based wage determination in the low-income labour market', *Oxford Economic Papers*, **27**, pp. 61–81.

Rodrik, D. (1995), 'Why is there multilateral lending?', CEPR Discussion Paper, No. 1207, London: CEPR.

Ruf, Francois and P.S. Siswoputantro (eds) (1995), *Cocoa Cycles. The Economics of Cocoa Supply*, Cambridge: Woodhead Publishing.

Ruttan, Vernon W. (1984), 'Social science knowledge and institutional change', *American Journal of Agricultural Economics,* **39** (December), pp. 549–59.

Sachs, Jeffrey and Wing Thye Woo (1994), 'Experiences in the transition to a market economy', *Journal of Comparative Economics,* **18**, pp. 271–75.

Sampson, G. (1996), 'Compatibility of regional and multilateral trading agreements: reforming the WTO process', *American Economic Review,* May.

Schrieke, B. (ed.) (1929), *The Effect of Western Influence on Native Civilizations in the Malay Archipelago*, Batavia (Jakarta): Royal Batavia Society of Arts and Sciences and J. Kolff and Co.

Schultz, Theodore W. (1968), 'Institutions and the rising economic value of Man', *American Journal of Agricultural Economics*, **50** (December), pp. 1113–22.

Scott, James C. (1976), *The Moral Economy of the Peasant*, New Haven: Yale University Press.

Sender, Henny (1991), 'Inside the Overseas Chinese network', *The Institutional Investor*, August, pp. 29–43.

Shleifer, A. and R. Vishny (1993), 'Corruption', *Quarterly Journal of Economics*, **108** (3), pp. 599–617.

Sjahrir and Brown, Colin (1992), 'Indonesian financial and trade policy deregulation: reform and response', in Andrew MacIntyre and Kanizhka Jayasuriya (eds), *The Dynamics of Economic Policy Reform in South-east Asia and the South-west Pacific*, Singapore: Oxford University Press.

Soesastro, Hadi (1989), 'The political economy of deregulation in Indonesia', *Asian Survey,* **24** (9) (September), pp. 853–69.

Squire, Lyn (1981), *Employment Policy in Developing Countries*, Oxford: Oxford University Press.

Stiglitz, Joseph E. (1976), 'The efficiency wage hypothesis, surplus labour and the distribution of income in LDCs', *Oxford Economic Papers*, **28**, pp. 185–207.

Stiglitz, Joseph E. (1986), 'The new development economics', *World Development*, **14** (2), pp. 257–65.

Stiglitz, Joseph E. (1998) 'Macroeconomic dimensions of the East Asian crisis', in *Financial Crises and Asia, CEPR Conference Report No. 6,* London: Centre for Economic Policy Research.

Sunetra Sungsuwan (1991), 'The JPPCC and the determination of Thailand's economic policies' (in Thai), MA thesis, Faculty of Economics, Bangkok: Thammasat University.

Tham, S.Y. (1994), 'The impact of AFTA on the Malaysian manufacturing sector:

the case of rubber products', a report submitted to the Thailand Development Research Institute Foundation, Bangkok, Thailand.

Thayer, Carlyle A., (1992), 'Political developments in Vietnam: from the Sixth to Seventh National Party Congress', Regime Change and Regime Maintenance in Asia and the Pacific Discussion Paper Series, No. 5, Department of Political and Social Change, Research School of Pacific and Asian Studies, Canberra: Australian National University.

Thee, K.W. (1977), *Plantation Agriculture and Export Growth. An Economic History of East Sumatra, 1863–1942*, Jakarta: National Institute of Economic and Social Research.

Thomas, K.D. (1957), *Smallholders' Rubber in Indonesia*, Institute of Economic and Social Research, School of Economics, University of Indonesia, Jakarta.

Turner, H.A. (1965), *Wage Trends, Wage Policies and Collective Bargaining: Problems for Underdeveloped Countries*, Occasional Paper No. 6, Cambridge: Cambridge University.

van Arcadie, Brian (1993), 'Managing the renewal process: the case of Vietnam', *Public Administration and Development*, **13** (4), pp. 435–51.

Veblen, T. (1919), *The Place of Science in Modern Civilisation and Other Essays*, New York: Huebsch.

Wardhana, Ali (1989), 'Structural adjustment in Indonesia: export and the "high-cost economy"', keynote address at the 24th Conference of South-East Asian Central Bank Governors, Bangkok, 25 January.

White, Benjamin (1976), 'Population, employment and involution in a Javanese village', *Development and Change*, **7**, pp. 267–90.

White, Benjamin et al. (1992), 'Workshops and factories: dynamics of production organisation and employment in West Java's rural footwear industries', paper presented at the Ninth Biennial Conference of the Asian Studies Association, 6–9 July.

Williamson, Oliver E. (1975), *Markets and Hierarchies: Analysis and Antitrust Implications*, New York: Free Press.

Williamson, Oliver E. (1985), *The Economic Institutions of Capitalism: Firms, Markets, Relational Contracting*, New York: Free Press.

Winch, P. (1963), *The Idea of Social Science and its Relation to Philosophy*, London: Routledge Kegan Paul.

Wiradi, Gunawan (1978), *Rural Development and Rural Institutions, Rural Dynamics*, Series No. 6, Bogor: Agro-Economic Survey.

Wong Siu-lun (1985), 'The Chinese family firm: a model', *British Journal of Sociology*, **36** (2), pp. 58–72.

Wong Siu-lun (1988), 'The applicability of Asian family values to other socio-cultural settings', in Peter Berger and Michael Hsiao Hsini-lung (eds), *In Search of an East Asian Development Model*, New Brunswick, N.J.:

Transaction Books.

Woodside, Alexander B. (1971), *Vietnam and the Chinese Model,* Cambridge: Harvard University Press.

Woodside, Alexander B. (1989), 'Peasants and the State in the aftermath of the Vietnamese revolution', *Peasant Studies,* **16** (Summer), pp. 283–97.

World Bank (1989), *Malaysia: Mixing Risks and Rewards in a Mixed Economy,* Washington, DC: World Bank.

World Bank (1992), 'Indonesia. Tree Crop Smallholder Development Project', Report No. 102–IND, Washington, DC: East Asia and Pacific Region Division.

World Bank (1995), *World Development Report: Workers in an Integrating World.* Washington, DC: International Bank for Reconstruction and Development.

World Bank (1997) *World Development Report 1997,* New York: Oxford University Press.

World Bank (1998), *World Development Report, 1998,* New York: Oxford University Press.

Wurfel, D. (1988), *Philippine Politics: Development and Decay.* Ithaca: Cornell University Press.

Yayasan Lembaga Bantuan Hukum Indonesia (YLBHI) (1992), *Demokrasi masih terbenam: catatan keadaan hak-hak asasi manusia di Indonesia 1991* ('Democracy still submerged: notes on human rights in Indonesia 1991'), Jakarta:YLBHI.

Zen, Z., C. Barlow, S. Mawardi, R. Gondowarsito and Uhendi Haris (1992), *The Market for Smallholder Rubber Planting Materials* (in Indonesian), Medan: Pusat Penelitian Perkebunan Sungei Putih.

Index

Aitken, H.G.J. 73
Alchian, A.A. 10, 12, 17
Alexander, J. 51
Alexander, P. 51
All-Indonesia Workers Organization (SOBSI) 43
Allen, G.C. 74
Anderson, T.L. 15
Aoki, T. 58, 63
APEC (Asia–Pacific Economic Cooperation) 115, 161, 162
Aquino, Corazon 133
Arndt, H. 159
ASEAN (Association of South East Asian Nations) 115
Asian crises 153-5
Asian financial crisis (1997) 150, 178-9
    and the International Monetary Fund (IMF) 151-5
    and the World Bank 157-8
Asian Newly Industrialized Economies (NIEs) 57
automobile (automotive) industry
    Malaysia 66-9
    Thailand 96-7
autonomous states, and principal-agent framework 19
Ayal, E. 74
Ayres, C. 3

Bank Duta, Indonesia 113, 115
Bardhan, P. 49, 135
Barlow, C. 5, 6, 31, 33, 35, 37, 175
Barton, G. 169
Barzel, Y. 19
Basu, K. 11
Battacharya, A. 106
Bauer, P.T. 14
Becker, G.S. 9
Beresford, M. 120, 125, 127

Bergsten 162
Bhangwati, J. 159
Binswanger, H.P. 26, 27, 49
Board of Trade, Thailand 92
Boeke, J.H. 28
Bogor Declaration 115, 116
Bogor summit 161
Booth, A. 49
Boserup, E. 27, 31
bounded rationality 9, 14
Bowie, A. 57
Breman, J. 52
Brennan, G. 38
Bretton Woods Institution 153, 157
Brittan, Leon 162
Brown, C. 106
Bumiputera, Malaysia 56, 57, 67, 68
bureaucratic polity, Thailand 86-7

'Cairns group' 150
Campos, J.E. 108, 177
Candra Asri, Indonesia 113
capitalism 74-5
Carrol, J.J. 74
case study approach to institutions 4
Chandler, A.D. 80, 81
Chartichai, General 94
Cheung, S.N.S. 19
Chinese commercial and financial networks 82-3
Chinese commercial practices, as an institutional factor 75-7
Chinese family firms 77-80, 84
Chinese Merchant Families in Iloilo: Commerce and Kin in a Philippine City 75
Chote, R. 152, 154
Christensen, S.R. 89, 100
Clarke, G. 169
cluster approach 58-60
    in Malaysian manufacturing 59, 69-70

collective action 4
collectivized rural economy, Vietnam
123–5
Collier, W. 50
Commons, J. 3
conglomerates, Southeast Asia 80
cooperatives, Vietnam 124–5, 126
'corruption puzzle' 135
costs of information and transactions 8
Crouch, H. 43

Dam van Nhue 131
Day, R.H. 15
de Dios, E.S. 6, 175, 177
de Venecia, Jose 141
de Vylder, S. 120, 128
Demsetz, H. 10, 12
Devarajan, S. 45
direct labour services 27
Direktorat Jenderal Perkebunan 28, 29,
35
disequilibrium 13–14, 17, 123, 126,
170–73
Donnithorne, A. 74
Doronila, A. 136
Dorward, A. 4
Drysdale, P. 162
'Dutch disease' 109

East Asian miracle 150
economic development, and
entrepreneurship 74–5
'economic groups', Latin America 80
economic theory of institutional change
8–22
electrical and electronics industry,
Malaysia 61–3
enclosure, England 16
Engels, F. 14
entrepreneurship 72, 81, 83, 172, 177
definitions 73–4
and economic development 74–5
and institutions, Southeast Asia
72–84
Estrada, Joseph 141
European Union 161, 162
Explorations in Entrepreneurial History
73
export promotion, Malaysia 56
externality problems 17, 171

factor prices, long-run changes 15–16
Fama, E. 12
familism, in Chinese economic
organization 79–80
family firms 79
Fealy, G. 169
Feeny, D. 15
Fforde, A.J. 6, 120, 123, 124, 125, 127,
128, 177
Field, A.J. 10, 27, 173
Fields, G. 44
financial crisis of 1997 3, 150, 151–5,
157–8, 178–9
financial markets 179–80
Findlay, R. 18, 134
Fischer, S. 151
Fitzgerald, V. 170
Fong, C.A. 56, 61, 62
foreign investment, Malaysia 56
free-rider problem 17, 21, 69, 124, 178
and open regionalism 162–4
Frohlich, N. 18

gama system 15
Gavin, M. 156
Geertz, C. 51, 74, 82
General Agreement on Tariffs and Trade
(GATT) 160
Thailand's membership 91
Uruguay Round 150, 160
Generalized System of Preferences 57
Ghanem, H. 45
Gilbert, C. 156, 157
global economic institutions 150–64
Golongan Karya party (GOLKAR) 43,
45
Goodpaster, G. 114
Goodwin, R.E. 38
Gouyon, A. 29
government
as an institution 178, 179
role in institutional change 173–7
government policy, change in 14
green revolution 48, 49–50, 51
group pattern of industrial organization
81–2
Gutierrez, E. 141, 143

Hadiz, P. 54
Harriss, J. 4

Hart, G. 49, 50
Harvard Centre for Entrepreneurial
Studies 73
Hawkins, E.D. 45
Hayami, Y. 14, 15, 16, 17, 18, 27, 37, 49,
50, 51
Heavy Industry Corporation of Malaysia
57, 66
Hewison, K. 86
Higgins, B. 75
Hill, P.J. 15
honour, in primitive societies 16
Hugo, G. 47, 52
human resources, in Malaysian industries
61-2, 64-5, 67
Hume, D. 8
Hunter, J. 4
Hutchcroft, P. 134

import substitution, Malaysia 55, 56
incomplete markets 28
Indonesia 5, 30, 168, 174, 176
    Agency for Research and Application
        of Technology 109
    balance of payments 111
    Bank Duta 113, 115
    Bogor Declaration 115, 116
    Candra Asri 113
    debt repayment 155
    deregulation 106
        trade and industrial 112
    deregulation and liberalization
        first phase 107-10
        second phase 110-15
        third phase 115-16
    economic growth 31, 44
    Economic Stabilization Council 108
    financial crisis 114, 116
    financial-sector liberalization 112-13
    Five-Year Development Plan 105
    foreign investment 109, 115
    government, and deregulation 105-17
    government-business relations 110
    import licensing system 110, 112
    import substitution 109
    institutional change 43-4
    institutional development 106-7
    institutional setting 106
    labour controls, efficiency and equity
        47-8

labour institutions 42-54
monopolies 116
Nahdatul Ulama 169
New Order government 5, 52, 105,
    107
oil boom 109-10
Pertamina 82, 108, 109, 111
Provisional People's Consultative
    Assembly 105
rubber 25
rural institutional change 42
'shop-keeper revolution' 82
trade unions 45, 46, 47
two-tier society 28
see also Java; Sumatra; Suharto
    regime
Indonesian Chinese 83-4
Indonesian Peasant Front (BTI) 43
industrial cluster development,
    institutional issues 60-69
industrial institutions, Malaysia 55-71
industrial labour, controls 44
industrial organization, group pattern
    81-2
innovation 123
institutional adaption 26
institutional adjustments 178
institutional arrangements 122, 169-70
    changes 16
    defined 10
    efficiency 11, 12
institutional change 26-8, 171
    economic approach 13-18
    economic policy in Thailand 85-102
    economic theory 8-22
    government role 173-7
    Indonesia 43-4
    induced institutional change
        dynamics 16-18
        in Java 49-51
    political constraints and influences
        172
    political economy 18-21
    theory of 5
    Vietnam 121-9
institutional choice set, changes 14, 30
institutional disequilibrium 17, 123, 126
    sources 13-14
institutional economics 4
institutional 'endogenization' 121

institutional issues, industrial cluster
  development 60-69
institutional setting, Indonesia 106
institutions
  defined 85
  efficiency 122
  and entrepreneurship, Southeast Asia
    72-84
  functions 9-13
  need for 9-10
  security function 9, 167
institutions of transition from central
  planning, Vietnam 118-31
International Bank for Reconstruction
  and Development (IBRD) 156
International Development Association
  (IDA) 156
International Monetary Fund (IMF) 6,
    91, 107, 116, 117, 170, 175-6, 180
  adjustment lending 152-3
  and the Asian financial crisis 151-55
  research analysis and policy advice
    151-2
  World Economic Outlook 151
Irwin, D. 159

Jackson, J. 160
Japan 79-80
  investment in Indonesia 109
Java
  induced institutional change 49-51
  labour contracts in rice farming
    48-52
  labour hiring institutions 27
  organized labour controls 42
  rice harvesting system 170
Johnson, H.G. 159
Jones, E. 11
just-in-time production technology 64

kedokan 50, 51
kelompok 30, 34
Kerkvliet, B. 123
Kikuchi, M. 14, 15, 16, 17, 18, 27, 37,
    49, 50, 51
Kilby, P. 73
Korea, rescue package 154
Krongkaew, M. 5, 101, 167, 172, 175
Krueger, A. 134
Kydd, J. 4

labour contracts in rice farming, Java
    48-52
labour hiring institutions, Java 27
labour institutions, Indonesia 42-54
labour market controls, Indonesia 45-6
Lai, Y.W. 62
land costs 31
land prices, in medieval Europe 15
Lande, C. 134
Langlois, R.N. 26, 70
Laothamatas, A. 87, 88
Latin America, 'economic groups' 80
Le Si Thiep 131
Leff, N.H. 75, 80, 81, 167
Leibenstein, H. 81
less developed countries (LDCs) 8
  states in 18, 21
Lewis, A. 48
Lewis, C.M. 4
Lim, S.C. 65
Limlingan, V.S. 76
Lin, J.Y. 3, 5, 6, 26, 27, 30, 33, 120, 129,
    167, 173, 174
Lin, J.Y., critique 122-3
linkages, in Malaysian industries 63,
    65-6, 68-9

McCloskey, D.N. 16
McCoy, A. 138
MacIntyre, A.J. 110, 113, 114
Mackie, J. 5, 72, 79, 167
Mahani, Z.A. 68
Malaysia 5
  automotive industry 66-9
    human resources 67
    linkages 68-9
    technology 67
  electrical and electronics industry
    61-3, 173
    human resources 61-2
    linkages 63
    technology 62
    training 61-2
  export promotion 56, 69
  First Industrial Master Plan 57
  foreign direct investment 57-8
  foreign investment 56
  foreign-direct-investment-led
    industrialization 57-8
  Heavy Industry Corporation 57

import substitution 55, 56
industrial institutions 55–71
industrialization 56–7, 57–8
manufacturing 55
 cluster approach 59, 60
 cluster development 55
 cluster formation 69–70
 institutional structure 55–60
 and multinationals 58, 69
National Development Policy 58
New Economic Policy 56, 57, 58
oil palm development schemes 37
Perwaja Steel 58
rubber products industry 63–6
 human resources 64–5
 linkages 65–6
 technology 65
 see also rubber industry
Second Industrial Master Plan 58, 64
Seventh Malaysia Plan 58
managerial discretionary behaviour 168
Manning, C. 5, 27, 44, 46, 47, 50, 52, 53, 174
manufacturing industry 15
Marcos, Ferdinand 133
market economies 119
market institutions 8
Marr, D. 120
Marx, K. 3, 14, 27, 136
Matthews, R.C. 11, 20
Mazumdar, D. 54
Metzner, J.K. 30
Mexico, standby programme 154
Mill, J.S. 8
minimum wage 44, 45
Mitsubishi 67, 68
monopsony 47
Morris-Suzuki, T. 63
Multi-Fibre Agreements 91
multinationals
 in Malaysian electrical and electronics industry 62
 in Malaysian manufacturing industry 69
Murtopo, A. 45
Myers, R. 82

Nabli, M.K. 4
NAFTA 161
Nahdatul Ulama, Indonesia 169

Nancy, C. 33
Narayanan, S. 62
Nelson, R.R. 17
Nelson Winter, S.G. 17
neo-Stalinist development model, Vietnam 120, 122, 123, 126
neoclassical economics 4, 8
networks (commercial and financial) 82–3
New Order 5, 52
 see also Suharto regime
Nogués 156
Nolledo, J. 133, 145
North, D.C. 12, 15, 17, 20, 27, 85, 171
Northeast Asia, Chinese family firms 78–9
Nozick, R. 18
Nugent, J.B. 4

Olson, M. Jr 17, 20
Omohondro, J.T. 75, 78
Ong, E.L. 64
open regionalism 6
 and the free-rider problem 162–4
 and the World Trade Organization (WTO) 160–64
Oppenheimer, J.A. 18
opportunistic behaviour 12
Overseas Chinese 72, 74, 75–7, 78

Paauw, D.S. 43
Paine, S.H. 120
Pancasila 43, 45, 48, 53, 174
Pangestu, M. 106
Panyarachun, Anand 94, 97, 100
Persson, T. 136
Pertamina (Indonesian state oil company) 82, 108, 109, 111
Perwaja Steel, Malaysia 58
Petcharee, T. 91
Philippine Rural Reconstruction Movement 169, 174
Philippines 6, 14, 15, 168, 171, 173, 175
 civil society institutions, growth 169
 civil-society changes 139–40
 Congress 142–4
 corruption 135, 137
 countrywide fund 142–4
 'democracy–authoritarianism' dichotomy 136–7

economic growth 132
executive 137, 144–6
    and legislature 137–8, 141
executive–legislative relations 132–48
factional politics 133–6
formal institutional changes 140–42
Marcos dictatorship 138
political system 132–3
pork-barrel politics 142–4
rent-seeking 134–6, 137, 138
Pincus, J. 49, 52
point-of-sale production technology 64
Polanyi, K. 16
policy failures 178–7
    sources 19–21
political economy of institutional change
    18–21
political entrepreneurs 17–18
political ingenuity 177
political reform 20–21
Pollak, R.A. 29
population increase 28
pork-barrel politics 142–4, 168, 169
Porter, M. 58
Portes, R. 164
Poulton, C. 4
Prayong, N. 97
preferential blocks 161
Prem Tinsulanon, General 93
primitive societies, honour 16
principal–agent framework, and
    autonomous states 19
private sector 180
product prices, long-run changes 15–16
Projects for the Rehabilitation of Export
    Crops 35
property managements 15
property rights 15, 18
    arrangements 15–16
    institutions 10–11
Proton cars 59, 66–9

Quezon, M. 138
Quraishi, A. 160

Ramli, R. 113, 114
Ramos, Fidel 141
Rangsun, T. 87, 89, 91, 94
Rasiah, R. 57, 58, 61, 62
rationality 9

research and development (R&D) 58–9
    in Malaysian electrical and electronics
        industry 62
rice production, Java 49–50, 51
Riggs, F.W. 85, 86
Rivera, T. 148
Robertson, A.F. 119
Robertson, P.L. 26, 70
Robison, R. 46
Rodrik, D. 153, 156
Root, L.H. 108, 177
Rosenzweig, M.R. 26, 27, 49
rubber industry
    Indonesia 25
    Malaysia 63–6
    smallholder rubber in Sumatra 28–32
rubber prices 31
Rubber Research Institute of Malaysia
    64, 65
Ruf, F. 30
rural institutional change, Indonesia 42
rural and regional development 180
Ruttan, V.W. 14

Sachs, J. 119
Sampson, G. 160
Santiago, Miriam 141
Schlicht, E. 11
Schrieke 30
Schultz, T. 3
Scott 49
security function of institutions 9, 167
Sender, H. 77
Seventh Malaysia Plan 58
Shleifer, A. 135, 137
Siswoputantro, P.S. 30
Sjahrir 106
smallholder block development schemes
    35–8
Smallholders Rubber Development
    Projects 35
Smith, A. 8
Snoh Unakul 93
social engineering 38
socialism 119
Soesastro, H. 6, 106, 110, 172, 174, 176,
    177
Southeast Asia
    conglomerates 80
    'Economic Miracle' 75

institutions and entrepreneurship
72-84
Squire, L. 54
state
defined 18
economic approaches to 18-19
and public policy 85
role in institutional change 173-7
see also government
states, in less developed countries 18, 21
Stiglitz, J.E. 154
subsistence ethic 16
sugar trade, Thailand 97-9
Suharto regime 42, 43, 44
Suharto, T.N.J. 105, 107, 115
Sumatra 5, 175
introduction of new technology 25
smallholder rubber 28-32
disequilibrium 30-32
private planting material nurseries
32-5
smallholder block development
schemes 35-8
Sundrum, R.M. 49
Sunetra Sungsuwan 93
Sutowo, I. 108

Taiwan 80
tebasan 50, 52
technology
as an industrialization strategy 70
changes 4, 14-15, 31
in Malaysian industries 61-2, 65, 67
Thai Bankers Association 94
Thailand 168, 174
automobile industry 96-7
balance of payments problems 91
Board of Trade 92
bureaucratic polity 86-7
business sector and economic policy-
making 92-4
business-oriented bureaucracy 99-101
capitalist class 87
corruption 169
economic policy 85-102
demand side 88-9
supply side 88
and the ethnic Chinese 86, 92
Farmers' Aid Funds 98
Federation of Thai Industries 92

financial crisis 152
First Plan 95
GATT membership 91
income inequality 101
Joint Public-Private Sector
Consultative Committee 92, 93-4
legal foundation of bureaucratic power
89-90
Ministry of Industry 98
National Economic and Social
Development Board (NESDB)
93
parliamentary system, weaknesses
90-91
policy-making, external forces 91-2
political system 85, 86-7
poverty 101
property rights 15-16
public debts 90
public enterprise privatization 95-6
Thai Bankers' Association 92
Tham, S.Y. 5, 66
Thanapornpan, R. 87
Thee, K.W. 33
Thierfelder, K. 45
Thomas, R.P. 15, 27
Tomich, T. 31, 35
trade liberalization 156
and World Trade Organization (WTO)
159-60
trade unions, Indonesia 45, 46, 47
transactions costs 13, 15, 48-9
transition from socialism to capitalism
119, 120
'Transitional Model', Vietnam 127-9
Tunisia 4
Turner, H.A. 54
Turton, A. 49

United States
constitution 12
public grazing land 15
Uruguay Round 150, 160

van Arcadie, B. 119
Veblen, T. 3
Vietnam 5, 171, 176
alternatives to socialism 125-7
collectivized rural economy 123-5
cooperatives 124-5, 126

CT-100 126, 127, 128, 129
First Five-year Plan 121, 125
history 120–21
household contracting 126, 127
institutional change 121–9
institutions of transition from central
    planning 118–31
reform package 127
rural collectivization 120
socioeconomic development 118
'Transitional Model' 127–9
Vines, D. 6, 162, 164
Vishny, R. 135, 137

Walras, L. 26
Wan, H. Jr 44
Wardhana, Ali 111
Weber, M. 18, 78
welfare 122
Wellisz, S. 134
White, B. 49
Williamson, O.E. 9

Wiradi, G. 51
Wolfensohn, J. 157
Wong Siu-Lun 78, 79
Woo, W.T. 119
Woodside, A.B. 120
World Bank 6, 35, 36, 48, 56, 91, 107,
    135, 150
and the Asian crisis 157–8
and development policies 155–8
lending 157
research, analysis and policy advice
    156–7
Strategic Compact 157–8
World Trade Organization (WTO) 6,
    150, 159-63
difficulties 160
and open regionalism 160–64
and trade liberalization 159–60
Wurfel, D. 133, 137

Zainal-Abidin, M. 5
Zen, Z. 33, 36